Richard B. Cheney and the Rise of the Imperial Vice Presidency

Richard B. Cheney and the Rise of the Imperial Vice Presidency

BRUCE P. MONTGOMERY

PRAEGER

Westport, Connecticut
London

Library of Congress Cataloging-in-Publication Data

Montgomery, Bruce P., 1955–
    Richard B. Cheney and the rise of the imperial vice presidency/
Bruce P. Montgomery.
        p. cm.
    Includes bibliographical references and index.
    ISBN 978-0-313-35620-9 (alk. paper)
    1. Cheney, Richard B. 2. United States—Politics and government—2001–
3. Vice-Presidents—United States. 4. Cheney, Richard B.—Political and social views.
5. Cheney, Richard B.—Influence. I. Title.
    E840.8.C43M66 2009
    973.931092—dc22
    [B]   2008041033

British Library Cataloguing in Publication Data is available.

Library of Congress Catalog Card Number: 2008041033
ISBN: 978-0-313-35620-9

First published in 2009

Praeger Publishers, 88 Post Road West, Westport, CT 06881
An imprint of Greenwood Publishing Group, Inc.
www.praeger.com

Printed in the United States of America

The paper used in this book complies with the
Permanent Paper Standard issued by the National
Information Standards Organization (Z39.48–1984).

10 9 8 7 6 5 4 3 2 1

Contents

Introduction

The origins of Richard B. Cheney's imperial vice presidency may be traced to his experiences during the turbulent times of the Nixon and Ford administrations. The Nixon years had invited a sweeping indictment against the presidency on numerous counts—campaign sabotage, burglary, bribery, extortion, fraud, destruction of evidence, domestic espionage, obstruction of justice, and abuse of power. The claims of unilateral authority in foreign affairs had pervaded and emboldened the domestic presidency, observed Arthur M. Schlesinger, Jr. "The all-purpose invocation of national security, the insistence on executive secrecy, the withholding of information from Congress, the refusal to spend funds appropriated by Congress, the attempted intimidation of the press, the use of the White House itself as a base for espionage and sabotage directed against political opponents—all signified the extension of the imperial presidency from foreign to domestic affairs."[1]

These actions, Schlesinger argued, constituted a revolutionary challenge to the separation of powers itself. They also ignited a furious congressional backlash resulting in the passage of many new laws to restore the balance of power and check unfettered executive authority. Cheney came to believe that the onslaught of these measures had imprisoned the presidency in a web of new regulation and laws that crippled its ability to act in the field of foreign policy. For Cheney, the presidency that had reached its zenith under Nixon was being imperiled under the presidency of Gerald R. Ford. Witnessing the congressional blitz of legislation to check executive power was a pivotal moment in the education of Cheney. He believed that the power of the presidency was being threatened and that America would be dangerously exposed unless it had a strong chief executive. David Gergen, a former White House staffer in the Ford administration, later noted that

Cheney emerged from that era committed to the idea of restoring the powers of the presidency.[2]

Cheney had witnessed the congressional backlash against the abuses of the Nixon years at the epicenter of the White House. In his meteoric rise to become the youngest chief of staff in American history, he became involved in many of the interbranch battles that engulfed the Ford presidency. After leaving the White House with the victory of Jimmy Carter in 1976, he returned to Washington politics as a conservative congressman from Wyoming. He quietly chafed under the domination of a mostly Democratic-controlled Congress, but nevertheless rose swiftly through the ranks of the Republican minority party in the House. He became a strong proponent of the Reagan administration's national security agenda, including massive defense spending and assisting the Contras against the Soviet-backed Sandinista government in Nicaragua. He also was an ardent supporter of the White House's efforts to bolster executive powers. At the conservative American Enterprise Institute in 1980, he publicly condemned Congress for unwisely restraining presidential power and called for its restoration. He declared that in past times of national peril—the Civil War, the Great Depression, or World War II—the nation had responded by giving the president extraordinary authority. The decade of the 1980s, he warned, would be one of those times when America would have to resort to force and would need a strong chief executive. His views on executive power were already well formed by this time and would only intensify in the coming years.

During his congressional years, his strongest expression on behalf of executive power came with the Iran-Contra scandal, perhaps the apex of his career in the House. As the ranking House Republican on the joint Senate-House Iran-Contra committee, Cheney came to the defense of the Reagan administration. He portrayed the Iran-Contra scandal not as a political crime, but as a fundamental dispute over policy. He oversaw the writing of the investigating committee's minority report, which delivered a full-throated assault on Congress's interference with the president's constitutional prerogatives on matters of national security. The report denounced the majority's findings of serious White House abuses as "hysterical" and condemned Congress for its inconsistent aid to the Contras, for passing laws that tied the president's hands in foreign affairs, for engaging in interbranch intimidation, and for overstepping its constitutional bounds by interfering with the White House. For the future vice president, the Iran-Contra investigation recalled the congressional "assaults" on the presidency during the 1970s. The experience magnified his almost theological conviction that the presidency had to be bolstered in a world fraught with dangerous risks to the nation's security.

As secretary of defense during the presidency of George H.W. Bush, Cheney battled Congress over such issues as defense budgets and weapons systems. A Cold Warrior, he remained cautious and wary of the sweeping changes taking place in the Soviet Union and the democratic revolutions in Eastern Europe. He endeavored to reshape American defense policy in a changing world where the threat of communism was rapidly vanishing and new security threats had yet to be clearly identified. He fought successful wars in Panama and Iraq, overcoming the lingering ghosts of Vietnam. When it came to ousting Iraqi forces from Kuwait in 1991, Cheney advised the president not to seek the support of Congress in launching the largest military undertaking since the Second World War. The advice represented his profound distrust, if not contempt, for the institution in which he served for almost a decade. In Cheney's view, recent American history seemed to involve the struggle between a strong presidency necessary in a deadly world and the naïve, untrustworthy, and sometimes disloyal constraints of Congress. His outlook exerted little influence in an administration that for the most part sought consultation with Congress and comity among the global community of nations.

By the time Cheney brought his hard-edged views of executive power into the administration of George W. Bush, in 2001, the vice presidency had undergone dramatic changes since the mid-1970s. The office had matured to enjoy a large and professional staff, a West Wing office, a separate line item in the executive budget, and an official residence at the Admiral's House at the Naval Observatory. Vice presidential activities had become far more substantial. Not only did vice presidents hold routine private sessions with presidents, but they also attended cabinet and National Security Council meetings. They received full intelligence briefings and access to presidential information. They lobbied on behalf of administration policies and programs, assumed leadership in the political party second only to the president, and carried out sensitive diplomatic missions. They served as important presidential advisors and liaisons to Congress and public interest groups. The vice presidency had come a long way since the days when John Nance Garner told Lyndon Johnson that the office "was not worth a pitcher of warm spit."

From the beginning of the Republic, the vice presidency has always been what the president wanted it to be. The Constitution gave the office remarkably few responsibilities aside from taking the president's place in case of death, disability, resignation, or removal from office and breaking tie votes in the Senate. The office only possessed as much power and prestige as the president was willing to give it. While the early presidents gave their vice presidents little to do, subsequent presidents in the twentieth century gradually lent stature to the office, attracting individuals of greater talent and establishing the office as a stepping stone to the presidency. "The vice president will be and is what the president wants him to be," Hubert Humphrey had said. Nothing more demonstrated this truism than the vice presidency of Richard B. Cheney, who far surpassed any of his predecessors in power and influence. By the time he took office, the vice presidency had assumed considerable importance in the operations of the White House. His predecessor, Al Gore, had become one of the epicenters of power in the executive branch in the Clinton administration, an indispensable advisor to the president.

Nonetheless, contemptuous of the vice presidency's traditional role, Cheney aimed to aggregate unprecedented powers in the office. The dramatic elevation of vice presidential authority derived from the president's willingness to delegate broad swaths of his presidential powers to his more experienced deputy. As a condition for accepting the vice presidency, Cheney arranged an improbable portfolio that would define the office in a new and wholly novel light—an imperial vice presidency. Cheney's portfolio involved the core issues of most concern to every president, including economic issues, intelligence and national security, energy, and the White House's legislative agenda. He managed the president's transition team after the GOP won the White House in the 2000 presidential election, populating the new administration with many of his close allies. He created an enormous shadow national security team. His reach was felt at the Cabinet and sub-Cabinet levels where his predecessors were rarely seen. Even before the terrorist attacks on September 11, 2001, he led the administration's charge to roll back what he perceived to be the legislative encroachments of the 1970s. He worked to cloak the White House in greater confidentiality.

But it was the terrorist attacks that truly transformed his vice presidency. After 9/11, Cheney and his longtime aide and legal counsel, David Addington, would become the animating force behind the "war on terror." In the vice president's view, the terrorist attacks created the urgent necessity of giving the president unrestrained authority to defend the nation. To battle the terrorist scourge, America would have to go to the "dark side," unleash the intelligence agencies, and use any means at its disposal. This outlook would define the central philosophy and legacy of the Bush presidency at home and abroad. Cheney and Addington aggressively drove sweeping legal changes through the White House, the Justice Department, and the Pentagon. They overshadowed the secretary of state, the national security advisor, and other senior White House aides. Their expansive interpretation of executive power would define the administration's extralegal policies on a range of critical issues—imprisoning suspected terrorists at Guantanamo Bay, Cuba, beyond sovereign law; rendition and secret prisons; harsh interrogation methods; and domestic warrantless wiretapping. Cheney wasted little time in beginning his legal revolution behind closed doors, igniting major controversies in and out of the administration at home and overseas.

He also became the major force behind the war with Iraq to eliminate Saddam Hussein's alleged weapons of mass destruction, an assumption that proved erroneous and produced major international ramifications for U.S. geostrategic interests. The vice president and other proponents of the war against Iraq had sounded the alarm of a rogue regime rearming with weapons of mass destruction, reconstituting its nuclear program, and having ties with the al Qaeda network that struck America on 9/11. They were convinced that Iraq posed a gathering and imminent threat. They drew parallels to the great threats of the twentieth century—to Hitlerism, militarism, and communism, all defeated by the free world and the might of America. Once again the United States was called to defend the safety of its people and the hopes of mankind. Yet, it was a mirage. After months of intensive searching throughout Iraq, American intelligence could find no evidence of wide-scale efforts to develop weapons of mass destruction. The vice president had predicted that American forces would be greeted as liberators and that the country could be turned over to civilian authorities after the 2003 invasion. But American troops found a suspicious population, Iraq's institutions collapsed, and sectarian fighting broke out. The United States fell into a years-long occupation as it battled a vicious insurgency. In the end, Cheney's authority derived from a president willing to delegate unprecedented powers to his vice president. Cheney managed to dominate events and shape world history like no vice president before him. The consequences of his actions and reach of his authority were extraordinary, but his powers relied on the president's willingness to take his advice. In the annals of the vice presidency, his tenure may be seen as a remarkable aberration. No president prior to George W. Bush was willing to give his vice president such enormous powers. Few, if any, may be willing to do so again.

One

The Vice Presidency

Although the Constitutional Convention of 1787 created the vice presidency almost as an afterthought, the framers did not intend it to be an insignificant office. They saw its occupant as truly the second citizen of the land. Under the Constitution, the vice president was to be the person winning the second largest number of electoral votes in the contest of the presidency. He was expected to have all the qualifications of a chief executive. Nonetheless, the Constitution established only two major responsibilities for the vice president: to take the president's place in case of death, disability, resignation, or removal from office and to preside over the Senate, casting a vote only to break a tie.[1] With so little responsibility assigned to it, the framers unwittingly doomed the vice presidency to near oblivion for almost two centuries.

As the nation's first vice president, John Adams served under George Washington for eight years, casting more tie-breaking votes than any subsequent vice president in American history. The small number of Senators often produced tie votes, allowing the combative and voluble Adams to participate in debates. It was not long before they silenced the vice president altogether, marooning him in the Senate. "It's to be sure a punishment to hear other men talk five hours every day," Adams complained to his wife, Abigail, "and not be at liberty to talk at all myself, especially as more than half I hear appears to me very young, inconsistent, and inexperienced." The situation represented a monumental irony, wrote the historian Joseph Ellis: "The man famous as the indefatigable orator of independence in the new government was obliged to remain silent in the legislative councils of the new government."[2]

Adams bitterly resented being ignominiously stranded in the Senate while debates raged around him regarding the direction of the republic. As Adams saw it, he was a man of action who should have been playing a central role in the great unfolding drama of securing the American Revolution. During the debates of the Continental Congress, he achieved fame as the "Atlas of Independence" for insisting on breaking away from England. He had persuaded Washington to lead the Continental Army, selected Jefferson to draft the Declaration of Independence, and led the Board of War and Ordinance for more than a year when fighting broke out. In 1777, Congress sent him to Paris to help Benjamin Franklin negotiate an alliance with France and then to work on a peace treaty ending the war. These and other endeavors earned him a reputation along with Madison for being "America's most sophisticated student of government." Instead, now he was the vice president, marginalized and muted, limited to breaking tie votes, while Hamilton and Madison occupied the limelight. "To make matters worse," wrote Ellis, "his duties in the Senate removed him from the deliberations of the cabinet." Washington almost never consulted him on policy matters, believing that the vice presidency was more a legislative than an executive office.[3]

Like in other matters, Washington's actions set precedent for his successors. For a long time, presidents supposed themselves constitutionally forbidden to involve their vice presidents in executive decisions. To do so, Washington believed, would violate the separation of powers. Adams himself appeared to endorse this constitutional view. "The executive authority is so wholly out of my sphere," he noted, "and it is so delicate a thing for me to meddle in, that I avoid it as much as possible." He nevertheless supported the Washington administration's principle initiatives, many of them controversial, involving Hamilton's financial plan, suppression of the Whiskey Rebellion, the Proclamation of Neutrality, and Jay's Treaty. Thus, he existed in limbo, muzzled and stranded in the Senate and outside the sphere of the executive. "It was difficult to think of the ever-combative, highly combustible champion of the American Revolution as extraneous and invisible, but that is what the vice presidency made him."[4]

No wonder that Adams lamented to his wife that "my country has in its wisdom contrived for me the most insignificant office that ever the invention of man contrived or his imagination conceived." Indeed, from the start, history had shown the vice presidency to be a job of spectacular frustration.[5] But questions about the office predated Adams. The constitutional framers never had a great commitment to the vice presidency, nor did it ever produce much enthusiasm at the ratifying convention. While some saw the vice presidency as unnecessary, others believed it belonged more to the legislative rather than the executive branch of government. James Monroe declared to the Virginia ratifying convention that there was no need for the office.[6] Some shared Connecticut delegate Roger Sherman's sentiment that "if the Vice-President were not to be President of the Senate, he would be without employment."[7] Elbridge Gerry, one of the signers of the Declaration of Independence, felt so strongly about the Constitution's vice presidential provision that he refused to sign the nation's founding document. The provision violated the separation of powers, he contended, and would create an executive branch spy in the Senate. "We might as well put the President himself at the head of the legislature," he stated. Despite Gerry's scruples on the matter, he later became vice president during Madison's second term. Hamilton defended the vice presidency as a means to cast tie-breaking votes in the Senate, but privately he complained to James Wilson that everyone was "aware of that defect in the constitution which renders it possible that the man intended for Vice President may in fact turn up President."[8] The First Congress debated whether the vice president should even receive a salary before deciding on the sum of $5,000 a year. Thus, conceived in doubt, if not suspicion, the vice presidency became the stepchild of the executive and legislative branches almost from the start. The Constitution provided the vice presidency with few official duties, sowing the seeds of an extraneous and invisible office.[9]

Nonetheless, the electoral system initially produced figures of remarkable stature until passage of the Twelfth Amendment in 1804, providing that electors vote separately for president and vice president. Before then, electors in their respective states would cast two votes for president. The candidate winning a majority would be named president and the runner-up, vice president. This system not only produced Adams for the vice presidency in the elections of 1789 and 1793, but also Thomas Jefferson in 1797. Both moved on to the presidency. The Twelfth Amendment stemmed from the electoral standoff between Aaron Burr and Jefferson. Burr's refusal to defer to Jefferson threw the election into the House of Representatives. After thirty-six ballots, Jefferson won. The states ratified the amendment to prevent such deadlocks in the future by providing for separate voting for the two offices. The amendment also assured that the president and vice president would be representatives of the same party. The framers of the Republic failed to foresee the inevitable rise and influence of opposing political parties on the constitutional system. By the time Jefferson was elected as Adams's vice president, both were members of opposing political parties that were degenerating into partisan warfare. Jefferson assumed the role of opposing the Federalist administration in which he served and endeavored to set up a Republican government in exile. As vice president, he in fact became the leader of the opposition party and was quick to erect a wall of separation from the presidency.[10]

While correcting the electoral system's early imperfections, the Twelfth Amendment sent the vice presidency into precipitous decline. No longer held by runners-up in presidential contests, the vice presidency became filled with what one scholar termed a "rogues gallery of personal and political failures."[11] The new process ended the prospect of attracting strong figures of talent. Senator Samuel White of Delaware summed up the consequences of the improvident amendment: "Character, talents, virtue, and merit will not be sought after, in the candidate. The question will not be asked, is he capable? Is he honest? But can he by his name, by his connexions [sic], best promote the election of a President?" Roger Griswold of Connecticut declared that the vice presidency was now "worse than useless," while other political leaders suggested abolishing the office altogether. Senator Jonathan Dayton observed that the reasons for creating the vice presidency were "frustrated by the amendment." It would be "preferable," he said, "to abolish the office."[12] The effort, however, failed by 19-12 in the Senate and by 85-27 in the House.

Many of these bleak predictions proved prophetic. After Adams, Jefferson, and Burr, the vice presidency became the resting place of inconsequential figures. Few could recall George Clinton and Daniel Tompkins, both New Yorkers, who served with easy indifference under Jefferson, Madison, and Monroe. John C. Calhoun's vice presidency stood in contrast to his immediate predecessors. The able and ambitious South Carolinian never ceased coveting the presidency, but his support for nullification effectively killed his chances for the office. In 1836, his successor and rival, Martin Van Buren, became the first vice president since Jefferson to win the presidency in his own right.[13]

In April 1841, John Tyler claimed the presidency when William Henry Harrison died a month after his inauguration, raising a potential constitutional crisis over the unprecedented question of succession. In the matter of succession, it remained unclear whether the Constitution provided for the vice president to serve in a caretaking capacity until another election could be held or whether he inherited the full powers of the office. Former President John Quincy Adams declared that Tyler's power grab violated both the "grammar and context of the Constitution." After all, no one ever intended, much less elected, Tyler for the executive chair. Nevertheless, Tyler took the oath of office, declaring himself president. Despite efforts at impeachment, his critics ultimately yielded to the fait accompli, and no one protested nine years later when Zachary Taylor died and was succeeded by Vice President Millard Fillmore.[14] The precedent of presidential succession received constitutional sanction in 1967, more than a century later when the states ratified the Twenty-fifth Amendment.[15]

The vice presidency remained an invisible office throughout the rest of the nineteenth century. Vice presidents were rarely invited to attend cabinet meetings or consulted on executive policies. A few vice presidents, including George Dallas, Levi Morton, and Garret Hobart, took their duties seriously, studying the Senate's rules and precedents and presiding effectively over the chamber. Most others like Henry Wilson, Grant's second vice president, spent his days as he wished. Wilson devoted his time to writing a three-volume history of slavery before dying in his Capitol office. Clinton, Gerry, Thomas A. Hendricks, and Hobart also died in office. William R. King, nominated as vice president with Franklin Pierce, was known to be in failing health, dying just six weeks after taking the oath of office. Few seemed to notice or even care.[16]

Anonymous and marginalized, vice presidents rarely became the chief executive on their own. Few men of stature sought to occupy the invisible office. Twenty-one vice presidents held the office between 1805 and 1899, but only Martin Van Buren won the presidency in his own right. Four others ascended to the White House following the death of elected chief executives. But their presidencies accomplished little. None received their party's nomination to seek an independent full term.[17] The "Vice Presidency was nothing," wrote Arthur Schlesinger, Jr.[18] It was "not a stepping stone to anything but oblivion," said Theodore Roosevelt after accepting the vice presidential nomination in 1900.[19]

EARLY TWENTIETH CENTURY

The vice presidency gradually gained stature in the twentieth century. The century's first vice president, Theodore Roosevelt, added luster to the office not seen since Calhoun. Roosevelt, who coveted the presidency, had no use for the second office. But Republican leaders convinced him he would enliven and bring stature to McKinley's campaign. Once ensconced, however, he hoped to use his term to study law.[20] He only had to endure six months of "oblivion" before McKinley caught an assassin's bullet in September 1901, propelling him into the White House. When he obtained a vice president of his own, Roosevelt showed little respect when it came to Charley Fairbanks. He entertained Washington with Finley Peter Dunne's witticism when remarking that he was going down in a submarine: "You really shouldn't do it—unless you take Fairbanks with you."[21]

Woodrow Wilson's vice president, Thomas Marshall, was quick to ridicule his own predicament. He once told the story of a woman who had two sons. One ran off to sea and the other became vice president. And neither was ever heard of again. On another occasion, he compared the predicament of a vice president to a "man in a cataleptic state: he cannot speak; he cannot move; he suffers no pain; and yet he is perfectly conscious of everything that is going on about him."[22] Marshall had more to do than most of his predecessors, presiding over the cabinet while Wilson negotiated the peace treaty in Versailles. But when Wilson suffered a debilitating stroke, Marshall dreaded inheriting the presidency either through Wilson's death or a congressional effort to replace the ailing president. Concerned that resignation would further incapacitate her husband, Mrs. Wilson assumed some of the president's clerical and administrative responsibilities without informing Marshall.[23]

On the whole, the vice presidency remained an office of great tedium until Franklin D. Roosevelt. The vast restructuring of the economy under the New Deal and America's emergence as a dominant world power during and after World War II perhaps inevitably raised the importance of the office. John Nance Garner, a former speaker of the house, exercised greater responsibilities than his predecessors—attending cabinet meetings, acting as legislative liaison to the Senate, and becoming the first vice president to travel abroad as the president's representative when he attended the inauguration of Manuel Quezon as president of the Philippines in 1935. Garner later won a degree of fame for telling vice presidential hopeful Lyndon Johnson more than twenty years later that the office "was not worth a pitcher of warm spit."[24] Roosevelt gave greater responsibilities to his second vice president, Henry A. Wallace. He not only chaired the Board of Economic Warfare and the Supply Priorities and Allocations Board, but also served on the Advisory Committee on Atomic Energy. Further, he served as Roosevelt's envoy to Latin America, Russia, and China. Both Garner and Wallace ran afoul of Roosevelt or his advisors. Garner openly opposed Roosevelt seeking a third term, viewing the New Deal as too liberal, and challenged Roosevelt for the 1940 nomination. Wallace not only clashed with powerful Roosevelt aides, but Secretary of State Cordell Hull opposed his involvement in foreign affairs. Moreover, Wallace had few friends in the Senate, limiting his influence in the chamber.[25]

Perhaps owing to these unhappy circumstances or his own illness, Roosevelt gave his third vice president, Harry S. Truman, little to do. Aware of Roosevelt's illness and initially loath to take the vice presidency, Truman remarked to a reporter that those who had succeeded dead presidents were scorned in office, had their hearts broken, and lost any semblance of respect in the public arena. "I don't want that to happen to me."[26] Before the president's death after just eighty-three days in office, Truman met with the president a few times, mostly about Senate affairs. He also attended cabinet meetings, "not that Roosevelt ever did much at his cabinet meetings," Truman recalled.[27] On the whole, he was kept in the dark—including the Allies' plans for the postwar world and the development of the atomic bomb. Truman brought his own vice president, Alben Barkley, a former Senate majority leader, more into the loop, inviting him to meetings of the cabinet. Moreover, with passage of the National Security Act of 1947, Congress made him a statutory member of the new National Security Council (NSC), the leading group that advised the president on national security matters. For the first time, the vice president, by law, became involved in formulating policy at the highest levels in the executive branch.[28]

EVOLUTION OF THE MODERN VICE PRESIDENCY

The vice presidency underwent its first real evolutionary leap during the Eisenhower administration. The office not only won more institutional responsibilities, but also higher visibility and respectability. In 1956, the *Congressional Quarterly* noted that the vice presidency had "reached its highest stage of development during the incumbency of Richard M. Nixon." Like his immediate predecessors, Nixon met with the cabinet and the NSC. But unlike them, he served as chairman in the president's absence, outranking the department secretaries. Eisenhower allowed Nixon to serve as a political advisor on matters ranging from dealings with Congress, to Senator Joseph McCarthy, to helping to resolve the 1959 steel strike. At Eisenhower's request, moreover, Nixon undertook the unenviable task of investigating allegations of misconduct by the president's White House chief of staff.[29]

Nixon also took the administration's case to the country and was a tireless campaigner for the Republican Party. In the 1954 congressional elections, he campaigned in 95 cities in 31 states, delivered 204 speeches, and met with the press more than 100 times—all in a period of 48 days. When it came to campaigning and defending the administration's positions, he served as an effective partisan, but critics denounced him as a "hatchet man." His foreign visits to fifty-four countries in eight years set a record for vice presidential travel and whetted his already growing interest in foreign affairs. Two were notable. In the spring of 1958, during a tour of Latin America, the motorcade taking Nixon and his wife to Caracas was attacked by a mob armed with rocks and pipes. The following year, Nixon engaged in the memorable "kitchen debate" with Soviet premier Nikita S. Krushchev at an American industrial and cultural exposition at Sokolniki Park in Moscow. Later broadcast on American television, the lively debate bolstered Nixon's Cold War credentials as an ardent anticommunist.[30]

Eisenhower also named Nixon to chair a president's commission to end racial discrimination in companies that held government contracts and a cabinet committee to formulate polices to tame inflation. Neither panel had much of a budget and enforcement power.[31] Nixon evidently held these assignments in low regard, ignoring them in his books and only mentioning them in passing in an extensive interview on his years as vice president.[32] The vice presidency may have risen in stature, but it still had no authority. Still, Nixon used his assignments creatively to become the most visible vice president in history. More than any of his predecessors, Nixon understood the potential of the office, especially in the new age of television and air travel. From debating Krushchev to collecting political IOUs, he used the office so artfully that he became the first sitting vice president in 100 years to be nominated as a presidential candidate. The office once again, since the time of Adams and Jefferson, became a useful springboard to the Oval Office.

Lyndon Johnson hoped to transform the office when he accepted the vice presidential nomination in 1960. Presiding over the Senate and casting rare tie-breaking votes was not his idea of how to achieve a record to win the presidency. But Johnson's plan to make himself a powerful vice president ran into overwhelming obstacles. Within days of taking office, Johnson proposed that Kennedy sign an executive order providing the vice president authority over several agencies as well as directing cabinet heads and department chiefs to give him copies of all documents provided to the president. Kennedy turned aside the power grab, but nevertheless saw Johnson as a useful political ally.

To mollify Johnson's enormous ego, Kennedy tried giving him the trappings of power. While rejecting Johnson's request for an office next to the president's, Kennedy assigned him a six-room suite on the second floor of the Executive Office Building next to the White House. Kennedy also invited Johnson to attend cabinet meetings, weekly sessions with House and Senate leaders, prepress conference hearings, and NSC meetings, as required by law. He named Johnson to head the new Committee on Equal Employment Opportunity (CEEO), chair the National Aeronautics and Space Council (NASC), and represent the president on trips abroad.[33] The president also sought Johnson's views on legislative and political problems, went out of his way to keep the vice president informed, and relied on Johnson's advice on civil rights. Johnson's push for a massive job-training and vocational education program convinced Kennedy to include it in his proposals.[34]

The vice president was seldom happy, however. He railed against the president for not relying enough on his legislative expertise on the Hill. He also had little use for making symbolic visits abroad. He complained that his activities in chairing the CEEO and the NASC would undercut his chances for the presidency. Kennedy attached vital importance to both issues, even if Johnson felt distinctly relegated to a secondary role. Besides these jobs, he had few formal assignments. Nevertheless, Kennedy imbued Johnson and the vice presidency with prestige by associating both with two of the most crucial issues of the day. If nothing else, Johnson's unhappy experience to expand the powers of the vice presidency proved that only the president had the transformative powers to enhance or diminish the vice presidency in the executive branch.

In November 1963, Johnson inherited the presidency after Kennedy's assassination, winning reelection in 1964. Johnson graced his vice president, Hubert H. Humphrey, with numerous responsibilities, even if some were trivial. The former Minnesota senator chaired a number of presidential councils, but these assignments did little to vest prestige in the office. Humphrey nevertheless energetically pursued them, promoting jobs for youths and the domestic travel and marine programs. While Humphrey's efforts were effective, his assignments never involved him in the major issues of the day. Humphrey also served as a political advisor, if only contributing intermittently to decision making or according to the whim of Johnson. Although Johnson occasionally invited Humphrey to the Oval Office for lengthy discussions, at other times the vice president was ignored, left out of important councils where major policy decisions were reached. Nonetheless, Johnson often relied on Humphrey's counsel on civil rights and on serving as a liaison to the civil rights community. But he played only a small role in deciding what to do about the escalating war in Vietnam, despite offering his advice in person and in memoranda. One of Johnson's press secretaries, George Christian, wrote that the "critical decisions on the war were made at the 'Tuesday lunch' and supplemental meetings, especially in the last two years of the Johnson Administration. Humphrey was only rarely a participant in these sessions."[35] Humphrey's experience proved a truism that applied to predecessors and successors alike—that the vice presidency was the creature or supplicant of the president. He had as much power and prestige as the president was willing to give him. Or, as Humphrey said: "The vice president will be and is what the president wants him to be. . . ."[36]

EMERGENCE OF A STRONG VICE PRESIDENCY

On the whole, the vice president remained outside the president's inner circle until the groundbreaking tenure of former Minnesota Senator Walter Mondale, who became a major policy advisor in the Oval Office. Mondale's predecessor, Nelson Rockefeller, also gained entry into the president's inner circle when Ford named him to lead the Domestic Council. In appointing Rockefeller vice chairman of the Domestic Council, the president placed him at the fulcrum of domestic policy making. But the assignment caused a backlash and the vice president fell victim to palace politics. Carter, however, considerably bolstered the statutory importance of the vice presidency by signing an executive order making the vice president second in the chain of command for the control of nuclear weapons, a responsibility that had rested with the secretary of state since 1958. The prestige of the office took another leap due to the remarkable compatibility between the two. Carter understood that previous forlorn marriages between presidents and vice presidents had produced little but strained relations, if not discord. He also knew that past vice presidents had been undermined by presidential aides and that the talents of leading political figures like Humphrey and Rockefeller had been utterly wasted in office.

Carter intended to make Mondale, who had more Washington experience, a fuller partner in his administration. The president gave Mondale an office inside the West Wing, the first time since Spiro Agnew, and integrated the staffs of the president and vice president into a working team. The proximity of the vice president's office next to the president's proved significant, as one vice presidential aide observed, since "Mondale didn't have to beg anyone to visit him in the West Wing." Further, Mondale brought his Senate staff with him and placed two of his aides at the number two posts at the national security and domestic councils. These moves assured his access to key information rather than having to rely solely on Carter's presidential aides. The granting of greater powers to the vice president, however, stirred resentment among some in the administration. Attorney General Griffin Bell complained that moving Mondale into the White House had been a mistake, providing the vice president too much influence in shaping the administration's policies. "He managed to do this because of his physical location in the West Wing of the White House," Bell said, "and because of placing some close aides in crucial posts in the policy-making apparatus."[37]

As part of Carter's inner circle, Mondale evaded many of the miseries of his predecessors. He avoided the minor functions, presidential commissions, and specific assignments with their false trappings of significance. From the beginning he worked on strengthening his advisory role to the president and focused on influencing internal White House operations as a generalist and troubleshooter. In this way, Mondale pioneered a new vice presidential role as a general advisor to the president.[38] Mondale was invited to attend all scheduled meetings, received the same daily intelligence information that the president got, and met routinely with senior staff and the NSC. The president and vice president also held private luncheons one day each week to discuss policy matters. Carter made sure that Mondale and his staff were never isolated from policy discussions. So protective was the president toward Mondale that he threatened to fire any staffer who assailed the vice president.

Carter heeded Mondale's advice on reversing spending cuts, establishing the Department of Education, and attempting to reach accommodation with the Soviet Union. Mondale also influenced policy on everything from decisions about the Shah of Iran and the American hostages in Tehran, to policies on electoral reform, job training, and hospital costs. If nothing else, the power of vice presidency derived solely from the bonds of trust established with the president, not from any inherent statutory or constitutional authority. In a constitutional democracy, it was perhaps odd that the authority of the second office would be held wholly hostage to such presidential whim. The office may have leapt in power and prestige, but it remained the president's to decide whether the vice presidency would be strong or weak, meaningful or utterly insignificant, depending on his own personal and capricious inclinations.

Although historically the vice presidency had been considered "everything from a spare tire to a pitcher of warm spit," Al Gore raised the office to unprecedented heights. Before Gore agreed to be Bill Clinton's running mate in 1992, he had risen rapidly in Congress, first by winning his father's old House seat in central Tennessee in 1976, then moving to the Senate in 1984 and winning reelection in 1990 by a landslide. In 1988, he made a respectable, if premature, run for the Democratic nomination. When Gore accepted the vice presidential nomination, he saw the office as a springboard to the White House. The success of his vice presidency depended on his strong chemistry with the president. In June 1992, when Clinton interviewed Senator Gore about joining him on the Democratic ticket, the two formed a fast bond, seeing the campaign and issues in the same light.[39]

After they won in November, but before the inaugural, Clinton set out to make his running mate a full partner in his administration. Representatives of the two worked out an unprecedented agreement that spelled out a degree of shared responsibility. The codification of their partnership amounted to a reinvention of the vice presidency. The agreement carried no legal authority, but the president stood by its terms. Clinton granted Gore enormous policy and personnel responsibilities. On taking office, Gore exerted considerable sway over environmental and technology policy. He headed the administration's reinventing government initiative to cut red tape and improve efficiency. He also assumed a prominent diplomatic role with Russia and the former Soviet republics, venturing beyond serving as a mere envoy to ceremonial events abroad. He named his principle advisors throughout the executive branch, developed the Telecommunications Act of 1996, winning congressional support to pass it, and built support for the North American Free Trade Agreement (NAFTA). He met with the president routinely, was in the information loop, and was considered one of the three power centers in the White House, next to the president and the First Lady. The opinions of Hillary Clinton and Gore were the only ones that seemed to count. "You always knew whether it was an important meeting when you saw whether Hillary and the vice president were there or not," said Robert Reich, the former labor secretary. "They were the president's two top advisors and everybody else played second fiddle. If they were there, it was an important meeting. If they weren't, it wasn't."[40]

Secretary of State Warren Christopher declared him "the most influential vice president in history." After just two years in office, the relationship between Clinton and Gore had deepened to where the president did not make any decision of significance without him. "I cannot imagine the president making a major decision before talking it through with the vice president," former presidential advisor George Stephanopoulos said at the time. He also served as the administration's quintessential troubleshooter and earned a reputation in the State Department as a leading player in foreign affairs. His active foreign policy role stemmed from Clinton's lack of passion for international affairs and Christopher's willingness to give up some of his authority to other agencies, leaving openings for Gore to conduct diplomacy.[41]

Many of Gore's breakthroughs for the vice presidency—negotiating the reach of his powers, assuming an important role in foreign affairs, and placing aides in influential positions—set new precedents or patterns for the office. Mondale had moved the vice president's office into the West Wing of the White House in proximity to the president's office, something that Johnson had failed to do and that had been taken away from Agnew. But Mondale did not have the broad influence exercised by Gore, who according to Paul Light, an expert on vice presidential power, had succeeded in "extending the model [of the office] to its ultimate degree." Gore was loyal to his boss, but he nevertheless cultivated his own power. One senior official called him "the strongest and steadiest advisor that the president has."[42]

The vice presidency had come a long way since the end of World War II. In many cases, vice presidents became the presumptive front runners of their party's presidential nomination. With the exception of Dan Quayle, the eight postwar vice presidents who pursued their party's nomination had won it. The office provided those seeking the highest office the opportunity of early fund raising and organization building. Their activities as party leaders, election campaigners, fund-raisers, and public advocates for the administration's policies enabled them to win friends among political activists who dominated the nominating process. Beyond positioning its inhabitants for the Oval Office, the vice presidency had become institutionalized, growing larger, more prominent, and attracting people of stature. From the mid-1970s when vice presidents resided in the Old Executive Office Building, arranged their own housing, and went begging for speech writers at the White House, the vice presidency had matured to enjoy a large and professional staff, a West Wing office, a separate line item in the executive budget, and an official residence at the Admiral's House at the Naval Observatory. Vice presidential activities also had become far more substantial. Not only did vice presidents now routinely hold private sessions with presidents, but also attended cabinet and NSC meetings. They received full intelligence briefings and access to presidential information. They lobbied on behalf of administration policies and programs, assumed leadership in the political party second only to the president, and carried out sensitive diplomatic missions. They served as important presidential advisors and liaisons to Congress and public interest groups.

The office remained a creature of the presidency, however. The position had risen in prestige, assuming newly engrained patterns of responsibilities and becoming more an executive rather than a legislative branch office, but it ultimately relied on the president's transformative powers to elevate or diminish the office. In the final analysis, the evolution of the office had shown that the vice presidency was what the president wanted it to be. "The vice president will be and is what the president wants him to be," Humphrey had said.

In a sense, nothing more demonstrated this principle than the vice presidency of Richard B. Cheney, who far surpassed his predecessors in power and influence in the administration of George W. Bush. By the time Cheney took office, the vice presidency had certainly assumed greater importance in the operations of the presidency. But Cheney proceeded to make the assertion of sweeping executive powers and the establishment of an imperial vice presidency the hallmarks of the George W. Bush presidency. The dramatic elevation of vice presidential authority derived from the president's inclination to delegate broad swaths of his presidential powers to his more experience deputy. When he became vice president, Cheney repeatedly spoke of his agenda of restoring the lost powers of the presidency by rolling back the unwise limits imposed by Congress after Vietnam and Watergate. The full measure of his views on executive supremacy not only had been forged by his experiences during the Nixon and Ford administrations, but also by his experience in the Democratically controlled Congress throughout most of the 1980s and in the wartime administration of George H.W. Bush as secretary of defense.

Following the September 11, 2001, terrorist attacks, Cheney became the lead agent on issues of national security and executive power. The 9/11 attacks transformed his vice presidency, already powerful, into the center of a white-hot debate over the administration's aggressive conduct of the war on terrorism and the dramatic expansion of presidential powers. The two issues were inextricably linked. Cheney believed that the United States was at a pivotal point in history, requiring a powerful commander in chief to combat the global scourge of global terrorism. "This is a battle," he had said, "for the future of civilization."[43] After the terrorist attacks, Cheney quickly emerged as the ideal wartime *consigliere* for the president. A hardened veteran of the executive branch with an encyclopedic knowledge of national security, he was able to take center stage in an administration led by an inexperienced president willing to delegate many details to his subordinates. Such circumstances gave him an enormous opportunity to work his will. Yet, his journey from being an affable, easygoing staffer in the Nixon White House to a powerful, hardened ideologue in the George W. Bush administration explains much about how he managed to transform a once modest post into an imperial vice presidency.

Two

The Nixon and Ford
Administrations

Cheney's march to the vice presidency began in 1968 when he won a fellowship from the American Political Science Association, which brought him to the staff of Congressman Bill Steiger, a Wisconsin Republican. Steiger first won election to the House in 1966 at the age of twenty-eight, becoming the youngest member of Congress. Although a Republican, Steiger became one of the leading power brokers in the overwhelmingly Democratic House. Cheney began his internship on January 3, 1969, just three weeks before the inauguration of Richard Nixon. On the same day, Steiger was sworn in for his second term. He involved the young intern in most operations of his office. Cheney's passion for politics, work ethic, and efficiency made a fast impression on Steiger, who wrote the executive director of the American Political Science Association that he was "exceptionally pleased with the help of Dick Cheney." Steiger and Cheney were roughly the same age, only three years apart. As the two became close friends, Steiger gave the congressional fellow considerable responsibility, making him virtually a staff aide. Steiger's most important committee assignment involved the committee on Health, Education, and Welfare (HEW), which oversaw the new giant federal agency created as part of President Lyndon Johnson's War on Poverty. From the time that it was recognized as a major political and social phenomenon in 1964, experts viewed urban poverty as an affliction that could be cured with massive infusions of jobs, education, goodwill, and welfare programs. Johnson's New Society program represented the kind of big government program that ran against the small-government, free-market philosophy of the Republican Party. As soon as 1970, much of the euphoria of the mid-1960s had waned with the recognition that urban poverty would be an enduring fact of American life. While working with Steiger's staff on HEW issues, Cheney received his first meaningful education regarding dealing with a major federal agency.[1]

Cheney soon caught the attention of Donald Rumsfeld, a former fighter pilot and four-term Republican congressman from the fashionable 13th District of Illinois north of Chicago who had just been named in April 1969 to run the Office of Economic Opportunity (OEO).[2] Like the HEW, the agency arose out of Johnson's War on Poverty. Johnson created the agency as a cabinet-level agency within the White House to signal its importance and assure its executive-level accountability. The agency intended to replace the ineffective state and municipal programs aimed at assisting the poor with a federal program that provided grants directly to community-based programs.[3] Cheney wrote an unsolicited memorandum to Rumsfeld, a friend of Steiger's, providing advice for his upcoming confirmation hearings. The strategy memo was "pretty nervy," Cheney recalled, "full of advice on what he ought to do, how he ought to conduct himself during the congressional hearings."[4] Steiger gave it to Rumsfeld who regarded it so favorably that he appointed Cheney as his executive assistant, beginning a political and ideological collaboration that would help educate Cheney in the ways of Washington.

Cheney accepted Rumsfeld's offer to be his assistant as the Nixon administration was seeking greater executive control over federal agencies, including the OEO. The agency's antipoverty programs were proving increasingly unpopular among conservatives, who accused it of inefficiency, political favoritism, and corruption. In 1970, *Newsweek* declared that for all the agency's good intentions for waging the war on poverty, the OEO amounted to a "costly, inefficient hydra that had been … marked for starvation by [President] Nixon."[5] Nixon singled it out for criticism during the 1968 presidential election and, after winning the presidency, wanted to abolish the agency. Conservatives particularly targeted the OEO's Office of Legal Services, which was created to provide free assistance to the poor. Soon after being established, the agency's poverty lawyers began prosecuting high-profile class action suits on behalf of minority groups. The successful suits against local, state, and federal agencies, police departments, corporations, and others angered Republicans and their donors who viewed the poverty lawyers as "tax-funded radicals." It was a problem and Nixon wanted Rumsfeld to fix it.[6]

In 1969, Nixon had given Rumsfeld the titles of director of the Office of Economic Opportunity and special assistant to the president. As the director of OEO, Nixon expected Rumsfeld to reorganize it out of existence. "The president sent Rumsfeld there to close it down," remembered Christine Todd Whitman, who began her political career at OEO and later became governor of New Jersey and administrator of the Environmental Protection Agency. "Some of us thought the programs were worth saving, but we were all aware that the agency's time was limited."[7] As one of his first policy moves, in 1969, Rumsfeld appointed Terry Lenzer, a twenty-nine-year-old former federal prosecutor and civil rights attorney, to run the Office of Legal Services. By this time, the office employed more than 2,000 lawyers in 850 neighborhood law offices around the country. Lenzer brought considerable energy to his job as chief of the OEO's legal services arm. He hoped to accelerate law reform in welfare, housing, health, consumer fraud, and municipal services. He stirred excitement among the agency's poverty lawyers by his intention to be an advocate on behalf of the poor inside the government.[8]

Lenzer's idealism and refusal to politicize the office, however, proved a political embarrassment for Rumsfeld. With Legal Service lawyers winning major cases on behalf of migrants, Southern blacks, Appalachian Whites, coal miners, Eskimos, and others, Lenzer drew fire from top White House aides— White House chief of staff H. R. Haldeman and domestic advisor John Ehrlichman—to purge attorneys who were aggressively prosecuting cases. The aides also criticized Rumsfeld for not doing enough to dismantle the agency's antipoverty programs and rein in Lenzer, who was resisting his boss's efforts to reorganize the OEO's legal services arm and gut the program.[9]

The reorganization plan called for shifting authority for hiring, funding, and policy direction from Lenzer, the national legal services director, to OEO's ten regional nonlawyer directors. When one of Lenzer's staff leaked word of the plan, it ignited opposition from the legal profession, including the staid American Bar Association—hardly the voice of radicalism. Critics charged that the plan aimed to politicize and destroy the program; it would subject field directors to powerful interests in their home states to quash controversial lawsuits on behalf of the poor. "The principle that we're fighting for is that the poor should have justice just as equal as those who can pay," said Maynard J. Toll, president of the National Legal Aid and Defender Association and a member on the Legal Services' Advisory Board. Regional OEO officials, he said, were more likely to waver on this principle than lawyers insulated from political pressures. With the public storm surrounding the proposal, Rumsfeld tried to defend it, but the reorganization plan was ultimately scuttled.[10]

Lenzer's days were numbered after the blowup. Nixon had been pressuring Rumsfeld to purge disloyal officials with the aim of exerting greater political control over the federal government—a message not lost on Cheney.

As Rumsfeld increasingly made his way into the inner councils of the White House as special assistant to the president, Cheney stepped in to assume greater responsibility at the OEO. He showed an aptitude as an efficient and strong manager. Skeptical about the legal services office, Cheney let Lenzer know that neither he nor anyone else at the White House supported his activism.[11]

After the midterm elections in November 1970, the OEO's morale problems came to a head when Rumsfeld summoned Lenzer and his deputy, Frank Jones, to his office. With Cheney at his side, Rumsfeld fired them both, later explaining to the press that the two were "either unwilling or unable" to carry out his policies and were exceeding their authority. Lenzer shot back that Rumsfeld and the Nixon administration were "caving into the political interests . . . who are determined to keep us from suing special interests close to them on behalf of the poor."[12] The incident drew fierce political criticism, made worse, reported a news weekly, after Rumsfeld was "caught misleading a Senate subcommittee about his plans to lessen the impact of OEO's legal activities." But Cheney—largely anonymous to the press—evaded the scathing criticism. By this time, Rumsfeld with Cheney as his executive assistant had already considerably reduced OEO's power. The Job Corps and Head Start had been spun off to two cabinet departments, and another poverty program, VISTA, was under review to be abolished entirely. For the young aide, the experiences at the OEO represented a step in his political education in how a president could impose his will over an insurgent federal bureaucracy supported by Congress.[13]

At the end of December 1970, Nixon appointed Rumsfeld full-time to his own staff as a presidential counselor, signaling his rising influence. At the time, he said that he would do anything Nixon wanted him to do. "If he wants me to do things," Rumsfeld said, "I do them."[14] One year later in December 1971, Nixon named him head of the Cost of Living Council (CLC), an agency created to tame inflation with wage and price controls. In the summer of 1971, inflation was spiking along with the concerns of American voters. Nixon presented an economic plan calling for domestic tax cuts, tax hikes on imports, abandoning the gold standard for the dollar, and freezing all prices and wages across the U.S. economy. The freeze comprised an antimarket plan for an administration that stood ideologically opposed to government intrusion. Nixon created the CLC to monitor the freeze, which was anticipated to be short-lived.[15] Cheney passed up a job at the Nixon reelection campaign to accept Rumsfeld's offer to be his director of operations at the CLC, monitoring the enforcement of wage and price controls. But as the program fell into chaos and politics, Cheney grew frustrated with the futility of trying to regulate wages and prices in an economy as vast as America's. He later recalled that he had become a "great skeptic about the whole notion of wage-price controls." The idea that "you could write detailed regulations that were going to govern all aspects of an economy as big as the U.S. economy [was] loopy," he said. The experience, he later recalled, moved him "radically in the free-market direction" and convinced him of "the importance of limited government."[16]

After repeatedly clashing with Haldeman and Ehrlichman, Rumsfeld asked Nixon for a foreign assignment. Nixon obliged, naming him the envoy to NATO in December 1972. Cheney declined his patron's offering to be his deputy in Brussels, forgoing the chance to gain foreign policy experience. For a brief period, Cheney's fate ran separate from his political and ideological mentor. With two daughters to support and his wife teaching at George Washington University, Cheney joined Bradley Woods, a small consulting firm in Washington. For eighteen months he mostly prepared research papers on Nixon's economic program and the energy business, while watching from afar as Nixon battled Congress over assertions of executive power and the disintegration of his presidency.[17]

While Nixon once appeared invulnerable, observed Henry Kissinger, his secretary of state and national security advisor, the president could do little to hold back the disclosures of his abuse of power—the "details of the original Watergate break-in and wiretapping; the burglary of the office of Daniel Ellsberg's psychiatrist; the cover-up; the use of government investigative agencies to harass political opponents; and the juvenile escapades, such as the so-called enemies list...."[18] Kissinger later recalled that the disintegration of the presidency had rendered Nixon into "stunned lethargy." At a time when he should have been at the "height of his success," everything now "was crashing around him." Nixon was increasingly being put on trial before the court of public opinion, the television cameras, and the nation's free institutions—the courts and Congress. He had been battling the release of selected tape recordings to the special prosecutor and congressional investigating committees. After Alexander Butterfield, a White House staffer, revealed the existence of the president's secret taping system in July 1973, it necessarily placed Nixon in the position of withholding evidence that "on the face of it could settle the various allegations once and for all." From then on, Nixon's fight to withhold evidence from the congressional investigating committees and the judiciary under the cloak of executive privilege and the separation of powers became the critical issue.[19]

At the same time, as the cancer of Watergate grew, Congress sought to curb Nixon's claims of executive power, passing laws that ordered him to stop the bombing campaigns in Laos and Cambodia. Even earlier, congressional members were already working on a measure to restrain Nixon's war powers, believing that the Vietnam tragedy stemmed from a usurpation of the war power by the president. After waging a three-year effort, Congress passed the War Powers Act in 1973 over Nixon's veto to reduce presidential discretion in committing American military forces. The law required the president to notify Congress whenever American troops were being committed to combat. It called for the troops to be withdrawn from foreign territory within 60 days unless Congress explicitly gave approval for them to remain. The act marked the worst legislative setback in Nixon's five years in office and was the first time in history that Congress had spelled out the war-making powers of the Congress and the president. The White House denounced the measure, declaring that it "seriously undermined this nation's ability to act decisively and convincingly in times of international crisis."[20]

Amid another war decades later, Cheney would characterize this era as the "low point" of executive power, denouncing the War Powers Resolution as unconstitutional because it made an overreaching "change in the institutional arrangements" between the legislative and executive branches. "I don't think you should restrict the president's authority to deploy military forces because of the Vietnam experience," he said.[21] With the constitutional crisis surrounding Watergate and public demands to end the war, Congress was just beginning to assert its constitutional powers in order to restrain an unfettered presidency. Then, on July 24, 1974, a unanimous Supreme Court ordered Nixon to turn over sixty-four tapes to special Watergate prosecutor Leon Jaworski. One of those recordings was the "smoking gun" tape of June 23, 1972, which implicated Nixon in the Watergate conspiracy and forced him to resign under threat of impeachment. The ruling marked a blow to the imperial presidency. Besides leading to Nixon's presidential ruin, the importance of the ruling lay in the principle that the judiciary had the final word in defining the reach of presidential power. Nixon had been claiming virtually unlimited authority, especially regarding national security, and that this power gave him the right to withhold his tape recordings even from criminal judicial proceedings. But the Court ruled that while the president was owed considerable deference, he was not above the law. Perhaps most important, the ruling "illustrated a crucial purpose for the separation of powers, and for the checks and balances it was devised to provide."[22]

CHENEY ENTERS THE FORD ADMINISTRATION

On the evening of August 8, 1974, Nixon gave a televised resignation speech to the nation, becoming the only American president in history to resign. That same evening, Cheney received an overseas call from Rumsfeld's secretary in Brussels asking him to meet his former boss at Dulles Airport in northern Virginia the next day. Rumsfeld's secretary gave no explanation, but Cheney understood that his career in public life was linked to Rumsfeld's and that it was about to enter a new phase in the administration of Gerald R. Ford. Rumsfeld, then still the NATO ambassador, was vacationing in Italy when he was asked by Philip Buchen, soon to be Ford's White House counsel, to lead the change in administrations. Soon after heading up the transition team on the ruins of the Nixon presidency, Ford made him White House chief of staff—or staff coordinator—after briefly considering him for vice president. Rumsfeld again hired his ambitious protégé to be his deputy and introduced him to the workings of the inner sanctum of the White House.[23]

The day following Rumsfeld's acceptance to be de facto chief of staff, he offered Cheney a power-sharing arrangement—part of his policy that everyone in the White House should have a deputy who could speak for him in his absence. The policy aimed to promote greater efficiency in the White House, and Cheney became not only Rumsfeld's deputy, but his alter ego. Cheney explained the nature of this arrangement years later in an interview with conservative journalist Stephen Hayes, a senior writer for the *Weekly Standard*: "The understanding when I took the job was that I would get access to the president and that I would be Rumsfeld's surrogate. When he wasn't around, I would be in a position to make decisions for him and to operate as though I had his job. We agreed at the outset that we would alternate trips. He would take one presidential trip and I would stay in the White House and run it; the next time, I'd go on the trip and he'd stay at the White House."[24] In this way, Rumsfeld gave his deputy frequent access to the president and to shared responsibility and power, which later prepared the way for Cheney's promotion as Rumsfeld's replacement.

Cheney assumed his initial post in the Ford administration at perhaps the nadir of the American modern presidency. The Watergate scandal had ignited a furious congressional backlash resulting in the passage of new laws to restore the balance of powers and check unbridled executive power. Cheney came to believe that these congressional actions had ensnarled the presidency in a web of regulation and laws that incapacitated its ability to move on matters of foreign policy.[25] From the White House's perspective, the presidency had become Gulliver in Lilliput, tied down with questionable laws and unable to act. For Cheney, the imperial presidency that reached its zenith under Nixon had been cut low and was now imperiled under Ford. Witnessing the erosion of presidential power "was a pivotal moment in the education of Dick Cheney," recalled David Gergen, a former White House staffer in the Ford administration. "Many of us felt strongly that the power of the presidency was threatened, that America could not lead in the world and couldn't get much done in Washington unless you had a more effective chief executive. Dick came out of that absolutely committed to the idea of restoring the powers of the presidency."[26] Indeed, it was a commitment that gathered increasing ideological force with Cheney's improbable but fateful march to become the nation's first imperial vice president.

Nonetheless, immediately following the nightmare of the Nixon years, President Ford himself became an active agent in curbing presidential powers with the aim of regaining the public trust. "For the first time in the memory of most people in Washington," reported the *New York Times* on August 17, 1974, "a President of the United States is actively seeking to restrain the prerogatives and power of his office." In his first days in office, Ford acted to reduce a staff swollen by his predecessors and to shift authority back to the cabinet. He also aimed to make the presidency more informal, open, and less imperial in tone and appearance. His intent was to reshape the office in substance and image to restore more of a balance of powers between the branches. He acted to assemble a more diverse cabinet with substantial but limited authority and a diverse staff in points of view and sensitive to congressional prerogatives. He also sought a less formal approach in making decisions with emphasis on free discussions instead of memorandums or conferences with limited participation. It represented a more traditional orientation that recalled the era before Johnson's use of the presidency's powers to wage war in Vietnam polarized the nation and the government.[27]

Ford's efforts to curb the executive drew considerable notice given his predecessor's aggressive moves to radically expand an already imperial presidency. During his presidency, Nixon sought to broaden and consolidate his powers on several fronts. Faced with what he considered a profligate Congress, Nixon transformed an occasional practice of former presidents into a tactic of confrontation. Presidents previously withheld appropriated funds mostly to defer, or spread out, spending rather than employing it as a political weapon to cut programs. Escalating budget deficits due to Johnson's Great Society programs and the Indochina war were raising concerns in Congress and the White House about the need to impose spending controls. Nixon's aggressive version of the impoundment tactic alarmed many in Congress, who considered it unprecedented in scope and severity—a power grab. During his 1972 reelection campaign, Nixon proposed that Congress give him unlimited authority to cut spending in whatever programs he chose. The request spurred fears not only that he would slash social programs treasured by liberals, but that it would constitute the greatest delegation ever to the president of Congress's constitutional authority to control spending. "The Constitutional right of the President of the United States to impound funds ... is absolutely clear," Nixon declared.[28] When Congress refused to grant him such expansive authority, Nixon claimed he had a presidential right of impoundment, withholding at least $15 billion by 1973—an astounding 20 percent of all discretionary spending. He also sought to abolish congressionally created programs by executive order. These and other actions outraged many members of Congress, who charged that Nixon aimed to strip the constitutional prerogative of the legislative branch over the power of the purse.[29]

Nixon also sought to dominate the federal bureaucracy of 2.5 million civil employees by placing a network of trusted loyalists in the cabinet and other key posts and directed by the Office of Management and Budget (OMB), a White House agency. He also moved to monopolize the regulatory agencies, created as arms of Congress, through appointing his ideological loyalists in posts throughout the government. As a further counterweight, he created a counter-bureaucracy in the Executive Office of the President (EOP), while expanding and empowering the White House staff. By 1972, the EOP grew to 5,600 employees compared to 1,400 in 1952. These moves aimed to counter the civil service-dominated agencies, which arose mostly under Democratic administrations. Nixon ran foreign policy through Kissinger and his National Security Council staff, while creating a parallel White House office, the Domestic Council, to oversee the domestic arena. With such actions, Nixon moved the modern presidency more dramatically than any of his predecessors toward creating all policy at the White House. Together with the secret air and land campaigns in Laos and Cambodia, domestic spying on protest groups, claims over the budgetary process, and other matters, many saw an unfettered and out-of-control presidency unmoored from the Constitution.[30]

After the Watergate disclosures, Congress forced Nixon to retreat on several fronts, including ending impoundments and adopting a more conciliatory stance. But the fundamental nature of his imperial presidency remained. He continued to set policy through the OMB and never granted much power or standing to Cabinet members who served as little more than administrators or figureheads. The president's large White House staff continued to reflect Nixon's reclusive nature and his preference for making decisions through formalized channels. The president's staff, which numbered a few assistants under Truman, expanded to about 500 under Nixon. This number did not include the OMB, whose own staff with administration-wide responsibilities comprised about 600. This was the apparatus that Ford inherited and wanted to alter, in part by restoring authority to the department heads to facilitate public access. By doing so, he hoped to restore the traditional system under which groups and congressional members could influence policy and obtain information about programs from the departments involved instead of through the more secretive executive offices of the president.[31]

But there was considerable skepticism about how far Ford was willing or how far he could go in reversing the decades-long gravitation of power to the White House. The Nixon years invited a sweeping indictment against the presidency on numerous counts—campaign sabotage, burglary, bribery, extortion, fraud, destruction of evidence, domestic espionage, obstruction of justice, and abuse of power involving everything from punishing political opponents with punitive tax audits, to withholding money appropriated by Congress, to secret air and ground warfare in Cambodia. The claims of unilateral authority in foreign affairs had pervaded and emboldened the domestic presidency, wrote Arthur M. Schlesinger, Jr., in his 1973 book, *The Imperial Presidency*. "The all-purpose invocation of 'national security,' the insistence on executive secrecy, the withholding of information from Congress, the refusal to spend funds appropriated by Congress, the attempted intimidation of the press, the use of the White House itself as a base for espionage and sabotage directed against the political opposition—all signified the extension of the imperial Presidency from foreign to domestic affairs." These actions, he contended, constituted a "revolutionary challenge to the separation of powers itself."[32]

In his first formal address to Congress on August 12, 1974, Ford tried to alleviate the great distrust surrounding the presidency by offering an olive branch. "As president, within the limits of basic principles, my motto towards the Congress is communication, conciliation, compromise, and cooperation," he said. While appreciating Ford's efforts at reconciliation, his administration was quickly overtaken by an emboldened Congress.[33] The congressional backlash against presidential power escalated just weeks after Ford assumed the presidency. On September 9, 1974, Ford gave ex-president Nixon a full and unconditional pardon, while the head of the General Services Administration, Arthur F. Sampson, signed an agreement giving Nixon title to his presidential tapes and records amid the continuing Watergate trials and investigations. The Nixon-Sampson agreement also allowed Nixon to destroy any of his furtive tape recordings after five years, with all of them to be destroyed after ten years or upon his death, whichever occurred first. These actions caused a furor on Capitol Hill, as well as among the press and large segments of the American public. The pardon and the Nixon-Sampson deal plunged Ford's month-old presidency deep into crisis, leading the *Wall Street Journal* to discern a "crisis of competence" and causing Ford to become the first president in memory to trigger a negative job rating by the end of his first month in office. Many of Ford's own supporters rued the timing of the pardon with the upcoming midterm elections. While the Senate passed a resolution urging the president to cease from issuing additional pardons until the judicial process had run its course, the House introduced more than a dozen bills and resolutions demanding an inquiry into Ford's actions. In Congress, there was also talk of a constitutional amendment to restrict the president's pardon power, as well as a short-lived movement to revive the impeachment process with the aim of compiling a record for posterity.[34]

CONGRESS ACTS AGAINST THE PRESIDENCY

Although Congress could do nothing to reverse the president's pardon of the disgraced ex-president—an act of supreme executive authority—it passed emergency legislation to abrogate the Nixon-Sampson deal. The Preservation Recordings and Materials Preservation Act directed the government to seize the former president's tapes and records for the continuing Watergate trials and investigations and to preserve them for posterity for fear he would create national amnesia regarding the worst deeds of his White House years. Accused of continuing Nixon's monumental cover-up, Ford's intentions of good will were overrun with suspicion and accusation. In a morose and defensive White House, even some among Ford's own staffers were beginning to think the worst. One stalwart Ford loyalist lamented that he "would not exclude the possibility that Ford made a verbal deal with Nixon for a pardon before Nixon resigned." Rumsfeld and Cheney had just entered the administration in their initial posts when Ford, seeking to calm the waters, agreed to testify before the House Judiciary Committee to explain his reasons for pardoning Nixon. The decision stunned not only congressional leaders, but also members of his White House staff. The departing chief of staff Al Haig pleaded with Ford not to humiliate the office of the presidency. The image of Ford humbling himself and the presidency before Congress made an indelible impression on Cheney who would always remember it. Ford's act offered "startling evidence" of just how far the imperial presidency had fallen from grace and the apex of power.[35]

In retrospect, Ford's pardon of Nixon helped the nation heal its divisions rather than prolong the Watergate episode with a long trial of the former president. But the act proved unwittingly disastrous for his administration and the Republican Party. What the Republicans "did not need," said a news magazine, "was precisely what Ford represented—the pardon of Richard Nixon and the resurrection of Watergate as a live issue in the campaign."[36] Across America, the Republicans labored amid a climate chilled by Watergate, inflation, recession, and an embittered discontent with politics.

The result was a landslide for the Democrats in the 1974 November mid-term elections. Ford had tried to exorcise the demons of Watergate and regain the public trust, but his party lost forty-eight seats in the House and five in the Senate, giving the already dominant Democrats a veto-proof majority. "When you screw up like we did, you have to pay the price," said one GOP strategist.[37] With the Republicans outgunned by virtually 2 to 1 in both chambers, an emboldened Congress embarked upon historic reforms that altered the balance of powers. A demoralized Ford administration could do little to hold back the sweeping legislative tide of reforms that aimed to constrain executive power. On matters involving war powers, government information, intelligence oversight, executive ethics, and impoundment, Congress reshaped the political landscape to imprison the executive and strengthen its own prerogatives. Cheney would never forget the spectacle of a weakened presidency in retreat before an activist Congress and would endeavor in the future to restore the lost executive powers of the Nixon administration.

The Ford administration's first major fight involved legislation to strengthen the Freedom of Information Act (FOIA). Passed in 1966, the law ushered in the great American experiment in open government. The landmark measure granted citizens the right to access all federal government information limited only by nine exemptions governing national security, private commercial or trade secrets, law enforcement, personal privacy, and other matters.[38] It represented a chink in the armor of the imperial presidency under Johnson, who signed the bill into law on July 4, 1966.[39] As a wave of openness swept over Washington, in early 1974 Congress introduced a bill to strengthen the FOIA, adding important provisions aimed at speeding up responses, providing for judicial review, reducing fees, and allowing the courts to review in camera classified information to determine whether it was being properly withheld under the law's nine exemptions. Following excessive delays and denials under the Johnson and Nixon administrations, Congress sought to bolster the law's effectiveness regarding the public's right to know and to serve as a bulwark against excessive government secrecy.[40] Even before Nixon's resignation, the House passed its version of the bill by the margin of 383 to 8, while the Senate's version passed by 64 to 7.[41] The overwhelming vote in favor of strengthening the key open government law indicated a major rejection of the pervasive secrecy of the Nixon administration. "We have seen too much secrecy in the past few years, and the American people are tired of it," said Democratic Senator Edward M. Kennedy of Massachusetts and a sponsor of the bill.[42]

After Nixon's resignation, Ford inherited the battle to bolster the freedom of information law. At first, Ford evinced reluctance at vetoing a measure that accorded with his aims to make the presidency more open and candid. But with the Cold War and national security ever present concerns, the bill drew immediate opposition from the major national security and intelligence agencies, the Pentagon, and the State Department. All of Ford's senior aides, including then-chief of staff Rumsfeld and even his deputy Dick Cheney, opposed the bill. The lone exception was Philip Buchen, the White House counsel and a longtime friend of the president.[43] Antonin Scalia, head of the Justice Department's Office of Legal Counsel and a future Supreme Court Justice, led the assault against the measure inside the administration. Scalia contended that the bill fundamentally violated the president's constitutional authority to protect information for purposes of national security and foreign policy. The act originally exempted national defense and foreign policy information, but one of the bill's seventeen provisions would permit a petitioner to ask a federal judge to review classified information to determine whether it should be made public. When vetoing the bill, Ford singled out this judicial review provision, among others, saying that it would damage national security and diplomatic relationships. The provision was seen as an unacceptable infringement on executive powers to classify and keep information secret. But in the aftermath of Watergate, these arguments made little headway with a hostile Congress that aimed to impose transparency and accountability on the executive branch. After Ford quashed the bill on October 17, 1974, both houses of Congress overrode his veto one month later. "There's a message to Ford," said Democratic Representative Wayne L. Hays of Ohio with bravado. "It is, get rid of some of those fellows who are giving you bum advice."[44]

As Ford struggled to develop policies that would regain public confidence, on December 22, 1974, Seymour M. Hersh of the *New York Times* published an explosive article that would undercut those efforts, prolong distrust in the presidency, and lead to a historic congressional investigation of the CIA's domestic intelligence activities. The article proved shocking for an agency that was born of the Cold War and that had been shielded by unprecedented governmental secrecy throughout most of its history. Before Hersh's revelations, the agency was already left vulnerable by recent disclosures about its involvement in Watergate and its role in the fall of the elected Marxist government in Chile. The article came just over a month after the Democrats won sweeping victories in the midterm elections, ushering in the most liberal Congress in memory. Citing "well-placed government sources," Hersh reported that the agency, "directly violating its charter," had conducted a "massive illegal domestic intelligence operation during the Nixon Administration against the antiwar movement and other dissident groups in the United States. . . ." The article charged that a special counterintelligence unit—reporting directly to Central Intelligence Agency (CIA) director Richard Helms—had compiled "files on at least 10,000 American citizens." Since the 1950s, said Hersh, the CIA also had engaged in "dozens of other illegal activities inside the United States, including break-ins, wiretapping, and the surreptitious inspection of mail." It was "highly coordinated," one *Times* source was quoted as saying. "People were targeted, information was collected on them, and it was all put on [computer] tape, just like the agency does with information about KGB agents."[45]

The chain of events leading to Hersh's expose began in early 1973 when Nixon appointed James R. Schlesinger as the new CIA director, replacing Richard Helms. After Schlesinger learned that operatives had carried out domestic break-ins on behalf of the Nixon White House, he ordered an investigation into past operations outside the CIA's charter. Carried out amid the gathering storm surrounding the Watergate investigation, the inquiry revealed details about illegal domestic wiretapping operations, failed assassination plots, mind-control experiments, and spying on journalists from the early years of the CIA. The agency came to refer to its file of misdeeds as the "family jewels." In July 1974, after Nixon appointed him secretary of defense, Schlesinger left the file to the next CIA director, William Colby.[46]

The revelations ignited a firestorm of controversy and congressional fury. The chairman of four Congressional committees announced investigations into the affair as Capitol Hill rang with calls for greater congressional control and reform of the agency. White House operatives made frantic efforts at damage control. Kissinger immediately pressed for a full report of the allegations from CIA director William Colby. On Christmas Eve, Colby sent a lengthy memo to Kissinger summarizing the findings of Schlesinger's investigation. After Watergate, both Ford and Kissinger thought the full record of the "family jewels" could destroy the agency, if the secrets were made public. For his part, Cheney wrote a memo to the president, urging the establishment of a special White House commission to investigate the CIA. Cheney reasoned that the commission offered the best way to thwart any "congressional efforts to further encroach on the executive branch." Cheney feared—as did others—that Congress would call for hearings that could prove damaging to the intelligence community, Ford's presidential standing, and the separation of powers. The young deputy chief of staff, who had no intelligence or national security experience, also urged releasing unclassified parts of Colby's report in response to Hersh's allegations.[47]

The disclosures set off a rapid chain of events that led to the most sweeping attacks on the presidency during the Ford years. On January 4, Ford discussed the matter in the Oval Office with Richard Helms, former CIA director and now his ambassador to Iran. "[W]e are in a mess," said Ford. "I automatically assume what you did was right, unless it's proven otherwise." Helms warned the president of the obvious. "A lot of dead cats will come out," he said. "I don't know everything which went on in the Agency. Maybe no one does. But I know enough to say that if the dead cats come out, I will participate."[48] Ford then took Cheney's advice, setting up a commission on January 14, 1975, under Vice President Nelson Rockefeller to investigate the domestic activities of the CIA. One day later, William Colby submitted a statement to the Senate Appropriations Committee, confirming that over the years the CIA had infiltrated domestic protest groups, carried out surveillance of U.S. citizens, opened people's mail, and amassed files on "about 10,000 citizens in the counterintelligence unit." According to Colby, the agency's domestic surveillance activities began in mid-1967 after President Johnson became concerned about domestic dissidence and appointed a National Advisory Commission on Civil Disorders. Afterward, on August 15, 1967, the CIA established a special unit within the agency's counterintelligence office to investigate "the possibility of foreign links"—or support from communist governments—to American antiwar groups.[49]

With such revelations, young deputy Cheney's plan of heading off congressional action with the Rockefeller Commission proved utterly futile. Colby's report seemed to substantiate many of the basic elements of Hersh's story, but left many unanswered questions, stiffening Congress's resolve to launch a thorough inquiry. The White House was soon facing eight separate congressional investigations and hearings on the CIA. The investigations were then combined into separate committee proceedings in each house. With the House focusing on failures of espionage and analysis, the Senate honed in on past abuses by the nation's intelligence agencies. Suddenly, the ghost world of intelligence was open to scrutiny as the inquiry into domestic spying widened into an inquiry of the whole invisible network of U.S. intelligence agencies.[50] The Senate panel created on January 27, 1975, under Idaho Democrat Frank Church—whom Kissinger later described as "our scourge on Vietnam and constant critic of 'deceitful' methods"—took center stage as it probed the sensational misdeeds and adventures of the country's vast and invisible spy network that arose after World War II.[51] With the Church committee demanding access to secret documents, the CIA's senior officers "feared personal and professional ruin," while the White House "feared political destruction."[52] The concerns were plausible, especially after allegations of past assassination plots against foreign leaders were leaked to CBS News in February 1975. To quash further publicity about the assassination plots, Cheney instructed the White House press secretary to stonewall press inquiries.[53]

In the succeeding months, the congressional investigating committees laid siege to the Ford administration with demands and requests for information. In an Oval meeting on October 13, 1975, the president and his senior aides discussed the rapidly evolving investigation. Colby told the president that any disclosure of documents that showed involvement in assassinations would be a "foreign policy disaster." To stop the Church committee from obtaining documents about sensitive covert operations, it was agreed that it would be better to have a political rather than legal confrontation. With that plan in mind, Ford shook up his national security staff at the end of October—an event that explains how Cheney unexpectedly rose to prominence in the inner sanctum of the White House. In what was immediately termed the Halloween Massacre, the president fired Secretary of Defense and former CIA director James Schlesinger and replaced him with Rumsfeld. Cheney took over Rumsfeld's post as White House chief of staff. Ford also stripped Kissinger of the National Security Council and eliminated a potential challenger for the 1976 presidential nomination by firing William Colby and appointing George H.W. Bush, the American envoy in Peking, as the next CIA director.[54] At the same time, Rockefeller, who represented the Republican liberal wing, withdrew as Ford's running mate for the 1976 presidential election—a sacrifice to the conservative wing of the Republican Party.[55]

After fifteen months of conducting the most sweeping investigation in the history of the U.S. Senate, including more than 800 interviews and hundreds of hearings, Church said that the agency was a "rogue elephant."[56] But as New York Times reporter and author Tim Weiner later wrote, the pronouncement had "badly missed the point by absolving the presidents who had driven the elephant."[57] During this period, Cheney penned a note to himself, expressing frustration over the administration's inability to respond coherently to the congressional investigations.[58] The administration was shell-shocked from the latest revelations and was cast in a position of reaction and response. The House and Senate probes, which produced a stream of newspaper headlines, resulted in the creation of intelligence oversight committees in both chambers and the passage of laws that required the president to inform the committees about intelligence operations. The days of the nation's intelligence community operating with unfettered freedom, neither checked by Congress nor the courts, but at the discretion of the presidency were over. The Church committee's findings that the intelligence abuses stemmed from unrestrained executive power outside the norms of constitutional checks and balances ultimately compelled Ford to take action.

Even before the Church committee wrapped up its investigation, Attorney General Edward Levi began drafting a proposal to regulate domestic spying for foreign intelligence purposes. Levi envisioned a secret court within the Justice Department that would oversee and issue warrants governing electronic surveillance on U.S. soil. The warrant proposal offered the virtue of protecting fundamental civil liberties while allowing the government to carry out domestic spying under judicial supervision. But several of Ford's presidential advisors, including Rumsfeld, Bush, Kissinger, and National Security Advisor Brent Scowcroft, opposed the idea. They believed that it would violate the president's inherent constitutional authority to gather intelligence on foreign suspects in the United States. Levi argued that after all the revelations of the Church committee, Congress would act no matter what. "Certain committees of Congress will move ahead with their own proposals to control electronic surveillance for foreign intelligence purposes, and only by submitting an Administration proposal can we effectively counter objectionable moves by Congress." Ultimately, Ford heeded Levi's advice, giving him approval to begin negotiations with Congress in crafting the measure. By this time, however, both the White House and Congress had turned their attention to the 1976 election.[59]

Nonetheless, on February 19, 1976, the president went on the initiative, issuing a thirty-six-page executive order restricting the power of intelligence agencies to intrude upon the lives and activities of American citizens. The order banned political assassination, created an Intelligence Oversight Board, limited domestic spying on Americans, imposed restrictive regulations on the collection and dissemination of information about U.S. citizens, and outlawed burglaries, drug tests on human subjects, and the illegal use of tax return information. It also limited the infiltration of any group—whether for intelligence purposes or to influence its activities—to those comprising largely foreign nationals or directly controlled by a foreign government. The presidential order covered the CIA, the National Security Agency, the Defense Intelligence Agency, and other agencies involved in the collection of foreign intelligence. The final Church committee report condemned the FBI even more strongly than the CIA, resulting in a separate set of guidelines for the agency.[60] Ford's presidential order may have represented a capitulation on executive power, but it also was politically astute. As Levi had already advised, it was better for the president to take preemptive action and look presidential than to have Congress formulate the rules and set them in stone by statute. Despite the massive disclosures of previous presidential abuses of the intelligence agencies, the executive order contained no assurances that the agencies would be protected from future presidential pressures or demands.[61] Former President George H.W. Bush, who served as director of the CIA during its time of crisis, later contended that the congressional investigations did long-lasting damage to the agency. They harmed the CIA's links to foreign intelligence services, which provided much of the information it gathered, and "caused many people abroad to pull away from cooperating with the CIA."[62]

In the spring of 1975, amid the intelligence investigations, the president suffered new humiliations at the hands of Congress. Breaking the 1973 cease-fire agreement negotiated by the Nixon administration, the North Vietnamese invaded the South, threatening to overrun Saigon. Kissinger pushed for conducting a massive airlift to rescue Vietnamese allies, but congressional statutes passed at the end of the war required that the administration seek approval from Congress. Congress feared that committing military forces for the action could produce major new fighting and casualties and gave permission only to use the military to evacuate any remaining Americans who were in Saigon. As the biggest helicopter lift of its kind in American history got underway in early May 1975, a scene of utter panic and chaos ensued, broadcast on American television, as South Vietnamese desperately fought to board the last helicopter flights out of the American embassy. Congress had restrained the presidency, but it also had likely saved an already war-fatigued nation from renewed fighting and further casualties in Southeast Asia.

Two weeks later Ford asserted his executive prerogatives against the War Powers Resolution by ordering the armed forces to rescue the merchant vessel *SS Mayaguez* from the Cambodians, without first consulting congressional leaders. The unarmed vessel had been seized in disputed waters by Khmer Rouge gunboats and forced to anchor off the small crescent island of Koh Tang. The rescue was portrayed as a heroic operation in the press. It was a "daring show of nerve and steel," a "classic show of gunboat diplomacy," reported *Newsweek*. A weary president initially expressed relief that it all went well. "We got them out, thank God. It went perfectly. It went just great." But the flush of success quickly paled after details of the disastrous rescue surfaced over the course of several weeks. Operating with poor intelligence, the air, sea, and land assault targeted the wrong island trying to rescue the crew of the captured freighter. The crew were not being held captive on Koh Tang, but on the Cambodian mainland. More tragic, the Cambodians had already announced that they were releasing the crew and ship before 200 marines stormed Koh Tang and remained under heavy fire for many hours, resulting in fifteen killed. Twenty-three others died in a helicopter crash. The American merchant marines were heading out to sea aboard a fishing boat when the military assault began on Koh Tang. After giving orders to commit military forces, Ford invited the most important members of Congress to the White House for a briefing on the rescue operation. The president's action met with the general approval of Senate and House leaders, Democrats and Republicans alike. But Ford "struck a raw nerve when he described the planned air strikes against Cambodian military facilities at Kompong Som and Ream on the mainland," recalled Ron Nessen, the president's press secretary.

Three of the Senate's leading members—Democratic leader Mike Mansfield, assistant Democratic leader Robert Byrd, and Chairman John McClellan of the appropriations committee—objected strongly to the air strikes on the mainland. Ford explained that the strikes were designed to prevent Cambodian forces from attacking U.S. marines. "But, with memories still fresh of the escalating air strikes ordered by Presidents Johnson and Nixon during the Indochina war," said Nessen, "the senators were not satisfied with Ford's explanation." Mansfield expressed his deep concern and uneasiness at "this near invasion of the Indochina mainland," while Byrd criticized the president for not consulting with Democratic leaders earlier about the air strikes. "Why weren't the leaders brought in when there was time for them to raise a word of caution?" Byrd asked. "We have a government of separation of powers," Ford responded. "In this case, as commander in chief, I had the responsibility and obligation to act." Ford's words epitomized the presidency's unwillingness to yield its powers over military affairs, but the episode also represented congressional determination not to take a subservient role to the White House in matters of war and peace.[63]

On May 25, 1975, *New York Times* reporter Seymour Hersh published another expose on a highly classified U.S. intelligence operation. For "nearly 15 years," wrote Hersh, "the Navy has been using specially equipped electronic submarines to spy . . . inside the three-mile limit of the Soviet Union and other nations." Under the code-name Holystone, the classified missions "have been credited by supporters with supplying vital information on the configuration, capabilities, noise patterns and missile-firing abilities of the Soviet marine fleet." Hersh said that opponents of the classified spy missions believed that the spying missions were jeopardizing détente with the Soviets and hoped to force change in intelligence policy by going public. "Many of the critics acknowledged that they agreed to discuss the operation in the hope of forcing changes in how intelligence was collected and utilized by the government," wrote Hersh.[64] The revelations of yet another classified operation ignited fury among Ford's senior aides. Cheney received instructions from Rumsfeld, who was traveling with the president in Europe, to draft the administration's response to Hersh's article. Among Cheney's proposals were threatening to prosecute the *New York Times* if they did not stop publishing classified information, launching an FBI investigation of the *New York Times* and Seymour Hersh, and seeking a search warrant to go after Hersh's notes. Cheney proposed these options in a meeting he called with Attorney General Edward Levi and White House counsel Philip Buchen. Levi jettisoned the proposals, ultimately persuading the White House to let the matter drop, rather than to stir up more publicity about it.[65]

Nonetheless, as Hersh's latest expose came amid the continuing congressional investigations of intelligence abuses, Cheney saw opportunity in exploiting the disclosure to ward off the probes. "Can we take advantage of it to bolster our position on the Church committee investigations to point out the need for limits on the scope of the investigations?" It was a naïve proposition. The Church committee was already on the trail of the NSA and CIA regarding a program launched after World War II involving the participation of U.S. communications companies—including the Bell System and Western Union—in the monitoring of communications between the United States and countries overseas. There were also ongoing media reports not only about the CIA's massive illegalities, but also about the transgressions of the FBI's counterintelligence program. The FBI's program had operated from 1956 to 1971, gathering intelligence on subversive organizations and individuals by various means—infiltration, warrantless wiretapping, break-ins, opening of mail, and examination of financial records. Moreover, as the congressional investigations would reveal, the NSA became involved in the action, conducting electronic surveillance of civil rights and antiwar groups and activists starting in 1967. Against this tidal wave of disclosures, each of which created a further imperative and momentum to discover the full extent of the illegalities, Cheney's question betrayed a peculiar unreality regarding the magnitude of the problems facing the Ford administration.[66]

Three

Chief of Staff

Cheney was more astute when it came to maneuvering within the Ford administration. As deputy chief of staff, Cheney witnessed Rumsfeld's efforts to curb the power of Kissinger and the NSC. Rumsfeld urged the president to assert greater control over foreign policy in both image and reality. In the ever feuding Ford White House, the battle to diminish Kissinger's firm grip over foreign policy produced a flood of news stories that he would be fired from his second job as head of the NSC.[1] Rumsfeld's efforts to diminish Kissinger's influence supported later allegations that he played Iago in persuading the president to strip Kissinger of the NSC. Rumsfeld and Cheney advocated a tougher line against the Soviets, opposing Kissinger's policy of détente. While Cheney lacked foreign policy experience, he was willing to oppose Kissinger on at least one issue. In order not to disrupt ongoing talks with the Soviets, Kissinger advised the president against inviting the Soviet dissident and Nobel Laureate Alexander Solzhenitsyn, an opponent of détente, to the White House. Cheney disagreed and wrote a July 8, 1975, memo expressing his "strong feeling" that the president should see Solzhenitsyn. "I can't think of a better way to demonstrate for the American people and for the world that détente with the Soviet Union ... in no way means that we've given up our fundamental principles concerning individual liberty and democracy," he wrote. "Meetings with Soviet Leaders are very important, but it is also important that we not contribute any more to the illusion that all of a sudden we're bosom-buddies with the Russians."[2]

In just over a year working at the White House, Cheney won the improbable appointment of chief of staff. He was now well positioned to promote or kill proposals that came to the president. He served as gate-keeper, determining who would see the president and when meetings or phone calls took place and for how long. At the time of his appointment, one news source noted that "Cheney had been carefully trained by Rumsfeld to assume these duties, possibly because Rumsfeld saw his own position as transitional and felt he would move out and up."[3] Rumsfeld reportedly never wanted the position in the first place, preferring instead a cabinet post with more independence and political visibility or even the vice presidency. Many also assumed that he wanted the presidency.[4] Rumsfeld may also have calculated that with his protégé now serving as Ford's private counselor, he could count on his former aide to push his positions to the president, giving him an advantage over rivals in the administration.

Cheney quickly made an impression as President Ford's new chief of staff. He wasted little time in assembling half a dozen young aides to bring order to the White House. At the time, David Gergen was one the young aides who went to work in the Ford administration and reported to the president through Cheney. "I must tell you that I, along with all of my colleagues, was enormously impressed by Dick Cheney at that time," Gergen recalled decades later after serving as a presidential advisor to Presidents Nixon, Ford, Reagan, and Clinton. "He was a first-rate chief of staff; he was a man of great integrity. President Ford came to rely on him heavily during the time." Nonetheless, Ford avoided centralizing power either in Rumsfeld's or Cheney's hands as Nixon did with Alexander Haig and to a lesser extend Haldeman, both of whom served as a kind of deputy president. Whereas Haig served as the chief contact between Nixon and his administration, as well as Congress, Ford aimed to deal regularly with a broad array of senior staff aides, all of whom would have equal access. In his memoirs, Ford wrote that Watergate "was made possible by a strong chief of staff and ambitious White House aides who were more powerful than members of the Cabinet. . . . I decided to give my Cabinet more control." For this reason, Ford decentral-ized the post and dropped the title "chief of staff," preferring instead "staff coordinator." After Nixon's mania for secrecy, Ford wanted to be less reclusive and open up his administration to differing points of view. This approach seemed a natural reflection of Ford's congenial nature and his twenty-five years in the House of Representatives.[5]

At only thirty-four, Cheney experienced a meteoric rise in influence with his move close to the center of power. Under Ford's decentralized approach, Cheney's role involved more one of administration and coordination. His job largely comprised assembling people's views and reporting them to the Oval Office as an honest broker or arbiter. He learned from Rumsfeld to deliver his own views orally to the president, not to leave a paper trail if he could help it. "Both of these guys were crafty," recalled James Cannon, who served with Cheney and Rumsfeld in the Ford administration. "You never spotted their fingerprints." This approach allowed Cheney to act quietly and avoid exposing his opinions to examination and criticism. It was a lesson perhaps learned from Nixon's fatal obsession with recording his own deeds to his later chagrin and political ruin.[6] He preferred anonymity, but managed to befriend some among the White House press corps. White House press secretary Ron Nessen recounted that Cheney brought a difference in management style from Rumsfeld. "The departure of Rumsfeld brought a pleasant improvement in the relationship among White House staff members," he noted. Three weeks after the departure of Rumsfeld, Nessen wrote a memo to himself, noting the change: "There has been a real change at the White House since Rumsfeld left, a change of mood, almost like a fresh breeze blowing through."[7] But one journalist who knew both Rumsfeld and Cheney socially remembered differently. "They were two little throat slitters," he recalled.[8]

In their roles as chief of staff, Rumsfeld and Cheney repeatedly clashed with Vice President Nelson Rockefeller, one of the heirs to the great Rockefeller fortune who served as governor of New York for 15 years. The sixty-six-year-old Rockefeller long wanted the presidency and repeatedly waved off any talk of the vice presidency by saying that he was not the type to be "stand-by equipment." He ran hard for the presidential nomination in 1964 and 1968. Until Nixon's resignation, he was again campaigning for the top job, making political trips around the country and evading questions about his plans for 1976. Even before then, Rockefeller had a long public career in national and international affairs, beginning with his appointment by President Franklin D. Roosevelt as Coordinator of Inter-American Affairs during World War II. In the Truman administration, he headed the president's Development Advisory Board, which recommended the Partners in Progress program that he claimed was the forerunner of U.S. foreign aid. Under Eisenhower's Republican administration, he served as undersecretary of Health, Education, and Welfare and later as a special assistant for foreign affairs to General Eisenhower. After agreeing to accept Ford's offer of the vice presidency, one longtime associate predicted that he would be a threat to the White House bureaucrats. "I think that when Nelson Rockefeller sees a problem he cannot help but think about the solutions to the problems— he's such a dynamic guy," he said. "I suspect in doing this he's going to step on the toes of some of the bureaucrats who have the line responsibility. I think his very enthusiasm, his ability will make him a 'threat.' He'll be a constant challenge just by simply being there." The press wondered whether Rockefeller would be satisfied with second place. He "will have no real power," said the *New York Times*. Even "more vital to a man as determinedly energetic and managerial as Nelson Rockefeller, he will have no real duties, either, unless Mr. Ford decides to give him some."[9]

Despite such doubts, Ford agreed to give Rockefeller a meaningful portfolio, making him chief domestic policy advisor as head of the Domestic Council, created under Nixon to steer domestic policy. It was an offer of a fuller partnership unique in the annals of the vice presidency that gave him a foothold in White House policy making. The appointment and his portfolio led to clashes with Rumsfeld and then Cheney, who saw him as a rival and opposed his moderate pragmatism and spirit of activism.[10] Rockefeller's record in the 1960s of assailing attempts to undo social welfare and civil rights programs and his reputation as a liberal maverick within the Republican establishment put him at odds with the rising conservative wing of the party. Cheney feared that the vice president would dominate domestic policy and open up the administration to conservative criticism in the 1976 GOP primary. Further, after inheriting a difficult economy, Ford sought to impose fiscal discipline, curbing new government programs—a fact that did not stop the dynamic Rockefeller from seeking to influence presidential affairs with new policy and program initiatives.

Ideologically opposed to Rockefeller's view of government, Rumsfeld and Cheney energetically worked to bury his initiatives in the federal bureaucracy. At a 1986 forum at the University of California involving former chiefs of staff, Cheney recalled that in the "Ford administration, we had major problems in managing the vice presidential relationship. . . . President Ford put the vice president in charge of all domestic policy making, put him in charge of the Domestic Council, gave him the assignment of creating policy, and let him staff the operation out." Whenever Rockefeller proposed one of his domestic policy initiatives, Cheney said, he considered it his responsibility to put "sand in the gears." "I was the SOB, and on a number of occasions, got involved in shouting matches with the vice president," Cheney recalled.[11] But at least initially, Rockefeller could not be contained, brushing Rumsfeld and Cheney aside to sell the president on his $100 billion Energy Independence Authority, which would develop more alternative energy sources and nuclear power. The *Wall Street Journal* later reported that Cheney "didn't have the clout or the impertinence to dissuade" Ford from signing onto the gigantic energy scheme, a forward-thinking plan to bring energy independence to the United States.[12]

To Rockefeller's associates, if not to the vice president himself, Rumsfeld and Cheney were the devils incarnate. They held Rumsfeld responsible for engineering Rockefeller's ouster from the 1976 ticket, as well as the upheaval surrounding Ford's shake-up of his national security hierarchy. The vice president never found acceptance by the ultra-conservatives who exercised increasing power within party circles. The president also was facing a stiffening challenge from former Governor Ronald Reagan of California—a conservative favorite—for the Republican presidential nomination. As Ford moved steadily closer to the right wing of the party to win the nomination, Rockefeller was increasingly regarded as a liability. With the acceptance of the energy plan, Ford was said to have lost the "hearts of the party's conservatives," if not the oil state of Texas itself. The "ideologues assumed that if he could sign this bill, he would sign anything."[13] In an Oval Office meeting with the president on October 28, 1975, Rockefeller agreed to withdraw his name from the ticket, accepting lame duck status and resulting in the end of his national political career. The vice president was hurt by the controversial removal, later remarking, "I didn't take myself off the ticket, you know—he asked me to do it." After years of dissembling about his decision to fire Rockefeller, Ford would say it was "one of the few cowardly things I did in my life."[14]

The nadir of Cheney's relationship with Rockefeller occurred at the Republican convention in August 1976. Rockefeller cursed Cheney for a couple of alleged slights—denying him his rightful place on the podium with Ford and shutting down the microphone during a Rockefeller speech. Rockefeller accused Cheney of sabotaging his exit from the national political stage and ordered him to tell Ford that he was "finished" with the president's campaign. But Rockefeller got his rightful place on the podium, the sound evidently cut off on its own, and the vice president campaigned for Ford and his replacement on the GOP ticket, Senator Bob Dole of Kansas.[15]

Cheney also ousted Howard H. (Bo) Calloway, a former secretary of the army, who initially ran Ford's 1976 race for the GOP nomination. Calloway became a liability when press reports alleged that he used his position as army secretary to pressure the Agriculture Department and the Forest Service to approve an expansion of his Crested Butte, Colorado, ski resort on federal land. Following months of allegations, Cheney finally fired him from the campaign. According to Reagan biographer Lou Cannon, Cheney then muffed the transition, offering the campaign chairmanship to Stuart Spencer, a strategist who turned it down and creating a "distraction that put the White House rather than the Reagan campaign on the defensive."[16] Nonetheless, Cheney emerged as a major force in the president's race for the GOP nomination. Ron Nessen, Ford's press secretary, recalled that by the time Ford had won the nomination and was mobilizing to face Jimmy Carter, the Democratic nominee for the presidency, there was "no question that Dick Cheney was firmly atop the White Chain of command. Cheney had taken on more and more power until he was running the White House staff and overseeing the campaign in an authoritative manner." It was a critical position for someone who had never run for political office, much less managed a presidential primary and a general election campaign.[17]

Despite Cheney's efforts to move the president to the right, Ronald Reagan decided to contest the president for the GOP nomination. At the same time, by the time Cheney began overseeing the campaign, it was already unraveling, beset by dissension among various White House factions that played out their disputes in the press. Ford's campaign managers pushed him to crack down on the feuding, with little result. Sensitivity over news leaks "rose almost to the paranoid level," observed Nessen, "particularly among Cheney's assistants, nicknamed the 'junior varsity'." At the center of the dissension were Cheney and his small circle of loyal aides who determined with whom the president met, where he went, what he did, and the kind of the ideas that reached him and the way those ideas were translated into policy. Cheney's White House critics, including senior presidential aides and advisors as well as other high administration officials, attacked him in a May 1976 *New York Times* article, complaining that his staff operation was "inept and inefficient and that those who run it are too immature for the responsibility involved as well as politically naïve." The stinging criticism came after Ford suffered a string of primary election losses to Reagan in early May 1976. One of the president's longtime associates charged that mistakes by the White House staff were jeopardizing Ford's chances for a full term in office. Another midlevel aide wished that "we had some of the old Haldeman discipline back," adding that "there are just too many mistakes."[18] Cheney's political enemies also assailed him in other news outlets, including a column by Robert Novak and Rowland Evans. The journalists reported that Cheney was being "blamed for a succession of campaign blunders."[19] Cheney and his staff disputed the charges against them, saying that they were giving the president the kind of White House operation that he wanted and that the mounting criticism was "part of the game."[20]

To a considerable extent, Ford's open management style fueled dissension among White House staffers as they jockeyed for power and influence. After less than two months in office, Ford's administration was already beset by feuding and press leaks among various factions—the Nixon holdovers, Ford's trusted friends from Grand Rapids, members of Ford's congressional and vice presidential staffs, and newer staffers such as Rumsfeld and Cheney. He told his senior aides that he was "damn sick and tired of a ship that has such leaky seams. We are being drowned by premature and obvious leaks."[21] But the president rarely had such blowups, nor did he ever get tough enough to stop the feuding and fire the worst offenders. Neither could the feuding be stopped by chiefs of staff Rumsfeld or Cheney, who used the press in their own Machiavellian adventures and were themselves the target of such attacks in the press. Senior party officials continued to criticize Cheney's handling of the president's campaign until the end, and some came to blame him for managing Ford to defeat. Cheney himself later admitted that the "1976 campaign was in many respects a series of crises all the way from New Hampshire [the first primary] in February of 1976 when we won by 1,300 votes to the convention in Kansas City with a lot of wins and losses in between, to the final outcome in November."[22]

In the end, Ford narrowly won his party's nomination, but lost the presidential race to Jimmy Carter. In conceding the close election, a despondent Ford asked Cheney to deliver the concession speech to the new president-elect. By the time Cheney left the White House, he had earned allies and detractors alike, perhaps inevitable for someone in his position. While he held the respect among people in and out of his inner circle of aides, other White House advisors believed he had been too inexperienced to be an effective leader. White House press secretary Ron Nessen sent a personal note to Cheney, praising him for his "extremely able handling" of his many duties during the general campaign. Jerry Jones, a former special assistant to Nixon and director of scheduling and advance under Ford, believed that both Rumsfeld and Cheney shone among an otherwise "mediocre" staff. And Ford's pollster, Bob Teeter, said, "Cheney turned out to be . . . one of the best—if not the best—chiefs of staff ever."[23]

Others disagreed. Bryce Harlow, a former Nixon staffer and an informal advisor to Ford, believed Cheney was too young and inexperienced to be chief of staff, a sentiment shared by Bob Hartmann, the president's chief speech writer who fought with and detested Cheney. Hartmann also dismissed him as too conservative. "Whenever his private ideology was exposed, he appeared somewhat to the right of Ford, Rumsfeld or, for that matter, Genghis Khan."[24] To James Cannon, who served on the president's Domestic Council, Cheney was neither a good organizer nor politically astute. "Too bad Rumsfeld did not stay for the campaign," he said, "Ford might have won a second term." Moreover, according to former Nixon counselor John Dean, Cheney not only was in over his head, but also had alienated many White House aides. He could neither contain the feuding among White House staffers, nor prevent them from attacking each other as well as himself in the press. "The people I knew who were still there were very disenchanted with Cheney," he said. "They felt he was in way over his head."[25]

Whether Cheney was too young and inexperienced no longer mattered. As chief of staff, he had gained valuable experience running the White House—an education that hardened him as a veteran infighter and that later served him well in Congress and in his eventual return to the executive branch years afterward. He had served in a caretaker presidency, kept a low profile compared to other former chiefs of staff like H. R. Haldeman, and left the White House politically unscathed and largely unknown outside Washington circles—a faceless and forgettable personality. In 1979, John Herbers of the *New York Times* wrote that both Rumsfeld and Cheney had left the Ford administration "unscathed, but with little likelihood the world would remember their White House doings."[26]

CONGRESS IMPOSES FURTHER CONSTRAINTS ON PRESIDENCY

During the later days of the Ford administration and throughout the Carter presidency, Congress continued to pass a web of laws to constrain the executive and strengthen its own prerogatives. Carter signed the bills into law, giving his imprimatur to the need to impose additional restraints on the presidency. To counter government secrecy, Congress passed the Government in Sunshine Act in 1976, requiring that most decision making by independent agencies operated by boards and commissions be conducted in open meetings.[27] The act built on an earlier 1972 law—the Federal Advisory Committee Act (FACA)—that brought greater disclosure to the activities of presidential task forces.[28]

Congress also moved to restrain the executive from spying on Americans without warrants. In 1976, the White House took the initiative when Attorney General Levi issued new rules barring the agency from investigating individuals or groups for merely advocating controversial positions—or otherwise exercising their First Amendment rights—unless they threatened violence.[29] President Carter strengthened the guidelines in 1978, requiring the attorney general to approve all domestic investigations and to assure that any information gathered would be used for lawful governmental purposes. Moreover, the order required the attorney general to approve any counterintelligence operations on U.S. soil.[30] Then Congress passed the Federal Intelligence Surveillance Act of 1978 (FISA), establishing judicial oversight over what presidents had previously claimed as their inherent executive power for forty years. The law required that intelligence agencies obtain a warrant any time they sought to monitor communications inside the country. Before doing so, an intelligence agency had to establish probable cause that the target of electronic surveillance was a foreign power or an agent of a foreign power. The law established a special court—the Foreign Intelligence Surveillance Court—that could grant authority to wiretap Americans after a showing of probable cause. When drafting the law, Congress made clear that the act constituted the "exclusive means" by which domestic spying could be lawfully carried out for foreign intelligence purposes.[31] But years later under the George W. Bush administration, Vice President Cheney and other executive officials would attack the law as an infringement on executive power and a grave threat to the war on terror.

To further restore public confidence in government, Congress passed the Ethics in Government Act and the independent counsel statute in 1978. The ethics law created safeguards against the abuse of the public trust by government officials. One of the core provisions of the ethics law was Title VI, later known as the Independent Counsel Act (ICA).[32] The ICA created the special counsel's office to investigate perjury, bribery, fraud, influence peddling, and other forms of corruption by White House aides and cabinet secretaries. Until the law's expiration in 1999, the use of independent counsels quickly became part of Washington political life.[33]

Like his predecessors, Carter fought Congress to protect and extend the presidency's prerogatives. Ultimately, some of these disputes established precedents that his successors sought to greatly expand. Carter opposed the initial drafting of the 1978 Presidential Records Act (PRA), which overturned the long-running tradition of private ownership of presidential records that dated to the beginning of the Republic. The act declared that the records of all presidents and vice presidents would be the property of the American people. The law allowed citizens to review all materials, including confidential communications with advisors, twelve years after a president left office. The measure also assured that the most sensitive records relating to national security, foreign relations, financial and trade secrets, and personnel privacy were exempt from disclosure.[34] The law represented another cornerstone post-Watergate reform to counter government secrecy, but the Carter administration viewed the law's twelve-year ceiling on restricting access as deeply flawed and unconstitutional regarding sensitive internal White House communications.[35] Congress disagreed that the law would unconstitutionally infringe on the president's right to exert privilege and moved to set the marker at twelve years after a president left office. Carter's aides lobbied strenuously for a bill that would exempt his presidential papers from the law. Ultimately, Congress relented and passed a modified version of the legislation that was signed by Carter as the Presidential Records Act of 1978. The law exempted Carter's presidential papers, but covered those of all his presidential successors.

The Carter administration also battled Congress over one of the provisions of the Inspector General Act of 1978. Congress passed the act to probe and ward off corruption, waste, and fraud by placing a cadre of inspector generals (IGs) within federal agencies. Against the objections of the attorney general and federal agencies, the law required that an IG's findings be reported not only to agency heads, but also to Congress and the public.[36] Moreover, Carter attacked legislative vetoes, allowing Congress to intervene in the executive's implementation of programs funded by the legislative branch. The legislative veto might be imposed by both houses, one chamber, or even by one committee. Between 1970 and 1980, Congress passed 423 legislative veto provisions, more than half after 1975. The provision presented a problem, as the Constitution only gave the presidency—not Congress—the power of the veto. The Carter administration finally attacked the constitutionality of the legislative veto in *Immigration and Naturalization Service v. Chadha*, leading the Supreme Court to strike down the provision in 1983. The decision resulted in nullifying congressional injunctions across numerous federal statutes. More important, the 1983 ruling marked a landmark victory for presidential power and a significant reversal after a decade of active constraint by Congress.[37]

The executive branch also periodically fought congressional requests for information by the General Accounting Office (GAO), Congress's investigating and auditing arm. Congress therefore passed legislation authorizing the GAO to pursue court actions to compel the disclosure of documents from the executive branch. The law also authorized the agency to use its newly granted legal powers against the president and his principal advisors. As a matter of compromise, Congress gave the White House the power to prohibit disclosure through a certification process if it deemed that release of information would impair government operations. The act marked another victory for congressional prerogatives, but it would come under assault years later, under the George W. Bush and administration.[38]

Another dispute involved control over international treaties. The 1970s had witnessed congressional action to curb the use of executive agreements with foreign countries that bypassed the Senate's constitutional two-thirds vote requirement for treaties. Presidents had long negotiated executive agreements—sometimes in secret—without congressional oversight or consent. By the mid-1920s, the conclusion of these agreements was already outnumbering treaties, a trend that rapidly accelerated during and after World War II, primarily regarding military commitments overseas. The use of executive agreements reached unprecedented levels with the secret diplomacy of the Nixon-Kissinger years, which kept Congress in the dark about the nature of these understandings. In 1972, Congress passed the Case-Zablocki Act, which required that any international agreement other than a treaty be submitted to Congress within sixty days after the agreement took effect. But revelations of Nixon's secret assurances to the South Vietnamese that the United States would come to its defense if the North violated the peace agreement led Congress to push for legislation in both houses that would make any executive agreement subject to its vote of approval. Congress sought to subject executive agreements to the same ratification process as treaties. In testimony before the Senate on May 15, 1975, Scalia denounced the legislation as an unwarranted usurpation of presidential power to carry out the country's foreign policy. In the end, the congressional effort to strengthen oversight over executive agreements failed, but it did have the effect of pushing the president toward being more consultative when negotiating executive agreements with foreign leaders.[39] Under Carter, the presidency continued the struggle to exert control over international treaties, leading to several cases before the Supreme Court.[40]

By the end of the decade, Congress had sought to bind the presidency to the Constitution, while altering the balance of power to its own institutional advantage. It constituted a historic resurgence aimed at reclaiming the powers of the purse and war-making authority. With its many legislative achievements, Congress aimed to establish a bulwark against two centuries of growing presidential power that culminated in the crimes of Richard Nixon. Lawmakers hoped to ensure that there would be no more secret wars, no more covert scandals, and no more secret agreements with foreign leaders. By 1976, journalists were already concluding that Congress was winning its running battle with the presidency in the aftermath of Watergate.[41] And by the early 1980s, others were arguing that by imprisoning the presidency in a spider web of laws and oversight arrangements, Congress had dangerously diminished the executive while proclaiming itself as the imperial branch. The altered political landscape, they argued, set too many limits on the presidency, undermined national security, and even upset the constitutional order. Some critics believed that Congress's arrogation of power had pushed America into a "constitutional crisis" and urged a restoration of presidential authority—an argument that was welcomed by the Reagan administration and that Cheney was already professing and would continue to voice years later.[42]

Four

Congressional Years

When Jimmy Carter was elected in 1976, Cheney went back to Wyoming, where he was raised, won a seat in Congress, and returned in 1978 to the nation's capital as one of the more seasoned and talented conservative young Republicans. He had worked in both the Nixon and Ford administrations and had an understanding of the House after having served as a legislative fellow in 1968 in the office of Bill Steiger, the Republican dealmaker on the Ways and Means Committee. Because of his previous experience in Washington, he was unfazed by the bewildering array of congressional committees and subcommittees that greeted most freshman representatives. Within a couple of days of his election, Cheney struck a deal regarding his committee assignments with House minority leader John Rhodes. During the Ford years, Cheney had worked closely with Rhodes to advance the administration's legislative agenda. Rhodes agreed to give Cheney a seat on the interior committee if he would also take a thankless assignment on the ethics committee, which probed the alleged wrongdoings of House colleagues. The interior assignment was an astute choice given that about one half of Wyoming was federal land with considerable natural resources.[1] By serving on the interior committee, Cheney could court wealthy Wyoming constituents by having a say over how the natural resources on that public land were used.

But world events soon turned his attention to national security issues. On November 4, 1979, hundreds of self-described students—followers of the Ayatollah Ruhollah Khomeini—seized the American embassy in Tehran. When the Iranian militants stormed the embassy for the second time in nine months, few Americans could have anticipated the crisis would last fourteen months. In exchange for the American captives in the embassy, the Iranian radicals demanded that the United States hand over the deposed Shah, Mohammad Reza Pahlavi, so that he could be put on trial for crimes against the Iranian people. The shah fled to Mexico in January 1979 amid the Iranian Revolution led by Ayatollah Khomeini, but traveled to a New York hospital for emergency treatment for cancer. The Iranian Prime Minister Mehdi Bazargan resigned in disgust, and Khomeini and his Revolutionary Council took full charge of the hostage crisis. Within days, the news media began carrying pictures of captive American diplomats and military personnel blindfolded with their hands bound behind their backs. As Khomeini threatened to put the American captives on trial as spies, Carter gave orders to start deportation proceedings against Iranian students living illegally in the United States, cut off direct imports of Iranian oil, and froze Iranian assets in American banks at home and overseas. Orders were given to the aircraft carrier Kitty Hawk and five escort ships to steam from the Philippines to the Arabian Sea. The taking of the hostages constituted an act of revenge for the CIA's 1953 coup in Iran. "But the legacy of that long-ago operation went far beyond the Americans' ordeal," wrote Tim Weiner in *Legacy of Ashes: The History of the CIA*. "The zeal of the Iranian revolution would haunt the next four presidents of the United States and kill hundreds of Americans in the Middle East. A blaze of glory for the covert operators of the CIA's greatest generation became a tragic conflagration for their heirs."[2]

Just over a month later, on December 24, 1979, the Carter administration faced another international crisis when the Soviets invaded Afghanistan to shore up their communist client state. As declassified intelligence later showed, American analysts and policy makers knew about the Soviets' extensive military preparations along the border regions of Afghanistan. But while some analysts could not agree on the implications of the Soviets' military activity, others dismissed the idea that a full-scale invasion would occur.[3] National Security Advisor Zbigniew Brzezinski informed the president that the invasion had precipitated a wider regional crisis with grave implications for the United States. Both Iran and Afghanistan were already in turmoil, and Pakistan was unstable internally. If the Soviets succeeded in Afghanistan, Brzezinski feared, the age-old dream of Moscow gaining direct access to the Indian Ocean might be fulfilled. The Iranian crisis had upset the balance of power in the region, possibly allowing a Soviet presence on the edge of the Arabian and Oman gulfs. Accordingly, Brzezinski wrote, "the Soviet intervention in Afghanistan poses for us an extremely grave challenge, both internationally and domestically." Brzezinski advised that the Soviet invasion and the regional instability could complicate any resolution of the Iranian crisis and ignite a confrontation with the Soviets. Further, with Iran destabilized, there was no bulwark against a Soviet drive to the warm waters of the Indian Ocean.[4] In response to the crisis, Carter ordered the CIA to arm the mujahideen in their war against the Soviets, starting a chain of events that led years later to the rise of Osama bin Laden and the Taliban. Cheney backed the policy of supporting the Afghan rebels, saying in a 1980 interview that it was "the best way to make the Russians pay, and it will also keep them tied down so that they cannot move into Iran."[5]

For more than a year, the stalemate in the Iranian hostage crisis dominated much of the news coverage, taking a heavy toll on Carter's reelection prospects against Ronald Reagan. As the crisis deepened surrounding the fate of the Americans, Carter took a tougher line short of military action, severing diplomatic ties with Tehran, banning Iranian imports, prohibiting Americans from traveling to Iran, and sending all military equipment ordered by Iran before the crisis back into U.S. stockpiles. Hard pressed for action, the president pressured reluctant allies into imposing what they considered costly and unproductive trade sanctions against Iran. Carter also threatened to boycott the 1980 summer Olympics, a position that Cheney reluctantly agreed with. But the first-term representative, who had no foreign policy experience, criticized the president's public statements that he would not use force to resolve the hostage crisis. In an April 17, 1979, interview with a Wyoming newspaper, the *Pinedale Roundup*, Cheney said that although Carter "might decide not to use force, he should not make his decision known. Once you remove the threat of force you remove any incentive for the Iranians to free the hostages. Every single President for the last half-century at some time has had to use force to safeguard American lives. This is Carter's test. It's his test."[6] But it appeared Cheney spoke prematurely. A week later, on April 24, 1979, Carter took action, ordering a special operations effort to rescue the hostages that ended in catastrophe. Three helicopters were crippled en route to the desert staging area, prompting Carter to abort the mission. When attempting to evacuate, a helicopter collided with a transport plane, killing eight commandos in the Iranian wasteland. Kohmeini threatened to kill the hostages if Carter tried another rescue effort and U.S. Secretary of State Cyrus Vance resigned in protest over the raid. Amid the controversy that followed, several in Congress criticized the president for ordering the rescue mission without consulting them first under the War Powers Resolution. Carter responded that the mission depended on secrecy—a position that did little to satisfy his critics, but Congress took no action to further constrain the president's war-making authority.

THE REAGAN PRESIDENCY

On November 4, 1980, Reagan and his vice president, George H.W. Bush, won the White House on a straight campaign platform that called for cutting the size, scope, and spending of the federal government, cutting taxes by a third, and the immediate and dramatic strengthening of the nation's defenses. Once considered by some to be a washed-up movie star and too far right to be president, Reagan's brand of conservatism swept Carter out of the White House by a vote of landslide dimensions. His counter-revolution, reported *Newsweek*, "shredded the old Democratic victory coalition, overwhelmed Carter by 51 to 41 percent at the polls and 483 to 49 in electoral votes, and led a resurgent Republican Party to control the Senate for the first time in a generation." The scale of Carter's defeat was in important measure a repudiation of his presidential impotence in the face of economic stagnation, inflation, and rising interest rates at home and the nation's sense of anxiety, humiliation, and rage over the Iranian hostage crisis overseas. Carter not only lost the Northeast and nearly every state between Minnesota and California, but even the South turned on its first president since the Civil War. In Reagan's wake, the GOP won the Senate for the first time since the heyday of Dwight Eisenhower in the 1950s, providing the Republicans with a working coalition and a mandate nearly as imposing as Lyndon Johnson's in 1964 or Richard Nixon's in 1972. Although the Democrats retained the House, they gave up 35 seats. Moreover, the GOP victory swept out of office several prominent liberals, including Senators George McGovern, Birch Baye, Warren Magnuson, John Culver, and even Frank Church, who led the Senate's investigation of the nation's intelligence agencies during the Ford administration. The journalist Anthony Lewis observed that perhaps an explanation could be advanced for each of these Democratic losses. "But the number of them—the sweep of the liberal disaster—makes it evident that a broader [conservative] trend was at work."[7]

As a final humiliation for the Carter presidency, the Iranians released the 52 captive Americans just hours after the inauguration of Ronald Reagan, who had kept safely aloof from the final throes of the negotiations. Just weeks later on January 27, in an emotionally charged ceremony on the South Lawn of the White House, Reagan welcomed home the hostages formerly held in Iran and delivered the outlines of a new and more forceful policy. "Those henceforth in the representation of this nation will be accorded every means of protection that America can offer," Reagan said. "Let terrorists be aware that when the rules of international behavior are violated, our policy will be one of swift and effective retribution." The statement echoed his campaign promise to bolster the nation's military and signaled a more muscular foreign policy that also would seek to throw off the legislative constraints that bound the presidency from acting with greater freedom abroad—positions that Cheney would fully embrace.[8]

During the 1980 elections, Cheney, who supported Reagan, ran unopposed in Wyoming's GOP congressional primary and won a second term in Congress against a weak Democratic opponent, Jim Rogers, owner of a small-town motel and lounge where he also worked as the bartender. Cheney returned to Washington and was quickly catapulted into a leadership role with the help of Bob Michel of Illinois, whom Cheney had known during the Ford administration when Michel was the House Republican whip. Michel was angling for House minority leader after John Rhodes announced that he would be resigning from the post after the Ninety-sixth Congress. Cheney threw his support behind Michel, who returned the favor by helping him win the chairmanship of the House Policy Committee, making him the fourth-ranking member of the Republican leadership. Along with Michel and Cheney, Jack Kemp of New York and Trent Lott of Mississippi also won leadership roles. Together the four representatives formed the heart of the new Republican leadership in the House, with Cheney supposedly serving as a moderating voice among the right-wing conservative leaders.[9] At least in the beginning of his congressional career, there was a question within Republican circles about Cheney's conservative credentials. He had served as a functionary in a moderate White House under Ford and in his first congressional term had cast at least one-third of his votes in favor of Carter's policies.[10] Yet, Cheney would become one of the Reagan administration's most ardent supporters as the White House sought to restore executive powers and roll back the legislative handiwork of Democratic Congresses of the 1970s.

As chair of the policy committee, Cheney played the House so adroitly that he quickly overshadowed Trent Lott to succeed minority leader Michel. "Cheney's rise to power," wrote journalists Lou Dubose and Jake Bernstein, "was so rapid that Lott, minority whip and heir apparent, understood that he had lost his lock on the leadership position." Crowded out by Cheney's rising influence, Lott left the House to run for a vacant Senate seat. But Cheney was only a rising star within a minority conference that exercised little power in the House. His entire career in the House occurred while the Democrats held an overwhelming governing majority and dominated the legislative process. "Not only was Cheney a member of a disaffected minority party, he was a minority member of a Democratic Congress that had reasserted its power by ending the career of Richard Nixon and imposing limits on the authority of Gerald Ford—the two presidents for whom Cheney had worked," noted Dubose and Bernstein. Despite his conservative ideology, he kept distant but cordial relations with Newt Gingrich and his band of conservative partisans who waged an effort to overthrow the Democrats in the House. He shared their frustration with minority status while serving as bridge between Gingrich's radical faction and the more guarded members led by leader Bob Michel. He also maintained cordial relations with the majority. He "was an institutionalist," said congressional scholar Norman Ornstein. "He cared about institutions. He had a good relationship with [Democratic majority leader and later speaker] Tom Foley. He really cared about how the institution worked." In fact, Cheney was enormously active in the House. Aside from his memberships on the interior and ethics committees, he became a member of the intelligence committee and joined the Wednesday Group, a discussion group of mostly moderate Republicans. Indeed, Cheney played all sides of the political spectrum, associating with moderate Republicans, maintaining contacts with Gingrich insurrectionists, while even for a time cultivating cordial relations with the majority across the aisle.[11]

Of Reagan's presidential victory, Cheney said the 1980 returns showed 1976 to have been "an aberration." Indeed, Reagan's victory and Republican sweep of the Senate reflected a general and profound turn to conservatism that began even before 1980. Some speculated that the Republicans might have won the White House in 1976 if not for the public revulsion at the crimes of Richard Nixon. The GOP victories in the Senate races showed something more profound at work than dissatisfaction with Jimmy Carter. The shift to Republican control of the Senate marked a sea change in the political landscape. It ushered in a new group of Senators from the far right, bolstered by superb organization, big money, and single-issue groups like the Moral Majority and other religious organizations preaching to millions that God favored a balanced budget, a stronger military, and a resurgent America. With control of the Senate and a firmer grip on the House through coalition with conservative Democrats, the Republicans emerged from the wilderness to win what they had not enjoyed for a long time—the responsibility of power in Washington.[12] "A tidal wave hit us from the Pacific, the Atlantic, the Caribbean and the Great lakes," House Speaker Thomas P. (Tip) O'Neill had said.

The "Reagan Revolution" would manifest itself in the most assertive presidency since the Nixon years. Cheney helped to defeat Reagan in the 1976 GOP primaries as part of Ford's presidential bid, but would now move with alacrity to forge close ties with the new administration—an effort that once again catapulted his rise to prominence. Just two weeks after the election, Cheney met with James Baker, the president's new chief of staff and a 1976 Ford campaign veteran. On November 18, 1980, Baker took notes as Cheney emphasized the imperative for the presidency to restore its executive powers lost after the Nixon administration.[13] Reagan's conservative revolution aimed to end fifty years of liberal big government by bleeding social and economic programs, slashing tax rates for individuals and businesses, and cutting the federal budget by tens of billions. The administration's untested economic program hoped to spur savings and investment, boost American industry, and usher in a new era of prosperity after the dark years of the 1970s. The Reagan agenda also called for appointing a conservative federal judiciary that would limit abortion, busing, and affirmative action. Reagan's foreign policy rested in the conviction that détente with the Soviet Union and the two SALT treaties had eroded American power. The Reagan administration pushed for a radical military buildup, the largest peacetime rearmament since World War II, as a sign of American resolve to confront the Soviet Union and its allies around the globe. The proposed buildup encompassing everything from the MX missile, the cruise missile, and the B-1 bomber to the 600-ship fleet aimed to redress perceived U.S. weakness in the face of Soviet military gains.

The administration's aggressive agenda was accompanied by an assertive presidential effort to throw off many of the legislative constraints of the 1970s. By the time Reagan entered office, some were arguing that the "imperial presidency" of the 1950s and 1960s had become radically transformed into the "imperiled presidency"—tied down and unable to act in response to rapidly changing developments in world affairs and on economic matters on the home front.[14] Indeed, conservative activists viewed the presidency as a casualty of congressional overreaching and in need of restoration of its executive powers. In a real sense, Reagan's agenda depended on a vigorous assertion of presidential power to impose his new economic order and a more muscular foreign policy. A collision between Reagan's ideological and activist agenda and the legislative binds of the 1970s passed by liberal Congresses seemed all but inevitable. But in an ironic and historic twist, the conservative Reaganites supported an unfettered executive that resembled the past Democratic presidencies of Franklin Roosevelt, Harry Truman, and Lyndon Johnson—all of whom endeavored to extend executive power and confronted opposition by Republicans whose ideology stemmed from a distrust of government power.[15] To the new generation of conservative activists, a strong and unfettered presidency was necessary for imposing lower taxes and traditional social values, building a more powerful military to confront communism, and overcoming the liberal status quo.

Although a leader in the House, Cheney also called for the restoration of executive powers—a position he argued shortly after winning his second term in a panel discussion at the American Enterprise Institute in December 1980. Organized around the theme of how to revitalize America, the panel discussion also involved Missouri Democrat Richard Gephardt and Georgians Wyche Fowler, a Democratic senator, and Newt Gingrich. Cheney called for the weakening of Congress. "A fundamental problem," he said, "has been the extent to which we have restrained presidential authority over the last several years. Consumed with the trauma of Watergate and Vietnam, we have tampered with the relationship between the executive branch and the Congress in ways designed primarily to avoid future abuses of power.... We have been concerned with the so-called myth of the imperial presidency." Cheney labeled Congress as the problem and called for the need to restore balance between the legislative and executive branches. Unlike Cheney, Gingrich took a salutary view of Congress, arguing for the need to strengthen, not weaken, Congress. "What we need is a stronger Congress, not a weaker Congress," Gingrich said. "The greatest danger of the Reagan administration is that conservatives will decide they can trust imperial presidents as long as they are right-wing when they are imperial."[16]

There was some irony and prophecy in the opposing comments by the two Republican representatives. While Cheney, a congressional leader, argued for the extension of presidential power at the expense of his own institution, Gingrich expressed, if not augured, the dilemma of a future Congress that would face a conservative George W. Bush presidency determined to re-create the imperial powers of the Nixon White House. Further, in a revealing statement of his already well-formed views on executive power, Cheney declared that in times of "great national peril in the past—during the Civil War, or during the Depression, or during World War II—we have basically responded, as a society, to those crises by having the president, whoever he was, assume extraordinary authority." Cheney warned that as in previous decades in American history, the United States would once again have to "resort to force someplace in the world" during the 1980s. "If you are as concerned as I am about the 1980s, we are talking about a situation again, when, at a minimum, we must reduce the trend of the last few years, or we will have undermined presidential authority rather than granted additional authority." By all means, Cheney said, Americans should heed the principles of democracy, freedom, individual liberty, and human rights, but these values should not "create a smoke screen in front of our own eyes when it comes time for us to assess the national self-interest and the interests of our allies overseas."[17] These words not only argued for extending presidential power, but suggested civil liberties must take a back seat to national security interests. It was a theme that he would strike several times over the next quarter of a century.

REAGAN REASSERTS EXECUTIVE POWER

Cheney's position echoed the Reagan administration's intent to reassert executive power and throw off the congressional constraints of the 1970s. The administration aimed both to control the federal bureaucracy and scuttle or reshape the laws passed to limit executive power. Harking back to the Nixon years, Reagan moved to politicize the federal agencies, placing hundreds of vetted loyalists across the bureaucracy. Like Nixon, this strategy meant to ensure that the administration's priorities would be carried out and prevent end-runs by bureaucrats around the White House and to Congress. The effort to dominate the federal bureaucracy hinged on taking full advantage of civil service reform passed in 1978 that granted presidents more authority in making high-level appointments. With this greater leeway, the president purged numerous career officials from key positions, replaced them with partisan loyalists, and imposed staffing cuts that wiped out entire offices of civil servants. Reagan also used his appointing power to bypass the Senate confirmation process, making as many as 250 recess appointments in eight years. Similarly, in the effort to reshape the federal bench, judicial appointees were vetted for their ideological conformity. The old public administration ideal of "neutral competence" was swept aside for ideological loyalty. Carter's merit-based screening process was "replaced in 1981 by a President's Committee on Federal Judicial Selection, which institutionalized close ideological review of candidates for the bench."[18]

The Reagan administration followed Nixon's lead in other ways, shifting policy making from the federal agencies back to the office of the presidency and reestablishing a hierarchical White House. Reagan also made wider use of executive orders, allowing him with the stroke of a pen to impose binding directives on members of the executive branch, shape regulatory action, restructure agencies or alter processes of decision making, and even formulate new policy in the grey areas where Congress had not legislated. Starting with the Reagan administration, presidents increasingly used executive orders to impose their will within the executive branch and bypass congressional oversight of the regulatory agencies.[19]

Less than a month after taking office in 1981, Reagan issued an executive order that constituted the centerpiece of his deregulatory drive. The directive ordered regulatory agencies to submit their rule-making proposals to the OMB for cost-benefit analysis and approval by the administration's partisan appointees. The strategy aimed to control and halt further regulation of the economy. Nixon had been the first to grant regulatory approval power to the OMB, but the strategy never took hold. In 1985, Reagan strengthened the presidential order with another version, giving it much greater force. Critics charged that the directive not only gave OMB officials, working under the White House, control over the rule-making process, but that numerous regulations were being scrapped, delayed, or watered down. With this new authority, one legal analysis concluded that the administration granted the OMB "virtually unbridled power to supervise or veto almost any agency's activity without public scrutiny." Even so, Congress did little to push back the executive's encroachment onto its institutional prerogatives and the OMB's newly granted power remained in effect through the George W. Bush presidency.[20]

Reagan also far surpassed Nixon in using signing statements to attack the constitutionality or legality of certain provisions of legislation he was signing into law. The presidential signing statement dated to James Monroe when he refused to enforce part of a bill for encroaching on his appointment powers.[21] But in his ever-running battle with congressional Democrats, Reagan began using them extensively as a line item veto disguised as constitutional commentary and indicating his intent to carry out only part of the laws passed by the legislative branch. While Reagan gave greater play to signing statements to veto provisions of laws he disagreed with, the Supreme Court's 1983 decision in *INS v. Chadha* struck down Congress's use of the one-chamber legislative veto to check executive power. It had become, Justice Byron White wrote, "a central means by which Congress secure[d] the accountability of executive and independent agencies." It was a double victory; the end of the legislative veto and the greater use of signing statements further empowered presidential authority at the expense of Congress.[22]

At the height of the Cold War and with national security an ever-present concern, Reagan officials vigorously battled Congress to roll back the Freedom of Information Act, contending that it was compromising national security secrets. The administration's fight to weaken the cornerstone open government act produced only modest changes that gave greater powers to the FBI and CIA to exempt select operational and investigative files from the law. The administration also issued a presidential order in April 1982, rewriting the classification system to assure that more rather than less information could be classified. In response, the House Committee on Government Operations issued a report, saying that the administration's explanations for its classification order were "not credible" and that there was "substantial doubt that the changes [to the classification system] could be justified." The White House proposed prison terms for those who leaked information, limited access to classified information, and restricted official contacts with the press. "This administration, like most administrations, is determined to dry up or otherwise manipulate and control information that enables members of Congress, the press and the public to understand what it is doing and why," said one critic.[23]

The administration's secrecy initiatives also sought to re-establish the primacy of executive privilege of former presidents against the 1978 Presidential Records Act, which asserted public dominion over the records of presidents and vice presidents. When drafting the act, Congress determined that an ex-president's right of executive privilege over his presidential materials expired after twelve years—a position that was opposed not only by Carter, but Reagan, who was the first president to be covered under the law. In 1986, the Office of Legal Counsel (OLC) issued an administrative rule ordering the U.S. archivist to bow to any claims of executive privilege by former President Nixon. The impetus behind the OLC's directive was not Nixon, but Reagan. By expanding executive privilege to suit the incumbent, the OLC hoped to lay the groundwork both for Reagan and the protection and courtesy of his presidential successors. Writing in the *Wall Street Journal*, historian Stanley Kutler noted that the "Reagan White House well realizes what stakes are involved in the future interpretation of the Presidential Records Act of 1978." The effort to adopt Nixon's extreme notion of executive privilege appeared to return the issue to "square one and 1973 when one of Nixon's lawyers flatly declared: It's for the president alone to say what is covered by executive privilege." The U.S. Court of Appeals overturned the Reagan administrative directive in 1988 on grounds that the U.S. archivist was not "constitutionally compelled" to obey a former president's claim of privilege.[24]

As the administration cloaked its activities in greater secrecy, Reagan also issued a pair of 1981 executive orders loosening Carter's constraints on the FBI and CIA. In 1983, Reagan's attorney general, Williams French Smith, overrode Levi's 1976 guidelines, watering down the evidentiary requirements before the FBI could launch full investigations. Another 1981 executive order liberated the CIA from Carter's legal constraints, empowering it to do almost anything around the world short of assassination and other strictly prohibited activities. The administration, moreover, freed the agency to carry out domestic counterintelligence in coordination with the FBI and shifted review authority from the national security advisor to the new director of the CIA, William Casey, whose talent lay in "bending rules to the breaking point." Within the first two months alone after taking office, the administration had already given Casey the "go-ahead for sweeping covert operations aimed at Central America, Nicaragua, Cuba, northern Africa, and South Africa."[25]

The Reagan Justice Department further pushed an obscure philosophy called the unitary executive theory, a concept championed by conservative lawyers to win back the lost powers of the presidency. The theory largely derived from two tenets in the Constitution: the "Oath" and "Take Care" clauses of Article II. The Oath clause requires the president to "faithfully execute the Office of the President and preserve, protect, and defend the Constitution of the United States."[26] The Take Care clause obligates the president to take care that the laws are faithfully executed.[27] Under the

Take Care clause, the president was obligated to assure that executive agencies under his purview were executing the laws according to his wishes—or so the unitary theory argued. According to the theory, the Constitution gave the president exclusive authority over everything in the executive branch, and any infringement on these powers was unconstitutional. It was therefore unconstitutional for Congress to pass any laws that gave executive branch officials independence from presidential authority or that interfered with his powers to remove such officials at will, despite the clear language of statutes to the contrary.

Under this theory, an independent counsel or members of the board of the Federal Reserve were wholly subservient to presidential authority and could be dismissed at the whim of the White House. Among the theory's most ardent supporters was Samuel Alito, then a Justice Department lawyer and later appointed a Supreme Court Justice by President George W. Bush. The theory dated to the 1970s when Congress and the courts responded to the sweeping abuses of power during the Nixon administration. With the congressional assault on executive power, lawyers in the Ford administration began seeking ways to safeguard presidential power. Leading the way was another future Supreme Court Justice, Antonin Scalia, who then headed Ford's Office of Legal Counsel. Under the leadership of Reagan's attorney general, Edwin Meese III, the Justice Department's conservative team produced an eighty-page treatise for bolstering presidential power. The report's cover letter gave a clarion call to reclaim the presidency's lost powers under the banner of the unitary executive—by refusing to enforce laws that unconstitutionally infringed on the presidency, vetoing legislation, using signing statements to generate a record of the president's constitutional interpretation of new legislation, and attacking the constitutionality of the War Powers Resolution, as well as other limits on executive powers.[28]

CHENEY: ALLY OF PRESIDENTIAL POWER

Faced with little opposition, Cheney would win repeated congressional reelections to the House until his resignation in March 1989. During this period, he continued his ascent to power, rising from the "fourth-ranking member of the leadership to become Bob Michel's number two"—his right-hand man.[29] He also won a seat on the House intelligence committee and later played a prominent role in the Iran-Contra hearings. Cheney aligned his voting record with the Reagan administration's "counter-revolution." On domestic affairs, he supported Reagan's radical package of massive tax cuts that won an 89-to-11 vote in the Republican Senate and cleared the Democratic House in a stunning 238-to-195 upset. The president's tax bill, even more than his $32.2 billion assault on the federal budget, was the instrument of what Treasury Secretary Donald T. Regan called a "conservative revolution" against fifty years of welfare statesmanship. Its key provisions included slashing individual income taxes by 25 percent between 1981 and 1983 and indexing them against inflation—a policy aimed at bleeding old social programs and curbing the possibility of new ones. The federal tax and budget cut victories came from a shotgun alliance between Republicans and conservative Democrats.

But Cheney's true interests lay in national security affairs and he would become one of the administration's most ardent congressional allies in projecting American power overseas and building up America's conventional and nuclear arms. During the Ford years, he had opposed the policy détente with the Soviet Union, which was continuing its post-Cuban Missile Crisis buildup—MIRVing (multiple independently targeting reentry vehicle) its missiles as well as introducing new and more powerful models.[30] Further, as White House chief of staff, Cheney had provided "instrumental support" to one of the CIA's outside intelligence panels—Team B—involved in examining the question of Soviet strategic objectives. Team B comprised one of three outside panels assigned to review the data and conclusions of the "A teams" within the CIA that were preparing the 1976 National Intelligence Estimate. With the blessing of Cheney and Rumsfeld, a private group set up by Paul Nitze, a longtime advocate for U.S. nuclear superiority, hand-picked Team B's outside hard-line analysts. In response to Nixon's policy of détente, Nitze and Albert Wohlsetter at the University of Chicago had formed the Committee to Maintain a Prudent Defense Policy, the first of several private organizations that aimed to subvert reducing the nuclear arsenal. The effort recruited young graduate students, among them Paul Wolfowitz and Richard Perle, unleashing "a team of sorcerer's apprentices whose trail of wreckage" would continue into the 21st century. Cheney's involvement, wrote Richard Rhodes in his book *Arsenals of Folly*, was the origin of his "alliance with the loose association of blusterous Manichean Democratic and Republican radicals who came to be called the neoconservatives."[31]

Richard Pipes, a former director of the Harvard Russian Research Center, directed the team, which produced a wildly distorted portrait of the Soviets as bent on nuclear superiority and world domination. According to the report, the Soviets were engaged in an intensified military effort to achieve nuclear as well as conventional superiority. "While hoping to crush the 'capitalist' realm by other than military means, the Soviet Union is nevertheless preparing for a Third World War as if it were unavoidable," said the report. "The intensity and scope of current Soviet military effort in peacetime is without parallel in twentieth century history, its only counterpart being

Nazi remilitarization of the 1930s. . . ." The report predicted that within ten years the Soviets might well achieve a degree of military superiority that "would permit a dramatically more aggressive pursuit of their hegemonic objectives, including direct military challenges to Western vital interests, in the belief that such superior military force can pressure the West to acquiesce or, if not, can be used to win a military contest at any level." It was an argument, based on paranoia and hyperbole, for vastly ramping up national defense spending to boost America's conventional and nuclear weapons programs and for contemplating the possibility of intercontinental nuclear war. Rhodes showed that Team B's conclusions were erroneous on every level and grossly inflated the Soviet nuclear threat, including the claim that a super-secret facility (later shown to be a rocket engine test site) was producing a nuclear-powered laser beam.[32] The practice of seeing exaggerated threats of weapons of mass destruction, unsubstantiated by evidence, would later be used by Vice President Dick Cheney to make a case for war against Iraq.

When Jimmy Carter summarily dismissed the report and disbanded the panel after his 1976 election, the nuclear conservatives formed the second incarnation of the Committee on the Present Danger (CPD) to raise public concern about the Soviet threat. The committee constituted a coalition of neoconservatives—mostly hawkish Democrats and aggressive Republican nationalists opposed to détente. Operating as a shadow foreign-policy cabinet, CPD members wrote position papers and opinion pieces, appeared on television news shows, and brokered news leaks from disgruntled hawks to news media outlets to build support for shoring up America's nuclear arsenal and assuming a more confrontational stance toward Moscow. After Reagan won the 1980 presidential election, some forty-six CPD members found a home in the new administration, many at senior foreign-policy-making levels—including CIA director William Casey, UN ambassador Jeane Kirkpatrick, Assistant Secretary of Defense Richard Perle, National Security Council Advisor Richard Pipes, and arms negotiators Max Kampelman and Paul Nitze.[33] The group's aggressive claims not only had portrayed Carter as a weak president unable to face down the Soviets, but continued to produce the intellectual underpinnings for Reagan's massive defense buildup at the expense of domestic programs.

Given his staunch opposition to détente and his early involvement in Team B, Cheney made for a natural congressional ally with the national security hard-liners in the Reagan administration. The projection of American power depended on a reinvigorated executive after the foreign policy humiliations of the Carter administration. Cheney supported Reagan's push for the controversial MX missile, a new land-based intercontinental missile that represented a technological leap in America's nuclear arsenal. First proposed in 1971 by the Strategic Air Command, the missile represented a key goal of the strategic modernization program to strengthen America's land-based nuclear deterrent. The MX had a range of approximately 4,000 miles; each missile carried ten 300-kiloton warheads that could destroy reinforced missile silos and command bunkers in the Soviet Union. To evade detection by Soviet satellites, the Pentagon proposed a variety of mobile basing systems— including launching by air from huge transport jets, shuttling them on trucks or rail cars among multiple protective shelters, or submerging them in lakes. The various proposals not only proved prohibitively expensive, but politically unpopular.[34]

In 1979, Carter's defense secretary Harold Brown championed the racetrack plan, which proposed shuttling 200 missiles along 10,000 miles of rails in and out of 4,600 shelters in Utah and Nevada. But the plan met vigorous opposition from conservative citizens of the western states, including farmers, ranchers, outdoorsmen, and leaders of the Mormon and Roman Catholic churches who objected on moral and environmental grounds. More important, critics argued that the shell game made no sense given the Soviets' capacity to build enough missiles with multiple warheads to hit every shelter, armed or empty. Reagan scrapped the plan in 1981 in favor of placing the missiles in super-hardened, dense silo clusters on the dubious hypothesis that incoming enemy missiles would destroy each other before hitting their targets. When the House rejected this option by a vote of 245 to 176 in December 1982, it handed the Reagan administration its first major defense policy defeat. Then in 1983, Reagan appointed a special eleven-member commission— led by Brent Scowcroft and including Donald Rumsfeld—to study how to revive the beleaguered MX. The commission recommended placing one hundred MX missiles in existing Minuteman III silos in eastern Wyoming and western Nebraska, even though these sites might be vulnerable to attack. The commission also proposed complementing the MX with smaller, single-warhead missiles called Midgetmen. With this proposal in hand, Reagan christened the MX the "Peacekeeper" and, along with the Midgetman, it became a big part of the administration's arms-control equation to bargain with the Soviets from a position of strength. In the end, however, only fifty were authorized for deployment at Warren Air Force Base, Wyoming.[35]

Even so, the MX plan faced congressional opposition from those who argued that it was too expensive, vulnerable to Soviet attack, and likely to upset the nuclear balance between the superpowers. In 1984, a confident Tip O'Neill predicted that the MX would never be deployed. Another congressional critic warned that the "MX is in its coffin, but we still have to drive the silver stake through its heart."[36] An old Wyoming friend of Cheney's—John Perry Barlow, who helped get him elected as the state's lone congressman—also opposed the plan and especially Cheney's role as congressional point man to deploy the MX beneath the Wyoming plains. Barlow later wrote that he once "conspired" with Cheney on the right side of environmental issues. "Working together, we were instrumental in closing down a copper smelter in Douglas, Arizona, that [sic] grandfathered effluents of which were causing acid rain in Wyoming's Wind River mountains," he wrote. "We were densely interactive allies in creating the Wyoming Wilderness Act. He used to go fishing on my ranch. We were friends." But not on the MX issue, which he viewed as a radical shift away from the theory of mutually assured destruction (MAD) toward a first strike policy. The MX would be targeted not at population centers but at Soviet ICBM sites. Because the U.S. missiles would be vulnerable in their silos, they would have to be launched first—based on a computer launch-on-warning system—to avoid being destroyed by enemy ICBMs. Barlow spent considerable time on Capitol Hill during the winters of 1981 and 1982, lobbying over a hundred congressmen and senators against the MX. "The only member of Congress who knew more about it than I did was Dick Cheney," Barlow said. Accompanying him on one of his "futile visits" to Cheney's office was veteran *Washington Post* columnist Mary McGrory. The columnist spent more than an hour listening to Barlow and Cheney argue over the arcane aspects of nuclear deterrence. "When we were leaving," Barlow recalled, "she who had seen a lot of politicians in her long day, turned to me and said, 'I think your guy Cheney is the most dangerous person I've ever seen up here.'"[37]

But Cheney's views and efforts to overcome the president's arms control opponents were little different from other congressional and administration anti-Soviet hard-liners, who had long argued for ramping up America's nuclear deterrent and contemplated the real possibility of nuclear war. Amid exploding budget deficits and runaway Pentagon spending, Reagan battled Congress over the controversial missile, winning funding in 1986 for only fifty MX missiles. The administration's defense buildup ignited an arms race with the Soviet Union that involved launching the Strategic Defense Initiative or "Star Wars," a futuristic endeavor to build ground- and space-based systems to defend the nation against a massive nuclear first strike. As an ardent supporter of Star Wars, Cheney believed the Soviets could not match American technological prowess and that it would force them to yield. In a sense, Cheney was right. According to some scholars and defense analysts, the Reagan administration spent the Soviets into oblivion. But the Soviet Union also collapsed for other reasons, including social, economic, and ideological stagnation and the revolutions in the satellite nations of Eastern Europe.[38]

As a longtime adherent of rolling back the spread of communism, Cheney backed the administration's efforts to assist the Contras against the

Soviet-backed Sandinista government in Nicaragua. Cheney often lent his assistance to National Security Council staffers in the White House in planning ways to out-maneuver Democratic opponents in funding the Contra rebels. Cheney later assailed Jim Wright, who in 1987 became speaker of the House, for meeting with Nicaraguan leaders to moderate American policy in Central America. According to Cheney, these meetings usurped the president's executive role in foreign affairs. Cheney also championed the administration's aggressive policy in projecting American power abroad, including the deployment of U.S. military forces in foreign lands. In 1982, he supported Reagan's decision to send 1,800 American marines to Beirut as part of a multinational peacekeeping force to help separate the warring Lebanese factions. But amid the sectarian strife, American forces went to war on the side of the Christians without knowing what they were getting into. U.S. jets were bombing Muslims, and American ships were firing one-ton shells into the hills of Lebanon. On October 23, 1983, terrorists drove a truck bomb into the American barracks at Beirut international airport, killing 241 American marines. The bombing ignited outbursts in Congress over Reagan's ill-defined mission in Lebanon. Democratic congressman Clarence Long of Maryland spoke for many when he denounced Reagan's policy in Beirut as being "based on the phony theory that if you put American uniformed men there, the enemy won't shoot at them. The theory has been blown up along with the Marine barracks." But Cheney argued that Congress was equally responsible, given that it had agreed to let the Marines remain in Lebanon after they had already been deployed to Beirut. With the backing of Speaker of the House Tip O'Neill and the Democratic leadership, the administration immediately beat back an attempt in the House to cut off funds for the Marines in Beirut, but four months after the bombing the Marines were ordered to start pulling out of Lebanon.[39]

Thirty-six hours after the Beirut tragedy, the United States turned its attention to a Marxist insurgency in Grenada, a tiny island in the Caribbean overrun by a Cuban brigade of military construction workers. When the island's leader, Maurice Bishop, was killed in a power struggle, the United States invaded to block the communist coup. Several Democrats predicted that the bloody tragedy in Lebanon and the invasion of Grenada would fuel public concerns that Reagan was reckless with the use of military force. Unlike Lebanon, the Grenada action provoked the House to pass a resolution, by an overwhelming vote of 403 to 23, to apply the War Powers Act to the U.S. Marines on the island and require their withdrawal within 60 days unless an extension was granted. Moreover, Speaker O'Neill appointed a delegation of fourteen House members, including Cheney, to investigate the situation in Grenada. O'Neill, who supported keeping troops in

Lebanon for fear of Syrian designs on Lebanon, assailed the president on Grenada: "You cannot justify any government, whether it's Russia or the United States, trampling on another nation." But Cheney extolled the invasion to reporters as a "selfless and courageous act by a great nation." The Grenadian people were grateful for being "rescued and liberated," he said, expressing unwavering support for the president's wartime powers.[40]

Seeing Cheney as perhaps the most ardent and knowledgeable congressional supporter of its national security agenda, the White House involved him in one of its Armageddon programs. With the nuclear arms race with the Soviets going at full speed, the Reagan administration began secretly flying Cheney out once a year for three or four days at a time to a remote location in the United States, such as an abandoned military base or bunker. During these clandestine ventures, neither anyone in Congress nor his own wife knew of his whereabouts. Joined by a team of forty to sixty federal officials and a single member of Reagan's cabinet, Cheney served as a principal figure in one of the administration's most highly classified programs. According to James Mann, author of *Rise of the Vulcans*, the program involved "furtively carrying out detailed planning exercises to establish a new American president and his staff, outside and beyond the specifications of the U.S. Constitution, in order to keep the federal government running during and after a nuclear war with the Soviet Union."[41]

The administration's secret continuity of government program involved a basic concept—if the American homeland was threatened with nuclear attack, three independent teams would leave Washington for three separate locations. Each team would be prepared to proclaim a new American president and set up a new government. If the Soviets were to locate and kill off one or more of the teams with a nuclear strike, the second or third team could assume control. Among the members of each team would be an experienced leader who could act as chief of staff and a single member of Reagan's cabinet who would serve as the next American president. Because some of these American "presidents" would have little experience in national security, they most likely would have "served as mere figureheads for their more experienced chiefs of staff, such as Cheney. . . ." The problem was that the program was deliberately and inherently extralegal and extraconstitutional; it set up a process for naming a new American president outside the bounds of the Constitution. The program not only disregarded the 1947 Presidential Succession Act, which put the two top congressional leaders in the line of succession after the vice president, but also included no contingency for reconstituting Congress. After all, one participant told Mann, "it would be easier to operate without them."[42]

Cheney once again came to the defense of the president's wartime powers after the Pentagon mounted a large nighttime air strike on Libya, its most devastating air assault since Vietnam. The April 1986 attack came in response to the bombing of a West Berlin discotheque popular with American soldiers, killing one U.S. serviceman. After U.S. intelligence intercepted Libyan government communications implicating Libya in the disco attack, Reagan ordered retaliatory air strikes on Tripoli and Benghazi. The disco bombing was the latest in a long string of Libyan-sponsored terrorist attacks on the West. From the burning of the U.S. embassy in Tripoli in 1979 to the terrorist assaults on the Rome and Vienna airports in December 1985, the administration accused Muammar Gaddafi of leaving a trail of blood and destruction. According to the United States, Gaddafi was one of the world's foremost sponsors of terrorism, financing groups from the radical Palestinian groups to outfits as distant as Colombia's M-19 guerrillas. Since 1980, the Libyan leader had carried out more than fifteen assassinations of anti-Gaddafi exiles in Italy, England, West Germany, and the United States and had called for attacking Americans in 1986 after the United States Navy clashed with Libyan patrol boats off the Gulf of Sidra. The U.S. air attack on Libya not only earned the ire of European allies for its unilateralism, but also of some lawmakers who argued that the administration was committing an act of war without consulting Congress under the War Powers Act. Just days before the air strike, Cheney appeared on the *MacNeil/Lehrer NewsHour*, all but mocking the voices on the Hill—"the cry for consultation in advance, let us in on the decision, we want to share responsibility." It seemed to Cheney that the Libyan episode was a "clear-cut case where the president as commander in chief . . . is justified in taking whatever action he deems appropriate and discussing the details with us after the fact."[43]

But the Libyan incident reflected a more assertive unilateralism that would sow the seeds and come to define Cheney's approach to international relations during the George W. Bush administration. Writing in *Time* magazine in April 1986, Strobe Talbott observed that the bombing attack against Libya was the most "dramatic example to date of an important theme in the foreign policy of the Reagan Administration: a determination to use American military power against enemies anywhere in the world, regardless of whether the United States has the support of its allies." The phrase "global unilateralism" came into vogue among critics and admirers of the administration's willingness to go it alone. In 1981, U.S. Navy fighter pilots had shot down two of Gaddafi's Soviet-built SU-22 fighters over the Gulf of Sidra. There was also the 1983 invasion of Grenada and the 1985 interception of an Egyptian airliner with the Achille Lauro hijackers aboard—all of which appeared to be mere dress rehearsals for the controversial bombing raid on Libya and the larger engagements to come. The administration's penchant for unilateralism also became apparent in its commitments for anti-communist guerrilla movements and the Strategic Defense Initiative conceived in 1983—a "deux ex-machina of global unilateralism: a made-in-the-U.S.A. system for effectively disarming the Soviet Union and any other threat to the United States."[44]

The Reagan Doctrine held that the United States should bypass wavering and sometimes unreliable allies in order to confront its enemies abroad and protect its national interests. These policies evoked sometimes nervous reactions among U.S. allies, who often questioned and resisted participating in American missions in far-flung corners of the world. But these policies caused even more anxiety among the Soviets, who were the principal targets of the American initiatives, leading Foreign Minister Eduard Shevardnadze to denounce the United States for its "neoglobalism." The Reagan Administration, wrote Talbott, had "given global unilateralism both doctrinal and operational standing that it did not have before," despite its having been around for decades. After World War II, the United States had assumed global interests and responsibilities to rebuild Europe and Japan and to contain the far-reaching ambitions and capabilities of the Soviet Union. The United States built regional alliances, endeavoring throughout the 1950s and 1960s to give its allies a sense of full partnership in America's mission. Even so, the allies resisted being drawn into America's major conflicts in Korea and Vietnam. In the 1970s and 1980s, the United States found itself at cross-purposes with allies over Iran and Central America and ran into differences over fighting terrorism. A number of conservative thinkers advocated tossing aside the niceties of bilateralism and multilateralism and adopting a more confrontational stance with the Soviets. Their radical form of global unilateralism advanced the idea that alliances and international bodies—including the United Nations, NATO, and others—were obstructing the vigorous defense of the national interest and should be discarded. Reagan stopped short of accepting this extreme advice in favor of consulting with allies in advance, welcoming their support if offered, but not making their backing a precondition for American action.[45] The go-it-alone approach would once again become policy with much greater consequences under Cheney and others who would plan and rationalize the invasion of Iraq.

Five

Iran-Contra

Nothing would define Cheney's view of executive powers and his terms in Congress more than his role in the Iran-Contra scandal. The beginnings of the scandal dated to 1982 when Congress passed the first Boland Amendment banning military aid to the Contras seeking the overthrow of the Soviet-supported Sandinista government in Nicaragua. Reagan challenged the amendment by claiming that his aims were to force the Sandinistas into a peace agreement with the rebels rather than to topple the Nicaraguan government. He directed his aides to find a way to get around the amendment and to continue to provide assistance to the Contras. The secret mining of three Nicaraguan harbors by the CIA with the aim of destroying what was left of the Nicaraguan economy led Congress to pass a tougher second Boland Amendment in 1984, ruling out all assistance to the Contras. Although the amendment banned the CIA from soliciting funds from third countries to aid the rebels, CIA director William Casey nevertheless arranged for Saudi Arabia and Taiwan to kick in millions of dollars, funneled through a Swiss bank account controlled by the agency. With the specter of growing Soviet influence in Central America—perhaps even another Cuba at the doorstep of the United States—Cheney saw the sweeping amendment as an infringement on the president's authority. It was a "killer amendment" that would compel the Contras "to lay down their arms," he argued. Nevertheless, the amendment became law and over the next several years, Cheney endeavored to have it repealed.[1]

At the same time, the administration's secret dealings with Iran began in June 1985 when National Security Advisor Robert McFarland and his staff proposed an initiative to cultivate moderate elements within Iran's leadership. McFarland proposed curbing Soviet influence in the oil-rich nation by supplying arms to Iran, one of the world's foremost sponsors of international terrorism. The Iranian initiative met repeated opposition by Secretary of Defense Caspar Weinberger and Secretary of State George Shultz, who warned Reagan that he might be committing an impeachable offense. Even so, under the guidance of CIA director William Casey, Reagan and the White House pushed ahead with the plan without telling Shultz. Reagan hoped the initiative would win the freedom of seven Americans held hostage by pro-Iranian Shiite groups in Lebanon—violating the administration's explicit policy of not dealing with terrorists and avoiding oversight of the House and Senate intelligence committees. In the summer of 1985, Reagan approved the first arms transaction, first using Israel as an intermediary and transferring 500 U.S. TOW antitank missiles to Iran in the hope that the American hostages would be set free. Although just one hostage was freed, the National Security Council (NSC) continued the rogue secret arms sales and diversion of profits to the Nicaraguan rebels without notifying Congress as required by law.[2]

The Iranian operation collapsed in early November 1986 when *Al-Shiraa*, a Lebanese weekly, broke the initial story on the secret arms shipments, precipitating the biggest constitutional crisis since Watergate. Following this and other disclosures, Reagan went on television and said, "We did not—repeat—did not trade weapons or anything else for hostages, nor will we." Then later that month, another underground operation came to light involving staffers in the NSC—Lieutenant Colonel Oliver North and Vice Admiral John Poindexter with the help of others in the CIA and the White House—who were diverting profits from the Iranian arms shipments to the Contras seeking the overthrow of the Sandinistas. While conspiring to evade the 1984 Boland Amendment, the NSC operatives hired private subcontractors to do much of the legwork and solicited private contributions from foreign leaders. Summoned to Congress, Casey denied that any funds for the Nicaraguan rebels had been solicited from foreign governments, while knowing that the Saudis had already agreed to give millions of dollars to the Contras at the request of the White House.[3]

The Iran-Contra affair had epitomized the Reagan administration's boldest expression yet of its aim to reassert presidential powers. The clandestine operation marked the high point of its struggle against the series of laws passed mostly in the 1970s to give Congress greater influence over foreign policy. These included the War Powers Act, passed over Nixon's veto in 1973 with the aim to prevent presidents from prosecuting undeclared wars; the amended Arms Control Act of 1976, intended to restrict the president's power to approve arms shipments to friendly countries; and the Intelligence

Oversight Act of 1980, meant to limit the president's broad authority to deploy secretly the intelligence agencies overseas. In 1981, a divided Congress was confronted with the ideological and activist Reagan Administration fiercely determined to reassert and guard its executive prerogatives. Reagan's landslide victory in the race for the presidency also had swept in a Republican majority in the Senate, providing the new administration with a working coalition and greater latitude to navigate around many of the most important laws. It was one thing for a mostly Democratic Congress to pass laws constraining the presidency during an era of reaction against executive abuse of power, but it was quite another for a divided Congress years later to marshal the political will to see them enforced against a popular president. On divisive foreign policy issues like the wars of Central America, Congress could rarely forge a consensus, falling into ideologically charged disputes, bitter recriminations, and political deadlock. The administration itself resorted to corrosive secrecy intended to conceal its activities from the public and Congress, resulting in the misuse of government institutions and the flouting of laws.[4]

Writing in the *New York Times*, Mark Danner, a staff writer at the *New Yorker* who wrote on foreign affairs, noted that the "supposedly 'secret' and 'illegal' aid to the Contras was in fact the product of political deadlock and cowardice on all sides." Although the president was committed to the Contras, the administration seemed unwilling to wage a campaign to persuade the public to fully support the cause. For its part, Congress had managed to pass the Boland Amendment, but proved too sharply divided and showed a willing and convenient blindness in accepting the administration's "bland assurances" that it was complying with the law. "In fact," said Danner, "the Administration's contempt for the law was shared by many in Congress. The entire matter was awash in hypocrisy."[5]

After the scandal broke and made international headlines, Congress with now Democratic majorities in the House and Senate proceeded to open hearings. Appointed the ranking House Republican on the joint Senate-House Iran-Contra committee, Cheney used his position to defend the president and his controversial policies in Central America, as well as to attack Congress. The initial debate among committee members involved how long the hearings should last. The Republicans pushed for abbreviated hearings, while the Democrats feared appearing partisan if they held exhaustive hearings that extended into the 1988 presidential election. The two sides struck an agreement on just a ten-month deadline to wrap up the investigation, a crucial mistake given that there was a considerable amount of evidence that had yet to be explored by the time the committee concluded its work. While some committee members wanted to extend the deadline to keep the investigation going, Cheney's view that the committee should adhere to the original schedule won the day, leaving many unanswered questions regarding what transpired.[6]

In his opening statements, Cheney set the tone and theme for his defense of executive power. "Some will argue that these events justify the imposition of additional restrictions on presidents to prohibit the possibility of similar occurrences for the future," he said. "In my opinion, that would be a mistake. In completing our task, we should seek above all to find ways to strengthen the capacity of future presidents and future Congresses to meet the often dangerous and difficult challenges that are bound to rise in the years ahead." Further, "One important question to be asked," he said, "is to what extent did the lack of a clear-cut policy by Congress contribute to the events we will be exploring in the weeks ahead?"[7]

During the hearings, moreover, Cheney often came to the president's defense. When Senator Daniel K. Inouye, the ranking majority senator on the investigating committee, said in a televised interview that a memo written by Poindexter suggested that he had briefed the president on the diversion of funds to finance secret operations other than the Nicaragua rebels, Cheney charged that the assertions were wholly unsupportable. Reagan insisted that he had never been told about any plans to use profits from the Iran arms sales to finance covert operations, and Cheney said that even if the president had read Poindexter's memo from "cover to cover," Reagan would "not have had any knowledge of an alleged diversion."[8] When Senator Orrin G. Hatch, the conservative Republican from Utah, raised the issue of pardoning Oliver North and John Poindexter from criminal prosecution by special prosecutor Lawrence E. Walsh, Cheney voiced support against Democratic opposition, though he thought the idea premature.[9] Further, when questioning Secretary of State George P. Shultz, who had opposed the interwoven Iran-Contra operations from the beginning, Cheney delivered a soliloquy reducing the Iran-Contra affair to a mere policy dispute. "There's a tendency for us to talk about a grave constitutional crisis," he said. "I look at the arguments about Watergate which some of my colleagues on this committee are fond of pulling out as a relevant analogy—and I must say I don't see any relevant comparison at all. I think the analogy is grossly overdone. . . . I just wonder if you would agree with my judgment that what we have here is a radically different set of circumstances, and not a political crime but rather fundamental disputes over policy."[10] But Shultz did not agree with Cheney's judgment, later repeatedly comparing the crisis to Watergate in his memoirs of his years as Reagan's secretary of state.[11]

At the close of the public hearings on the Iran-Contra affair on August 4, 1987, the Senate committee's chairman, Daniel Inouye, a wounded veteran of World War II, said that he saw the affair as a "chilling story, a story of deceit and duplicity and the arrogant disregard of the rule of law." Inouye had been especially disturbed by the claims of North and Poindexter that survival in a "dangerous world" often required measures beyond the bounds of the normal processes of government. "That," he said, "is an excuse for autocracy, not for policy. . . ." Whatever the case, the senator said, he found no virtue in the vision of government seen by North and Poindexter—that of a "secret government, accountable to not a single elected official" and "free from all checks and balances and free from the law itself." The House panel's chair, Lee H. Hamilton, an Indiana Democrat, sounded many of the same themes: "Too little accountability for decisions and actions taken in the name of elected officials; too much secrecy and deception in government; too little regard for the rule of law. . . ." One of the Republican committee leaders, Senator Warren Rudman, denounced the scandal as antithetical to "our democratic system of government." Alone among the four leaders who read full closing statements, Cheney attacked Congress as the problem. Its "vacillation" over appropriating funds for the Contras threatened the viability of the Nicaraguan insurgency and the "congressional track record" of disclosing government secrets forced the operation to go underground in order to roll back communism on America's doorstep in Central America and win the release of the hostages in Lebanon. Congress, he implied, could not be trusted with protecting the nation's secrets and should not usurp the executive's prerogatives in foreign affairs. Cheney urged his colleagues to "resist the temptation" to impose "further restrictions on the power and flexibility of future presidents."[12]

But it was in the final minority report where Cheney and his compatriots gave a full-throated attack on Congress's interference with the president's prerogatives in the foreign policy arena. Prepared on behalf of Cheney and seven other Republicans on the congressional Iran-Contra committees, the report called the majority report's charges of serious White House abuses of powers "hysterical." It reads "as if it were a weapon in the ongoing guerrilla warfare" between Congress and the White House, the minority report said. The errors made by the Reagan Administration in the Iran-Contra affair were "mistakes in judgment and nothing more," it said. "There was no constitutional crisis, no systematic disrespect for the rule of law, no grand conspiracy and no Administration-wide dishonesty or cover-up." The report condemned Congress for its inconsistent aid to the Contras, for passing laws that tied the president's hands in foreign affairs, for engaging in "interbranch intimidation," and for overstepping its constitutional bounds by interfering with the White House. The Reagan administration's major error was failing to fully protect its inherent constitutional powers. The report referred to the Federalist papers—Hamilton's support for "energy in the executive"—in denouncing the Democratic-controlled Congress for usurping the executive's prerogatives.[13]

Citing as precedent a 1936 Supreme Court ruling in *United States v. Curtis-Wright Export Corporation*, the report—above all—argued for unbridled executive discretion over foreign policy. After all, the Court referred to the "exclusive power of the president as the sole organ of the federal government in the field of international relations."[14] The minority said that history "leaves little, if any doubt that the president was expected to have the primary roles of conducting the foreign policy of the United States." Further, the report declared that any congressional action to limit presidential power over foreign policy should be viewed with considerable "skepticism." If such actions interfered with the "core presidential foreign policy functions, they should be struck down." Nevertheless, the *Curtis-Wright* decision addressed what Princeton University professor Sean Wilentz said was a "presidential claim of constitutional power to act in the absence of an act passed by Congress, not in violation of such an act."[15]

Among those who shaped the writing of the minority report and came to work closely with Cheney was a young, dour staff attorney, David S. Addington, a conservative hard-liner on national security issues. The son of a traditional Catholic military family, Addington had moved frequently as a young boy. His father, an army electrical engineer, was assigned to a variety of posts, including Saudi Arabia and Washington, D.C., where he worked with the joint chiefs of staff. Addington's father had earned a Bronze Star in World War II, served in Korea, and reached the rank of brigadier general before he retired in 1970, when David was thirteen. David Addington attended public high school in Albuquerque, New Mexico, where he graduated in 1974, the year that Nixon resigned. He then attended the U.S. Naval Academy in Annapolis, Maryland, for a year before dropping out and returning home where he worked in a fast food restaurant. He returned to college, however, graduating from Georgetown University in 1978 from the School of Foreign Service, earned a law degree in 1981 from Duke, and went to work for the CIA's general counsel's office. A former agency lawyer who knew Addington at the time described him as a strong opponent of the intelligence reforms of the 1970s. "Addington was too young to be shaped by the Vietnam War," he said. "He was shaped by the postwar, post-Watergate years instead. He's a believer that in foreign policy the executive is meant to be quite powerful." These views were shared by Cheney, who as chief of staff during the Ford years believed that the White House had capitulated too quickly on a range of executive-power issues to an assertive Congress.[16]

Addington was a staffer on the House Intelligence Community before becoming a member of the minority's legal staff. Like Cheney, Addington was an evolving executive supremacist regarding intelligence and foreign policy matters. Unlike Cheney, Addington also was a lawyer who aggressively sought to ground his views about the primacy of the executive in national security affairs in the Constitution. The minority report was chiefly authored by Michael J. Malbin, a former resident fellow of the American Enterprise Institute who was recruited by Cheney, but it also reflected Addington's constitutional theories on the inherent and exclusive right of the president to conduct foreign policy without congressional approval. It was a position that Cheney could appreciate as the two came to form a powerful team that would later find a place in the White House more than a decade later.[17]

The minority's views varied radically from those of the majority report, signed by eighteen House and Senate committee members, including three Republicans. The majority report condemned the "cabal of zealots" inside the White House for cynically subverting the rule of law and the Constitution. The small group of senior officials viewed "knowledge of their actions by others in the Government as a threat to their objectives," said the report. They informed neither the secretary of state nor the Congress and the American people of their actions. They destroyed official documents and lied to Cabinet officials, to the public, and to elected representatives in Congress when threatened with exposure. They "testified that they even withheld key facts from the President," the report noted. "Deniability replaced accountability," said the report, and confusion, deception, secrecy, and disdain for the law became the inevitable products of an attempt to avoid the open democratic processes of government. The covert program of support for the Contras "evaded the Constitution's most significant check on Executive power: the President can spend funds on a program only if he can convince Congress to appropriate the money." The report noted that the U.S. Constitution gave "important powers to both the President and the Congress in the making of foreign policy" and that the president was "the chief architect of foreign affairs in consultation with the Congress." But foreign policy could not work unless the branches worked together. "Yet, in the Iran-Contra Affair," said the report, "Administration officials holding no elected office repeatedly evidenced disrespect for Congress' efforts to perform its Constitutional oversight role in foreign policy." At the beginning of the Republic, the Founders had replaced the idea of monarchy with the rule of law—a principle that the president had failed to instill in his staff. In summing up its conclusions, the report cited Supreme Court Justice Louis Brandeis: "Our Government is the potent, the omnipresent teacher. For good or ill, it teaches the whole people by its example. Crime is contagious. If the Government becomes a law-breaker, it breeds contempt for the law, it invites every man to become a law unto himself, it invites anarchy." While the scathing report would later be echoed by the findings of the special prosecutor in 1993, the minority report quickly vanished from the public mind after briefly making headlines in the national press. It was dismissed by Republican Senator Warren Rudman, a signatory to the majority report, as "pathetic."[18]

The Iran-Contra hearings seemed to mark a watershed event for Cheney, deepening his antipathy for what he viewed as Congress's persistent encroachments onto the presidency's domain in foreign policy. The scandal and cover-up had threatened to topple the Reagan administration, a possibility that Cheney and his allies had done everything to avoid. He reflected the evolution of his thinking in a 1988 opinion piece in the *Wall Street Journal*. The editorial came before his successful effort in the House to block a Senate bill that would require presidents to notify Congress of any covert operations within forty-eight hours. It was the type of action that Cheney warned against in his closing remarks in the Iran-Contra hearings. The bill, said Cheney, constituted a "typical example of 'never again' thinking by Congress. To make sure the last disaster will never again repeat itself, Congress is willing to deprive future presidents of all possible discretion under conditions Congress cannot possibly foresee."[19]

The real dispute over the bill, he said, was over the scope of the president's inherent constitutional power. Cheney argued that Congress could exert its constitutional prerogatives over appropriating money to the executive branch, but it should avoid exercising this authority to invade the presidency's inherent power to conduct foreign intelligence operations. The presidency needed the flexibility to initiate operations as long as such actions were limited to the resources already available to the president. But if "Congress ever tries to insist on advance approval, that would surely be overturned as a legislative veto." Cheney proposed amending the Intelligence Oversight Act that would permit the two branches to recognize each other's appropriate constitutional role. But the proposal was an unequivocal argument for unilateral presidential action. "The president should retain the constitutional power to initiate a covert action," he suggested, "even if some members of Congress consider the operation controversial." Further, he advised that requiring the 48-hour notification might be acceptable if there was an escape clause for the president to invoke unilaterally in exceptional circumstances. Beyond this proposal, Cheney took a swipe at Congress, suggesting a 48-hour reporting requirement in reverse—mandating that members of Congress report their interactions and communications with foreign governments to the State Department within 48 hours after they occur. The proposal was more rhetorical than serious, but he aimed to reinforce his point that his own institution needed to retreat within its own constitutional bounds and improve its own untrustworthy and overreaching conduct.[20]

Six

The Secretary of Defense

In 1988, George Herbert Walker Bush, Reagan's vice president and the former CIA chief under Ford, won the presidency over Massachusetts Governor Michael Dukakis. Unlike President Reagan in 1981, Bush faced a strengthened Democratic Party on Capitol Hill. Reagan's victory had swept in a Republican-controlled Senate, giving his presidency a working coalition in Congress and causing the Democrats, having suffered heavy loses, to retreat in timidity. But in 1988, the Republicans lost ground in both houses, as the Democrats defied history and strengthened their majorities in the House and Senate while losing the presidency. The Senate minority leader, Bob Dole of Kansas, predicted that the situation would "spell trouble right from day one for George Bush."[1] In his acceptance speech in early November 1988, the president-elect took a conciliatory tone, saying he would do his "level best to reach out and work constructively with the United States Congress."[2]

In November 1988, while Bush talked of the need to consult and respect Congress, the Justice Department under his new attorney general wasted little time in attacking congressional power on foreign policy. The occasion came amid the prosecution of Oliver North for conspiring to deceive and obstruct Congress in its foreign policy responsibilities. In the pretrial hearings, the Justice Department intervened to assail the independent counsel, Lawrence E. Walsh. According to the department, by supporting the conspiracy charge, Walsh was conceding too much constitutional authority to Congress. "The President has plenary authority to represent the United States and to pursue its interests outside the borders of the country . . ." said a department legal memorandum. It argued that Congress faced "formidable constitutional limitations" in seeking to obtain information on covert operations such as North's dealings with terrorists in Iran. The memorandum constituted a sweeping claim of exclusive presidential power, arguing that Congress had no real role in the making of foreign policy. Once again, the 1936 Supreme Court opinion *Curtis-Wright* was cited—the decision that spoke of the "very delicate, plenary, and exclusive power of the president as the sole organ of the Federal Government in the field of international relations." But that case involved congressional authorization for presidential action. Further, the memorandum ignored Justice Robert H. Jackson's precedent-setting 1952 opinion rejecting President Harry Truman's claim that his foreign affairs powers allowed him to seize the nation's steel mills. The Constitution, he said, "enjoins upon its branches separateness but interdependence, autonomy but reciprocity." The Iran-Contra affair was a "particularly strange setting for an assertion that Congress can be excluded from any meaningful role in the making and checking of foreign policy," wrote Anthony Lewis of the *New York Times*. "For it is an extreme example of what can go wrong when we forget the fundamental premise of our Constitution, the need for checks and balances on power."[3]

Eight months later in July 1989, the new head of the Justice Department's Office of Legal Counsel, William P. Barr, sent out another warning regarding congressional threats to executive power. In a memorandum directed to general counsels of executive agencies, Barr outlined a series of ways in which Congress had commonly sought to encroach on executive prerogatives. Among other things, these included improper demands for sensitive executive branch information and infringement on the president's right to conduct foreign policy. Barr based his memo on the principles of the unitary executive theory, arguing that the Constitution directed the executive branch to speak with one voice. He warned the general counsels to be alert to any legislative efforts that would encroach on the president's power to fire executive branch officials at will. The memo stood in stark opposition to the June 1988 Supreme Court decision that upheld the independent counsel statute. In that case, the Justice Department claimed that the independent counsel law constituted an unconstitutional encroachment on the president's powers over the unitary executive. But the Court ruled in favor of Congress's power to establish officials in the executive branch who were beyond the reach and wholly independent of the president.[4] It was a stinging defeat for the unitary executive theory. Nevertheless, Barr advised that efforts should be made to limit the effect of the opinion by claiming that it only applied to independent counsels and not to other executive branch officials.[5]

In many respects, the Barr memo was a remarkable statement for defying congressional authority, if not denying the Supreme Court itself. It marked the first time that the Office of Legal Counsel had "publicly articulated a policy of resisting Congress," observed Georgia State law professor Neill Kinkopf. The Barr memo staked out an "expansive view of presidential power while asserting positions that contradicted recent Supreme Court precedent." Instead of "fading away as ill-conceived and legally dubious, however, the memo ideas persisted and evolved within the Republican Party and conservative legal circles like the Federalist Society."[6]

As Bush moved to assemble his national security team, a skirmish broke out over the nomination of former Senator John G. Tower of Texas as defense secretary. The nomination ran into stiff congressional opposition when Tower's personal life came under scrutiny amid charges of womanizing, alcohol abuse, and questionable ties to defense contractors. GOP leaders in the Senate and the White House battled to keep Tower's nomination alive before it went down by a vote of 53 to 47. It marked the first time since 1959, when the Senate rejected Lewis L. Straus for secretary of commerce, that a president's cabinet nomination had been denied. Never before then, in the nearly 200 years of the Republic, had the Senate rejected an incoming president's choice for his cabinet. Some saw the fight over Tower as part of the struggle between the branches for supremacy, similar to the War Powers Act restricting the president's discretion in waging undeclared wars. Senator Pete Wilson, a California Republican, said the Democratic majority had "corrupted, contaminated, and hijacked" the confirmation process, setting an "ugly, new, evil, dangerous precedent." Cheney may have agreed that the opposition party had invaded the prerogatives of the presidency, but he also knew that the White House needed someone who could work with Congress. Tower's bad twist of fate was Cheney's opportunity.[7]

Just one day after Tower's rejection in the Senate, Bush acted swiftly to transcend the fiasco, which had cast a shadow over most of his first fifty days in office, by nominating Cheney as his new secretary of defense. At the time, Cheney was preparing a conference paper to be delivered at the conservative American Enterprise Institute on congressional overreaching and aggrandizement of executive power. In the paper, he argued for exclusive presidential power in conducting foreign affairs and repealing the War Powers Resolution as unworkable and unconstitutional. Echoing many of his previous remarks, Cheney said Congress was untrustworthy when it came to national security and foreign policy, was indecisive and short-term minded, and was unsuited to overseeing or reaching consensus on covert operations that were better left to the executive branch. In the real world of profound national security threats, the president had to have complete latitude regarding foreign policy and launching military attacks against foreign enemies. Under Cheney's scheme of enhanced presidential power and a lesser role for Congress, lawmakers could still check executive power by cutting off funds for ongoing operations in the appropriations process. After agreeing to replace Tower as the new secretary of defense, Cheney withdrew from the conference and never delivered his caustic remarks.[8] Cheney's nomination met with warm and unanimous approval. The *New York Times* praised Cheney as "smart, generally knowledgeable about national security, very conservative, a party loyalist, honorable and exceedingly popular among Democrats and Republicans."[9] Sam Nunn, the Georgian Democrat who led the fight against Tower's nomination, hailed Cheney as a "man of honor and integrity." And Thomas S. Foley, House majority leader and Democrat of Washington, said Cheney's nomination was a "splendid choice, a man of great experience and capacity. . . ."[10]

Although Cheney had a record of solid support for Reagan's vast military buildup, he had never been a leading congressional voice on military affairs. His pragmatism, willingness to compromise, and nonconfrontational style won the confidence of liberals and conservatives alike. The nomination came just months after he won his sixth term in Congress and was elected minority whip, the GOP's number two position in the House. Further, he was a member of the House Select Committee on Intelligence, was the ranking Republican on its Program and Budget Authorization Subcommittee, was the ranking Republican in the House investigation of the Iran-Contra affair, and had a reputation as a leading Republican expert on intelligence affairs. Since winning his first election as Wyoming's lone congressman in 1978, he had voted for every effort to boost military spending. The American Security Council, a conservative organization, had given him a 100 percent rating on military-related votes. He had backed every military cause, from the MX missile, to production of weapons using poison gas, to the space shield against missiles. He fought on the House floor for aid to the Nicaraguan, Angolan, and Afghan rebels fighting Soviet-backed governments. He had voted for a treaty banning medium-range nuclear missiles, but also voted for production of new chemical weapons and against a nuclear test ban or a freeze on nuclear weapons production. Gordon Adams, director of a liberal Defense project, noted Cheney's political skill in being "able to walk a very good line . . . between some very tough conservative positions and an ability to deal with people who are not as conservative as he is."[11]

White House aides found Cheney attractive in two respects: as a consummate Washington insider who had a reputation for loyalty and as a team player with many of the president's top officials and as a link to Congress, where he had served since 1979. Cheney also was the choice of Brent Scowcroft, Bush's national security advisor who worked with Cheney in the Ford administration. Scowcroft later recalled that after the John Tower debacle,

"We needed a secretary of defense very badly." It was already March, he said, "and we just couldn't make policy with a big gap there. So we needed somebody fast. That meant it had to be somebody from Congress because otherwise we'd go through long hearings. And then I automatically went to Cheney."[12]

Amid the positive reviews, some questioned whether Cheney would be able to stand up to the services and the Joint Chiefs of Staff. After quickly being confirmed by the Senate Armed Services Committee, the new defense secretary swiftly put any such questions to rest. In less than a week after taking the oath of office in mid-March, Cheney moved to establish his control over the military. In an extraordinary public rebuke, he sharply criticized the Air Force chief of staff for holding congressional discussions without his approval on a major strategic issue. Responding to a question at his first news conference, Cheney accused General Larry D. Welch of "freelancing" regarding his discussions about options for modernizing land-based nuclear missiles with leading members of Congress. The rebuke came after the *Washington Post* reported on Welch's discussions with Congress. Cheney's reprimand of the four-star general, who was considered a contender for Chairman of the Joint Chiefs of Staff, was striking given that senior officers routinely met with members of Congress and that such rebukes were almost always done in private. Welch had cleared his congressional discussions with the acting secretary of the Air Force, but he was an easy target. Several high-ranking officers in the military believed that Cheney had used Welch as an example to send the message that he was in charge. The incident also reflected the same abhorrence of leaks and tendency for inner-circle councils that were his hallmarks as chief of staff to President Ford and as a senior Republican on the House Intelligence Committee.[13]

In his new post and with little administrative experience, Cheney surrounded himself with able staffers who could assure his success and control over the Pentagon. He made his initial choices for top Pentagon jobs in tight secrecy, bringing in many of his former congressional aides and loyalists. He named David Gribben, his former chief of staff in the House, as his new chief of staff at the Pentagon. Pete Williams, who served as Cheney's congressional press person, was appointed the defense department's spokesman. More important, Cheney named former Iran-Contra staffer and trusted congressional aide David Addington his personal assistant. In doing so, he gave Addington an office next to his, moving out a uniformed officer and reviving the post of Special Assistant, vacant since the Reagan administration. Addington was known to be smart, highly capable, and forceful. He quickly became Cheney's indispensable aide, deeply involved in issues and always in the background as he ran a highly efficient operation on behalf of the defense secretary. Addington was the starting point for every decision;

he met with and vetted the opinions of Pentagon officials, even the Joint Chiefs, before making decisions and bringing them to Cheney. By "force of personality," he took "charge and dealt with the details." Despite Cheney's efforts to specialize in national security matters while in Congress, he and Addington had the virtue of knowing they had much to learn about the intricacies of defense issues, and they were willing to listen. His five draft deferments as a young man during the Vietnam War stirred little animosity at the Pentagon, where he quickly earned a reputation for being a strong administrator who had good relations with Congress—a fact highly valued by military officials throughout the defense department.[14]

Cheney also kept Tower's choice of Paul Wolfowitz, the anti-Soviet hard-liner, to be undersecretary of defense for policy, the Pentagon's senior policy-making position. After six years focusing on Asia, Wolfowitz would once again have responsibility for arms control, the Middle East, and the Persian Gulf—the areas in which he specialized early in his career. It was an appointment that would form a lasting partnership between the two. Together, Cheney and Wolfowitz were a hawkish counterbalance to the pragmatic tendencies of Bush, Scowcroft, and Secretary of State James Baker. Cheney also recruited Colin Powell as the next chairman of the Joint Chiefs of Staff after Admiral William Crowe announced his retirement. Powell had served as Reagan's national security advisor before returning in 1989 to the military as head of the U.S. Forces Command, which oversaw the nearly one million Army troops in the United States. President Bush favored Powell to lead the Joint Chiefs, but the general had some doubts about serving under Cheney. He saw Cheney's fervent defense of Oliver North's rogue Iran-Contra schemes as support for military officers operating as free agents. Although the press ran stories that Powell would make history as the first black chairman, he brought significant credentials to the job. As national security advisor, Powell had gained broad foreign affairs experience and had spent more time in National Security Council meetings than either Cheney or perhaps even Baker, who had served as Reagan's treasury secretary. It was a fortuitous appointment for Powell. He would be the first chairman of the Joint Chiefs of Staff to serve a full term under the 1986 Goldwater-Nichols Act, which centralized authority through the chairman of the Joint Chiefs as opposed to the service chiefs. The law designated the chairman as the principal military advisor to the president, empowering him to speak for the entire military. Before, the chairman was merely the first among equals, limited to briefing the president and the secretary of defense on the consensus view of the service chiefs of the U.S. armed forces.[15]

Neither Cheney nor anyone else in Washington had any idea of the monumental changes to come with the startling retreat and collapse of the

Soviet empire. As early as 1947, George Kennan suggested that Soviet power "bears within it the seeds of its own decay." More than anything else, the internal forces of inertia, wastefulness, and corruption inherent in the Soviet system propelled the Kremlin's abandonment of Eastern Europe and its own ultimate collapse. On November 10, 1989, East Germans tore down the Cold War's most enduring symbol—the Berlin Wall—after weeks of unrest. In the following weeks, with the acquiescence of Moscow, democratic revolutions swept through the other communist countries of Eastern Europe. In Czechoslovakia, the one-time reformer Alexander Dubcek, whose efforts to achieve "socialism with a human face" was crushed by Soviet tanks in 1968, reemerged to lead the National Parliament, and dissident playwright Vaclav Havel was elected president. The fallen Romanian dictator, Nicolae Ceausescu, was executed by firing squad as the Soviets stood by and did nothing. Bush acknowledged the rapid pace of events in his February 1990 State of the Union address as he called for a reduction of U.S. and Soviet forces in Europe. The ever-cautious Cheney faced pressure to cut the defense budget in the face of huge federal deficits, withdraw forces from Europe, and reshape a military and defense strategy that had served for more than 40 years to deter or defeat a Soviet invasion of Western Europe. In this new era when Moscow no longer seemed a threat to the West and its global interests, Cheney would have to struggle with how and when to project military power abroad.

PANAMA

Cheney's first test came with the December 1989 invasion of Panama, the largest military operation since the Vietnam War. The episode ended with the surrender of the Panamanian dictator, Manuel Antonio Noriega, who was brought to the United States and convicted for criminal drug running. The United States had many years of experience with Noriega. As early as 1972, an American antinarcotics official proposed assassinating Noriega to curb the rising drug trade through Panama. The suggestion not only was rejected, but the CIA put Noriega, then head of Panama's intelligence service, on the payroll. Prominent among his bosses was George H.W. Bush, who was director of the CIA in 1976. In late 1983, Vice President Bush asked Noriega to pass a message to Fidel Castro, warning him not to interfere with the U.S. invasion of Grenada. Noriega also won Washington's appreciation by allowing the training of U.S.-backed Nicaraguan rebels on Panamanian soil. But the Panamanian dictator played a double game, funneling arms to the Sandinistas and to Marxist rebels in Colombia and El Salvador, providing CIA information to Cuba, and earning millions by helping Colombian drug lords run massive shipments of cocaine into the United

States. As late as 1987, the Reagan Administration was claiming that Noriega had been cooperative with U.S. antidrug efforts, but less than a year later, two federal grand juries in Florida indicted him on drug-running charges. Harsh economic sanctions were imposed to erode Noriega's base of support among his defense forces and government officials in Panama. Undaunted, the dictator's troops and supporters trashed free elections with blood and fraud and started harassing American citizens and military personnel. A failed coup against Noriega in October 1989 drew a storm of criticism in Congress for the Bush administration's inaction in giving support. The administration, aware of Latin sensitivity to unilateral U.S. interference, sought multilateral action through the Organization of American States, to little avail. On December 15, 1989, Panama's National Assembly proclaimed Noriega "maximum leader for national liberation" and declared that a "state of war" existed with the United States. One day later, after Panamanian troops shot and killed an American soldier, wounded another, and detained and mistreated a third and his wife, the Bush administration launched the invasion.[16]

With an invasion force of about 27,000 troops, the United States quickly took control of Panama. The United States also used radar-evading F-117 stealth fighter bombers for the first time, leading Les Aspen, chairman of the House Armed Services Committee, to denounce it as "show biz."[17] The invasion came after the CIA's covert agents dissuaded Bush from moving on yet another undercover operation, advising that only a full-scale invasion could remove Noriega. But some of the agency's most experienced Latin American operatives were loath to challenge the Panamanian strongman, and Bush complained that he was getting better intelligence from CNN than the CIA. Furious and with little confidence in the agency, the president from then on made plans to overthrow Noriega in close collaboration with Cheney, "whose skepticism about the agency deepened with every passing day."[18]

The invasion came against the backdrop of the peaceful revolutions in Eastern Europe and the advancing disintegration of the Soviet Union, which condemned the Panamanian operation. In the run-up to the invasion, Cheney wasted little time in exerting control. He dismissed General Frederick Woerner of the Southern Command, in charge of U.S. forces in Panama, for having "gone native" or soft on using U.S. forces to solve the Noriega crisis. He scrutinized the details of the invasion plans, questioned the intended use of the stealth fighter planes, limiting their involvement to just two bombing runs, and restricted press coverage of the Panamanian attack. After the operation, a report commissioned by the Pentagon criticized Cheney for excessive secrecy, which prevented reporters from covering crucial engagements in the invasion of Panama. Cheney had personally decided not to activate the press pool until after the start of the invasion and shut down a plan by public affairs officials at the U.S. Southern Command in Panama to let reporters who were already in the country cover the opening hours of the attack.[19]

The reasons for the invasion, said Bush, were to defend democracy in Panama, combat drug trafficking, safeguard American lives, and protect the integrity of the Panama Canal treaties. Unlike the Grenada invasion that aimed to stem the spread of communism in the American hemisphere, the Panama operation constituted a distinctly post-Cold War action. "With Panama," wrote James Mann, "America sent its troops for the purpose of restoring democracy and overthrowing a leader whose behavior was abhorrent"—the same rationale for the American war effort against Saddam Hussein in Iraq.[20] But there were other forerunners of the later invasion of Iraq—the use of unilateral force after failing to convince an international body to take multilateral action, the installation of a regime that owed its power to the United States, the effort to rebuild an economy that was in devastating decline after economic sanctions were imposed, and the attempt to train and rebuild a security force that would not turn on the civilian population. Nevertheless, the United States avoided the worst-case scenario of getting bogged down in a guerilla war in Panama. By February 13, 1990, the United States had already met its objectives of removing Noriega and establishing a semblance of democracy and had withdrawn all its forces, excepting a small contingent of just under the 13,597 troops that had been stationed in Panama before the invasion.[21]

Congress expressed broad support for the invasion, and Bush said at a news conference shortly after launching the attack that he would officially notify Congress of the operations under the War Powers Act, which required formal justification whenever the United States used force abroad. But Marlin Fitzwater, his White House spokesman, was quick to say that while the administration had kept Congress abreast of developments, it did not plan any formal invocation of the law. "We continue to maintain that the War Powers Act is unconstitutional," he said. Although Bush reported to Congress under the War Powers Act on December 21, 1989, the day following the invasion, he stayed clear of citing section 4(a) (1), the provision triggering the 60-day time limit requiring the president to terminate hostilities or seek congressional authorization for continued action.[22] The Panama action never did raise much concern in Congress about the War Powers Resolution. Its popularity among the American public and members of Congress, as well as the quick and successful nature of the operation within the 60-day time limit, seemed to foreclose any debate. On February 7, 1990, after the conclusion of hostilities, the House passed a resolution stating that the president had acted "decisively and appropriately in ordering the United

States forces to intervene in Panama."[23] While Bush indicated a readiness to consult with Congress, however, Cheney went on the attack. He assailed Congress for infringing on the president's authority to carry out foreign affairs and the Panamanian operation. Congressional members were "literally calling agencies downtown, or even people in Panama," he complained. "That creates all kinds of problems. [They] certainly complicate our lives when they run out and make public pronouncements in front of the press, knowing only half of what there is to know." The remarks indicated much of what he always considered wrong with the legislative branch—its out of control encroachments onto the executive's foreign policy prerogatives and its inability to keep secrets.[24]

With Cheney at the helm, the Panamanian invasion represented the Pentagon's growing confidence and willingness to use military power unilaterally. Even before Panama, Cheney had already indicated a greater willingness to use force after barely two months in office. He had approved plans for possible retaliation for the December 21, 1988, terrorist bombing of Pan AM Flight 103, which exploded into flames above Lockerbie, Scotland, killing 270.[25] By the time he had reached the Pentagon, he had been involved in many of America's military adventures since the Vietnam War. He had been in the Ford White House during the Mayaguez incident, was in Congress when the 1983 Beirut bombing occurred, supported the invasion of Grenada, backed aid and military assistance to the Nicaraguan rebels, and strongly favored huge defense increases to counter the Soviets. With Panama, he indicated a greater inclination to wage much larger military campaigns. Indeed, from Carter's disastrous Iranian rescue mission to the successful Panamanian invasion, the Pentagon under Cheney's recent watch and the White House had a changed outlook. The invasion broke the "mindset of the American people about the use of force in the post-Vietnam era," said Secretary of State James Baker III. "Panama established an emotional predicate that permitted us to build the public support so essential for the success of Operation Desert Storm some thirteen months later."[26] The short Panamanian war appeared to be a mere dress rehearsal for the much larger Desert Storm operation to come. In recalling the Panamanian episode, Cheney said that it was "interesting because it was a trial run to some extent. It was the first time the president and administration used force and exercised our authorities to launch a military operation. And it was good practice, in effect, for what you have to go through to do that kind of thing."[27] Most of the press accounts credited the success of the Panamanian operation to Colin Powell, the new chairman of the Joint Chiefs of Staff, who not only forged a working collaboration with Cheney, but quickly overshadowed him. His performance on Panama won him praise among his Pentagon colleagues and celebrity status among the media. He was clearly "in charge," said *Newsday*. "In a brilliant if violent thrust, Powell proved his military mettle."[28]

DESSERT STORM

Cheney and the Bush administration faced a far greater challenge in repelling Saddam Hussein's invasion and occupation of Kuwait. The road to war was littered with equivocation and miscalculation. American officials were hardly oblivious to Saddam's malevolence in the years preceding Iraq's invasion. He had attacked Iranian troops with chemical weapons and gassed the Kurds in his own country. Using chemical weapons, Iraqi forces killed an estimated 5,000 Kurdish people in Halabja alone.[29] In the late 1980s, Saddam also began developing nuclear and biological weapons and built long-range missiles and artillery to deliver weapons of mass destruction. In March 1990, British and U.S. officials caught Iraqi agents trying to smuggle nuclear trigger devices into Iraq and threatening to "let our fire eat half of Israel" if the Jewish state attacked Iraq. Saddam's threat led Representative Howard Berman on the House Foreign Affairs Committee to introduce a bill imposing trade sanctions on Iraq. The White House opposed the legislation not only because it usurped its foreign policy powers, but also because the administration considered Saddam useful in the Middle East balance of power politics. The Bush Administration, like Reagan's before it, saw secular Iraq as a possible countervailing force against Haffez Assad of Syria and the spread of fundamentalism emanating from the clerics in Iran, Iraq's arch enemy. Saddam "may have been a monster," said one administration official, "but he was our monster."[30]

During the bloody eight-year Iran-Iraq war, America also had favored Iraq by providing military intelligence and high-technology export licenses, which Saddam tried to exploit in his quest to build weapons of mass destruction. The Americans also removed Iraq from the list of state sponsors of terrorism and sought to maintain commercial ties between the two countries, with the United Sates selling almost $1 billion of agricultural goods to Iraq every year. Despite Saddam's efforts to obtain nuclear weapons capability, the Bush administration muted its public statements for fear of disrupting relations with Saddam. At the same time, U.S. intelligence was never able to penetrate the Iraqi police state and had little direct knowledge either of Saddam's inner circle, or its intentions. After the Iran-Iraq war ended in 1988, U.S. officials expected that Saddam would concentrate on the reconstruction of the country, demobilize the army, and refrain from further military adventures for the foreseeable future. Nevertheless, Iraq was never the administration's main concern. Until the invasion of Kuwait, the White House was preoccupied with the dramatic events sweeping through the Soviet Union and Eastern Europe.[31]

In the spring of 1990, Saddam once again began mobilizing his military forces. But the CIA not only overlooked it, but prepared a national intelligence estimate for the White House, stating that Iraq's armed forces were too exhausted and depleted from the war with Iran to launch any wars in the near future. Israeli intelligence warned Cheney and CIA director William Webster otherwise on July 20, 1990. According to the Israelis, Saddam not only aimed to obtain nuclear weapons technology, but posed an imminent threat that went beyond Israel to Kuwait and Saudi Arabia. The warning went unheeded even after July 24, 1990, when Webster reported to the White House that satellite images showed tens of thousands of Iraqi troops massing on the Kuwaiti border. On the following day, as Saddam secretly prepared to invade Kuwait, U.S. ambassador to Iraq, April Glaspie, met with the Iraqi leader in Baghdad in one of the critical junctions leading up to the crisis. Saddam called the unprecedented meeting to feel out what the Americans would do if he moved against Kuwait. What he heard was more than satisfactory. Glaspie urged Saddam to seek a peaceful resolution while reassuring him that the United States had "no opinion on the Arab-Arab" conflicts, like your border disagreement with Kuwait." She reported that she was under "instructions to seek better relations with Iraq." The meeting bolstered Saddam's impression that the Americans would tolerate, in the interest of Iraqi-American relations, his designs against the Kuwaitis. On July 31, the CIA downplayed the possibility of an invasion, an assessment supported by the Egyptians, Saudis, and Kuwaitis. At most, they said, Iraq's war scare aimed to intimidate Kuwait into handing over an island in the Persian Gulf and maybe an oil field straddled by the Iraq-Kuwait border. King Hussein of Jordan offered the president further reassurance: "On the Iraqi side," he said, "they send their best regards and highest esteem to you sir." Not until August 1 did U.S. intelligence warn of an imminent Iraqi invasion. The next day, on August 2, Iraqi forces invaded and occupied Kuwait within six hours, causing the Kuwaiti royal family and government to flee to Saudi Arabia.[32]

Amid recriminations about who lost Kuwait, Bush declared that the invasion would not stand. Nevertheless, with the Cold War winding down and America carrying the burden of redefining its role in world affairs, Bush struggled to forge a clear consensus both at home and overseas on the limits and uses of U.S. power. With skillful diplomacy, the president and Secretary of State James Baker led the United Nations and assembled a coalition of countries around the world, organizing and gaining international support and authorization for action against Iraq. If the Bush Administration had to go to war, it preferred to do so with full international backing under Article 42 of the UN Charter, which permitted the Security Council to authorize collective action. Secretary of State Baker later recalled that the administration wanted to make certain that since the United States would be operating under UN auspices, that it would "have sufficient authority to use force. . . . We had been able to cobble together a rather unprecedented international coalition," he said. "I had the feeling that the United Nations was working in the way in which the founders had intended." It was important, said Baker, that the action against Saddam Hussein not be seen as a "cowboy operation."[33]

On August 10, the Arab League summit agreed to send forces to defend Saudi Arabia against a possible Iraqi attack. Egypt, Morocco, and Syria sent more than 60,000 troops, which took part in the ground phase of the liberation of Kuwait that began on February 24, 1991. The United States also enlisted a coalition of other nations in condemning Saddam's actions, calling for Iraqi withdrawal from Kuwait, freezing Iraqi and Kuwaiti assets, banning weapons sales to Iraq, imposing a comprehensive trade embargo, and defraying U.S. deployment costs. The Netherlands, Belgium, France, Italy, Britain, Greece, and Spain, even the Soviet Union and others, sent ships to enforce the embargo against Iraq. At the same time, France, Britain, Pakistan, Bangladesh, Senegal, Niger, Bulgaria, Canada, and Afghan rebels sent air and ground forces to protect Saudi Arabia—while Japan, West Germany, the European Community, South Korea, and the Gulf Cooperation Council (Saudi Arabia, Kuwait, Oman, the United Arab Emirates, Qatar, and Bahrain) pledged more than $50 billion to support the Pentagon's massive deployment of troops and to compensate Egypt, Jordan, and Turkey for lost revenue stemming from the embargo.[34] The administration's adroit diplomacy, earning international credibility, if not admiration, stood in stark contrast to America's go-it-alone approach in the 2003 invasion of Iraq.

While the president maneuvered deftly on the international stage, his dealings with fractious members of Congress were less sure footed. As the international crisis worsened, lawmakers began to worry about the trend toward war. Les Aspin, the influential chairman of the House Armed Services Committee, declared that the president had no mandate to go to war. By October 1990, Congress already had limited Bush's freedom of action. It had rejected Cheney's effort to spend, without congressional oversight, the billions of dollars that allies had donated to the gulf operation and halted his massive $21 billion arms sale to Saudi Arabia. It perhaps said more about Bush's predilection for foreign policy over domestic politics that he was quicker in getting approval for the use of force from the UN than from the U.S. Congress. On November 29, 1990, by a 12-2 vote, with only Cuba and

Yemen in dissent and China abstaining, the UN Security Council approved a resolution authorizing the use of force if Saddam failed to leave Kuwait by January 15, 1991. The vote showed a surprising international resolve that would have been impossible during the Cold War when the communist nations would reflexively veto any move by the free world. "Freed from the stasis of the Cold War," said *Newsweek*, "Bush had achieved what the founders of the United Nations had only dreamed of: collective security against the forces of aggression." James Baker concurred. "I think it was a historic vote," he later recalled in 1996. "It was one of the few times that the Security Council had met at the foreign minister level for one thing and it was really one of the very few times that the Security Council had authorized through a Security Council resolution, the use of military force. . . ."[35]

Even so, as the United States was pouring tens of thousands of troops into the Gulf to persuade Hussein to back down or face overwhelming force, Bush struggled to convince Congress that a free Kuwait was worth dying for. The gulf crisis revived questions about presidential power and the constitutional authority to wage war. Throughout the fall of 1990, Congress had yet to authorize the use of force to repel Iraqi forces from Kuwait. The great debate in Congress centered on whether it should pass legislation establishing policy to wait for economic sanctions to force Iraq to withdraw from Kuwait or whether it should give the president authority to use military force. At issue was war powers, the debate almost as old as the Republic between the presidency and Congress over the authority to commit armed forces and wage war. As various legislators questioned Bush's massive military buildup, fifty-three lawmakers filed suit in federal court seeking to enjoin the president from starting the war without congressional authorization. Although Article I of the Constitution gave Congress the authority to declare war, Article II anointed the president as commander-in-chief of U.S. armed forces. Congress passed the War Powers Act in 1973 to assure that it had a say in the commitment of the armed forces. While President Bush challenged the constitutionality of the act, he also quasi complied with the law and maintained comity with the legislative branch by informing Congress of the deployment of the military.[36]

Against Cheney's advice, on January 8, 1991, Bush requested a congressional resolution in support of the use of force against Saddam Hussein. Cheney advised bypassing Congress altogether to begin hostilities. It was unnecessary and far too risky, he said, to ask the Democratic-controlled Congress for authorization to launch the war. Cheney later recalled that he "was not enthusiastic about going to Congress for an additional grant of authority. I was concerned that they might well vote 'no' and that would make life more difficult for us."[37] The advice followed remarks he made on a Sunday morning talk show in November 1990. Appearing on *Meet the Press*, Cheney disparaged Congress as a "great debating society" and ill-equipped to make important decisions on matters of war and peace.[38] Nonetheless, the president believed that a congressional resolution was crucial to demonstrate unified U.S. support for the international effort. After the bluntest and most open debate on the issues of war and peace since World War II, Congress ultimately gave Bush a de facto declaration of war. By margins of sixty-seven votes in the House and five in the Senate, Congress authorized Bush to use force to liberate Kuwait, despite vigorous arguments by Democrats to give international sanctions more time to work. In the end, members in both houses realized that failing to give the president a resolution of support would have disastrous consequences for U.S. policy in the Gulf and the international coalition against Saddam Hussein. Bush also recognized the imperative of demonstrating the will of a unified nation to the international community and Iraq. Conversely, Cheney's approach to bypass Congress when mobilizing and committing the largest invasion forces since World War II might well have caused the international coalition to question American unity and resolve.[39]

The day after Bush's request for a congressional resolution in support of the use of force, Secretary of State Baker announced the failure of his meeting with Iraqi foreign minister, Tariq Aziz, to resolve the crisis. The idea for the meeting of last resort came from Bush, who wanted to be seen in the court of history as having done everything possible in the pursuit of peace. According to Baker, "the meeting with Tariq Aziz in Geneva permitted us to achieve congressional support for something that the president was determined to do. . . ." The president aimed to go forward no matter what, but it was considerably better to have "the support of the peoples' elected representatives in Congress" and the "support of the American people." Even Sam Nunn, the powerful Democratic chairman of the Senate Armed Services Committee who challenged the administration's timetable for going to war, recognized that congressional opposition to the use of force collapsed after Baker's meeting with Aziz.[40]

From the beginning, Cheney played a strong hand in the crisis leading up to war. He stood among the key decision makers—including the president and National Security Advisor Brent Scowcroft—who were the most aggressive in pushing a military option. Baker was less eager to use force, preferred sanctions and a negotiated solution, and led the effort to assemble an international coalition against Saddam. Nevertheless, he was a loyalist and was committed to implementing whatever Bush decided. Powell opposed going to war in favor of containing Saddam Hussein with economic sanctions, putting him at odds with Cheney. Although the administration presented to the public an image of firmness and unanimity among the president's top advisors, the reality was one of doubt and tension. On August 3, the day after the invasion, Bush and his top advisors discussed the status of the unfolding crisis. Saddam had already advanced the ploy that the invasion and occupation of Kuwait would be temporary. Blinded by self-deception, America's Arab allies believed that there would be an Arab solution. With little debate, the meeting produced a decision to defend Saudi Arabia from Iraqi attack. Powell then asked whether U.S. forces should also liberate Kuwait. The president gave no response to Powell's question. The shadow of Vietnam hung over the meeting: the old fear of another escalating war with no exit. Cheney later confronted Powell for transgressing on his political turf. "Look," Powell recalls Cheney saying, "you just do military options. Don't be the secretary of state or the secretary of defense or the national security advisor. You just do military options." But Powell had the ghosts of Vietnam and Beirut running through his mind—the lack of clear military and political objectives and public support that resulted in defeat and catastrophe. "Perhaps I was the ghost of Vietnam, the ghost of Beirut, and I think as the senior military advisor to the President of the United States and the Secretary of Defense it was my responsibility not only to provide for military options but to help them shape clear political objectives for the military to help achieve," he recalled. "There had been cases in our past, particularly in the Vietnam period, when senior leaders, military leaders, did not force civilians to make those kinds of clear choices, and it caused me to be the skunk at the picnic. . . ."[41]

In discussing whether to go to war, Cheney argued that allowing Saddam to take over Kuwait would immediately transform Iraq into an oil superpower. International sanctions would fail, he contended, as the other countries in need of oil would break ranks. The president and Scowcroft agreed with Cheney, but Powell quietly pushed within the administration for economic sanctions and a strategy of containment. Haunted by the specter of Vietnam, Powell aimed to assert the kind of independence that he felt senior military leaders should have exerted during the war in Southeast Asia. He later explained that as a "midlevel career officer, I had been appalled at the docility of the Joint Chiefs of Staff, fighting the war in Vietnam without ever pressing the political leaders to lay out clear objectives for them."[42] But Cheney had no such qualms, and soon came into conflict with Powell regarding the details of the war plan to liberate Kuwait.

Although the administration hoped the crisis could be solved diplomatically or through sanctions, the president intended to do whatever it took to free Kuwait. "This will not stand," the president vowed only a few days after Iraq invaded Kuwait. Soon after, the president dispatched Cheney on a critical mission to meet with King Fahd to urge the acceptance of American forces in Saudi Arabia. Accompanied by Paul Wolfowitz and General H. Norman Schwarzkopf, Cheney warned the king that the Iraqis were massing on his border. If the king wanted U.S. assistance, Cheney said, the Saudis "did not have the luxury of waiting until Saddam began an invasion of Saudi Arabia because then it would be too late." Cheney's blunt talk produced the desired effect, quickly persuading the Saudis to accept U.S. forces in the Kingdom. With Iraqi forces a mere 200–250 miles from Saudi bases, air fields, and port facilities, Cheney cautioned the administration and the Pentagon not to talk openly of war lest it provoke Saddam to take preemptive action. When Air Force chief of staff Michael J. Dugan openly spoke to the press of his war plans, Cheney promptly ousted him, sending a stern warning throughout the Pentagon. At the outset, the Americans had only a small contingent of forces in Saudi Arabia, including the ready brigade of the 82nd Airborne Division and a wing of F-15s from Langley in Virginia. By the end of September, the Pentagon had moved enough U.S. forces to protect the Kingdom.[43]

By October, while continuing the buildup of U.S. forces in the region, Cheney leaned hard on military planners to draft a viable war plan to liberate Kuwait. The job of drafting the plan was left to General H. Norman Schwarzkopf, head of U.S. Central Command and commander of U.S. forces in the theater of operations. With limited U.S. forces in the region, Schwarzkopf did not have enough troops to defend Saudi Arabia while launching a major flanking attack. Instead, the general proposed a head-on, frontal assault against Iraqi fortifications in Kuwait. Powell presented the plan to Bush, Scowcroft, Cheney, and others at a White House meeting on October 11. "It was a terrible plan," Scowcroft recounted. "It called for a frontal assault, right up to the Iraqi strength," and ran the risk of substantial American casualties.[44] Cheney had no use for it either, recalling that he found it "unimaginative in terms of the ground war because I felt it did risk the possibility that we would not be successful, that we would get bogged down trying to attack the Iraqi fortifications head-on, that we'd suffer a lot of casualties, but there weren't many options given the size force we had." As the United States deployed forces starting in early August and into September, Saddam was also building up his forces in Kuwait. By the time the United States finished the first phase of deployment, it had about 200,000 troops in the theater facing more than 500,000 Iraqi troops across the border. Schwarzkopf also never liked the idea of a frontal assault and recommended that it not be implemented, but with limited forces in the field, he believed it was the only option if the order were immediately given to move offensively.[45]

Without Powell's knowledge, Cheney and his aide Wolfowitz began pursuing an alternative war plan in league with Henry S. Rowen, an academic from the Stanford Business School and Hoover Institution, the conservative think tank. On leave from Stanford, Rowen worked under Wolfowitz as assistant secretary of defense for international security affairs. Rowen drafted a new plan based on an obscure episode during World War II involving an Iraqi rebellion against British occupation. The British had quashed the insurrection in 1941 by quickly moving reinforcements overland from the territory now known as Jordan eastward across the desert to Baghdad. There was no reason why American and allied forces could not perform a similar feat by invading Iraq with air support from the west and threaten the Iraqi capital. At the same time, the forces in western Iraq could prevent Saddam from firing SCUD missiles at Israel, a real concern given that if the Israelis entered the conflict in self-defense it might fray the Arab coalition. According to Rowen's plan, Saddam would have to withdraw forces from Kuwait to protect Baghdad, making these troops vulnerable to air attack. If Saddam did not withdraw troops, the Iraqi capital would be open to allied attack, compelling Saddam to sue for peace.[46]

After vetoing Schwarzkopf's plan, Cheney sent Powell to the Gulf to meet with the general and determine what the military needed to defeat Saddam. In Powell's absence, Cheney presented Rowen's war plan, called Operation Scorpion, to the president and the national security advisor. This furtive maneuvering among Bush's top leaders set up an extraordinary situation. Behind the public façade of unity, Powell was quietly pushing his strategy of containment in opposition to the secretary of defense, while Cheney was secretly crusading for an alternative war plan that bypassed the chairman of the joint chiefs. Cheney's alternative war plan never went far. Schwarzkopf pointed out the impossibility of supplying troops hundreds of miles away in western Iraq—too distant from friendly forces. But the plan did provoke the considerable ire of Schwarzkopf. "I wondered whether Cheney had succumbed to the phenomenon I'd observed among some secretaries of the army," he wrote later. "Put a civilian in charge of professional military men and before long he's no longer satisfied with setting policy but wants to outgeneral the generals." Cheney, however, recalled that he had an ulterior motive in mind when pushing the Rowen plan. After rejecting Schwarzkopf's proposal for a frontal assault, he aimed to send "the signal to everybody, the joint staff, out in the field and central command" that he meant business and that unless they gave him a viable war plan, he would impose one.[47]

Powell and his war planners proposed the earlier concept of a flanking attack, sweeping around the Iraqis from the west. This left-hook strategy, however, depended on deploying far more troops, equipment, aircraft, and warships than the first plan. Cheney understood how much was at stake in the Gulf. After Vietnam and the lesser debacles surrounding the Marine barracks bombing in Beirut and the failed hostage rescue attempt in Iran, he believed the military could not sustain any more defeats. "If we screw this up," he said privately to Prince Bandar, the Saudi ambassador to the United States, "the military is finished in this society." Not wanting blame for a major fiasco, Cheney backed Powell's request for overwhelming military force. "I did not want to be in a position where the civilians had denied our military leaders the resources they said they needed to do the job," he recalled. When they came in with a fairly long shopping list ... instead of debating it, I said 'yes.'" So did the president. Bush "never once questioned the size of the force we wanted to commit," said Cheney. "He immediately agreed to a quarter million reserves. We said we wanted the VII Corps out of Germany, no problem, he immediately agreed to all of that so that I think that there was no excuse possible for anybody in the military to say that the civilian side of the house had not supported them. We gave them absolutely everything they asked for and then said, 'Now you must get on with the job.'"[48]

The new war plan accorded with Powell's doctrine of having a clear military objective, using overwhelming force, winning decisively, and exiting. These principles accorded with the thinking of former Secretary of Defense Caspar Weinberger in the early 1980s when Powell served as his military advisor. The United States began the war with an intensive air campaign, launched a flanking attack, and routed Iraqi forces in six weeks. On February 27, 1991, President Bush announced to the nation from the Oval Office that Kuwait had been liberated. He declared that after consulting with the secretary of defense, the chairman of the joint chiefs, and coalition partners, he was suspending combat operations starting at midnight Eastern Standard Time.[49] On March 6, the president was greeted on Capitol Hill by a three-minute ovation from lawmakers on both sides of the aisle in a joint session of Congress. It was a testament to his efforts to build consensus and unify the country. The speaker of the House, Representative Thomas S. Foley, Democrat of Washington, introduced Bush by giving him "our warmest congratulations on the brilliant victory of the Desert Storm operation." The speech, concluding a half-year of extraordinary diplomatic and military maneuvers, was a time for the president to bask in accolades for his skill in assembling a disparate international coalition, winning congressional support, and executing a swift and triumphant war. "As President, I can report to the nation: Aggression is defeated. The war is over," he declared. The *New York Times* reported that Bush had been invited to Capitol Hill for a celebration; "politicians here wanted to capture and promote the feeling that the nation had moved beyond the gloomy sense of America's decline as a world and economic power, as well as years stained by political scandal and marred Presidencies."[50]

But just as important were the tributes that came from other nations. As the United States marched on Kuwait, "most of the world stood up and cheered," said *Newsweek*. "In London and Tokyo, in Berlin and even Moscow, America was seen as a giant again—its military might beyond compare, its diplomacy sure-handed, its self-confidence restored. The U.S. victory was a dizzying spectacle, and the world could be forgiven a certain giddiness. . . ." Above all, the president and his secretary of state had shown a spirit for worldwide consultation. It was no accident that they moved swiftly to mobilize the United Nations in the gulf crisis, getting the Security Council to vote for war powers even before the U.S. Congress. "The United Nations," said the news magazine, "came out of this episode with a justifiable burst of pride."[51]

Nonetheless, Saddam Hussein had survived the allies' victorious war and the open rebellions in the Kurdish north and the Shiite south that followed. On February 14, two weeks before the end of the war, Bush urged the Iraqis to overthrow Saddam, igniting the mass uprisings. On orders from Saddam Hussein, Iraq's military leaders quickly sued for peace at Safwan near the Iraq-Kuwait border. Saddam Hussein's grip on power was tenuous at best immediately following the war, but he quickly regained control and brutally crushed the rebellions, massacring thousands. The Shiites felt utterly abandoned by the Americans, but the administration had no intention of going into Iraq.

At the end of the war, a sense of foreboding cast a pall over the jubilation in the Gulf States and the United States The question was whether the allies would once again have to go to war against Saddam Hussein. Bush and his senior military commanders had elected not to march on Baghdad to destroy Saddam's regime. Authorized by the United Nations only to expel Iran from Kuwait, the allies drove on to Nasiriya and the highway to Baghdad, 150 miles from the largely undefended Iraqi capital, before ending hostilities. American officials considered any effort to prolong the conflict by imposing a new regime in Baghdad politically unwise. Not only would it be militarily risky and destroy the international coalition, but it would inevitably alienate Arab opinion. Moreover, U.S. officials were cognizant of Iraq's Shiite majority and the prospect of another fundamentalist government—besides Iran—bordering the Gulf. "It's far easier to deal with a tame Saddam than with an unknown quantity," said one high-ranking official.[52] Still, the question persisted in various circles why the allies did not "finish the job" by pressing on to Baghdad.

The most reasoned answer regarding the first Bush administration's unwillingness to march on Baghdad came from Cheney. In an August 1992 speech at the Discovery Institute in Seattle, Cheney explained that "we made the decision not to go on to Baghdad because that was never part of our objective. It wasn't what the country signed up for, it wasn't what the Congress signed up for, it wasn't what the coalition was put together to do." The allies had achieved their military objections to expel Iraq from Kuwait, said Cheney. Saddam Hussein had lost two-thirds of his army, half of his air force, most of his weapons of mass destruction, and no longer posed any threat to neighboring countries. Moreover, the military challenges and risks would have been considerable. If "we'd gone on to Baghdad," he said, "we would have wanted to send a lot of force. One of the lessons we learned was don't do anything in a halfhearted fashion. When we committed the forces to Kuwait, we sent a lot of forces to make certain they could do the job." Cheney went on to say that a march on Baghdad would have involved moving from fighting in a desert environment where the enemy could be identified. "If you go into the streets of Baghdad, that changes dramatically," he stated. "All of a sudden you've got a battle you're fighting in a major built-up city, a lot of civilians are around, significant limitations on our ability to use our most effective technologies and techniques." Once Saddam Hussein and his government had been taken down, he pointed out, "then the question is what do you put in its place? You know, you then have accepted the responsibility for governing Iraq."

What kind of government would be established? Cheney asked. "Is it going to be a Kurdish government, or a Shia government, or a Sunni government, or maybe a government based on the old Baathist party, or some mixture thereof?" By this time, Cheney explained, the effort would have "lost the support of the Arab coalition that was so crucial to our operations over there because none of them signed on for the United States to go occupy Iraq. I would guess if we had gone in there, I would still have forces in Baghdad there today, we'd be running the country. We would not have been able to get everybody out and bring everybody home." Finally, Cheney underscored the question of significant additional casualties. During the Gulf war, 146 Americans were killed in action. "And the question in my mind is how many additional American casualties is Saddam worth? And the answer is not very damned many."[53] Cheney later reiterated some of these points in an interview with the PBS news program *Frontline*. The administration was "worried about Iraq coming apart," he said. "Now you can say, well you should have gone to Baghdad and gotten Saddam. I don't think so. I think if we had done that we would have been bogged down there for a very long period of time with the real possibility we might not have succeeded."[54] Cheney's statements throughout the 1990s had brilliantly outlined the daunting military and political obstacles to invading and occupying Iraq—words that ironically he and the president's son, George W. Bush, who would later become the country's chief executive, failed to heed when the United States all but unilaterally invaded and occupied Iraq, took down Saddam Hussein and his Baathist regime, unleashed violent sectarian passions, bogged down the American military in a protracted insurrection, and earned international discredit. The principles that President George H.W. Bush and Secretary of State James Baker had laid down for mobilizing international support and winning a worldwide coalition to roll back naked aggression were swept aside as irrelevant and outdated.

Wolfowitz endorsed Cheney's analysis in an article he wrote after the end of the war. If the allies had gone to Baghdad, "[n]othing could have insured Saddam Hussein's removal from power short of a full-scale occupation of Iraq," he wrote. "Even if easy initially, it is unclear how or when it would have ended."[55] He later expounded on this point in a 1997 essay, asserting that a new regime in Iraq "would have become the United States' responsibility. Conceivably, this could have led the United States into a more or less permanent occupation of a country that could not govern itself, but where the rule of a foreign occupier would be increasingly resented." Bush administration officials, he wrote, were aware of the "bloody stalemate into which General MacArthur had dragged our country during the Korean War by his reckless pursuit north to the Yalu River following his stunning success at Inhon."[56]

The war had further deepened Cheney's skepticism about the CIA. After the cessation of hostilities, a UN Special Commission went looking for chemical, biological, and nuclear weapons inside Iraq. The commission's investigators involved CIA agents under the UN flag. It was well known that Saddam Hussein had been aggressively pursuing nuclear weapons capability for years, raising concerns among U.S. officials. In the hunt for weapons of mass destruction inside Iraq, Richard Clarke, a staffer for the National Security Council, recalled that inspectors had discovered the heart of Saddam's nuclear weapons directorate in a raid on the Iraqi agriculture ministry. "We went there, broke down doors, blew off locks, got into the sanctum sanctorum," Clarke recounted. "The Iraqis immediately reacted, surrounded the facility and prevented the UN inspectors from getting out. We thought that might happen, too, so we had given them satellite telephones. They translated the nuclear reports on-site into English from the Arabic and read them to us over the satellite telephones." In August 1990, the CIA's National Intelligence Estimate put Iraq at least five years away from a bomb, but the new on-site evidence revised estimates downward to only nine to eighteen months before Saddam detonated his first nuclear weapon.[57]

"CIA totally missed it," said Clarke. "We had bombed everything we could bomb in Iraq, but missed an enormous nuclear-weapons development facility. . . . Dick Cheney looked at that report and said, 'Here's what the Iraqis themselves are saying: that there's this huge facility that was never hit during the war; that they were very close to making a nuclear bomb, and CIA didn't know it,'" Clarke stated. "I'm sure he said to himself, 'I can never trust the CIA again to tell me when a country is about to make a nuclear bomb.'" According to Clarke, there was "no doubt that Dick Cheney who comes back into office nine years later has that as one of the things burnt into his memory: 'Iraq wants a nuclear weapon. Iraq was that close to getting a nuclear weapon. And CIA hadn't a clue.'"[58]

In early January 1991, the defense secretary had advised Bush not to seek support from Congress in launching the war, claiming that the president possessed all the constitutional authority he needed. With the war underway, Cheney also had battled Congress on other issues. After taking office, Cheney faced the runaway spending on weapons systems from the Reagan years. He quickly took on the Pentagon brass and defense contractors, canceling the Navy's A-12 fighter jet that ran $1 billion over budget and months behind schedule, cutting production of the long-range, radar-evading B-2 Stealth Bomber from 132 to 20, and targeting the problem-plagued V-22 Osprey helicopter for elimination. His efforts to kill the V-22 ran into powerful opposition from the Texas and Pennsylvania congressional delegations. When Congress appropriated money for the V-22 over his opposition, Cheney refused to spend the funds. It recalled Nixon's efforts to impound appropriated funds for programs he disliked, stripping Congress of its constitutional power of the purse. Congress had responded by passing a 1974 impoundment law to prohibit such presidential power grabs in the future. Cheney nevertheless ignored the law, but later felt pressure from a provision passed by the House Armed Service Committee to cut 5 percent a month from defense spending until the defense secretary restored funding for the Osprey.[59]

Cheney's power grab also involved efforts to exert more political control over the uniformed military. As war quickly approached in the Gulf, a dispute arose between William James Haynes II, the army's civilian general counsel and a protégé of Addington's, and the army's leading uniformed lawyer, a two-star general, regarding whose office should have authority over legal issues that might arise from the war. The clash between the two was an extension of Cheney's effort in 1991 to get Congress to pass legislation that would strip the independence of military lawyers and put them under the authority of civilian political appointees. Although Congress rejected Cheney's proposal, his deputy, Addington, issued an administrative directive instituting the changes. Addington's actions on this and other matters in support of his boss and in defiance of Congress angered lawmakers on the Senate Armed Services Committee. In his 1992 confirmation hearing to become the Pentagon's general counsel, committee members voiced their considerable irritation at the efforts to bypass Congress. "How many ways are there around evading the will of Congress?" asked Democratic Senator Carl Levin of Michigan. "How many different legal theories do you have?" The Senate ultimately confirmed Addington with the assurance that the Pentagon would restore the independence of military lawyers and spend the appropriated funds for the V-22. Addington's reign as the Pentagon's chief lawyer was short lived. In November 1992, Arkansas Governor Bill Clinton defeated Bush for the presidency, marking the end of Cheney's career at the Pentagon.[60]

Cheney left the administration with a soaring public reputation. Despite their differences on the Gulf War, Cheney and Powell had waged successfully the largest military campaign since World War II. The *Los Angeles Times* ran a story referring to Cheney as a possible presidential candidate. He was honored along with Powell and Schwarzkopf in a ticker tape parade down Broadway in Manhattan—recalling the honors once given to Charles Lindbergh and Douglas MacArthur. Mayor David Dinkins gave them the keys to the city.[61] Cheney had run the Pentagon with a strong hand during two wars—Panama and the Gulf War—determined in both to vanquish the ghosts of Vietnam and avoid the burden and blame of lost conflicts. He had castigated and fired generals, while giving others the support and latitude they needed to win conflicts. He had reprimanded the vice president for asserting power he did not possess for calling a meeting of the National Security Council when the president was abroad.[62] He had established himself as an imperial office holder, emerging from these wars tested and steeled with a glowing public persona, honored and bathed in accolades, even while being overshadowed by the more charismatic Powell. He also had worked to redefine the Pentagon's mission, often battling Congress over defense budgets and weapons systems, during a time of sweeping democratic revolutions in Eastern Europe and the dissolution of the Soviet Union. By the end of the first Bush administration, he was at the apex of his public life.

Throughout his tenure at the Pentagon he had regarded the Democratic-controlled Congress contemptuously, making it clear to the president that he should not seek its support to launch the largest military undertaking since the Second World War. Cheney had long ago concluded that Congress often functioned as little more than a vexing gaggle of interests that regularly encroached on the presidency's rightful constitutional authority. In Cheney's view, recent American history involved the struggle between a strong presidency necessary in a brutish world and the naïve, untrustworthy, and at times disloyal constraints of Congress. His outlook, however, exerted little influence in an administration in which the president and secretary of state sought comity between the branches and among the global community of nations. On "just about every debate on a hard question of national security inside the Bush administration," said *Washington Post* national security reporter Barton Gellman, "Cheney was the outlier, and he usually lost because [former Secretary of State James] Baker and Scowcroft both had closer relationships with the president, and because the president himself was inclined to highly pragmatic positions. So when Dick Cheney wanted to sink some Iraqi tankers long before the UN authorized that, they said, 'No hang on a second. You're going to blow any chance of getting a resolution.'" There were many cases of Cheney advocating a "very strong, edge of the envelope view on executive power, and the previous presidents that he worked for didn't buy it," recounted Gellman. Cheney saw himself as a realist, more realistic about the world than any of his adversaries and critics. According to Gellman, Cheney believed that most people underestimated the risks to the well being and security of the United States. "If you want to fight the bad guys, you have to take the gloves off. So his views about what a president can do and what a president should do are very much in synch," said Gellman.[63] If Cheney had been president, an unrestrained unilateralism at home and abroad might have ruled the day; it certainly did eight years later when he returned to office as the most powerful vice president in American history.

Seven

In and Out of the Wilderness

During his Pentagon years after the end of the Cold War, Cheney oversaw reductions in the Defense Department budget, including cuts in troop strength, bases, and weapons systems. Faced with constant opposition from Capitol Hill, he derided lawmakers as a "bunch of annoying gnats." As defense secretary, Cheney showed stiff resistance to change, expressed suspicion of the dramatic changes in the Soviet Union and Eastern Europe, and even after the fall of the Berlin Wall and the breakup of the USSR, argued for continued military superiority. But he knew that he had to begin reshaping the size and mission of the Pentagon, including cuts that would produce a "peace dividend," before Congress seized the initiative. Those battles ended when he returned to private life after the Republicans lost in the 1992 presidential election to former Arkansas Governor Bill Clinton. Despite Bush's glorious Gulf War victory, the American economy had undergone two rounds of recession in 1990 and 1991, unemployment stood at nearly 8 percent, and many Americans believed Bush was more interested in foreign policy than repairing the economy. With the economy a major concern, in November 1992, Clinton won the White House with 43 percent of the popular vote, marking the first time in twelve years the Democrats would control the executive branch.

With Clinton's presidential victory, Cheney left the federal government for the American Enterprise Institute, a conservative-leaning Washington think tank. Since holding office in the Ford administration, he had been out of public life for only two years, in 1977 and 1978. But he spent most of that time raising money and running for Congress. Almost immediately, he considered running for the GOP presidential nomination in 1996. In late January 1993, after Clinton's inauguration, Cheney was asked on *Larry King Live* whether he might run. He said that he was considering it. "Obviously," he said, "I've worked for three presidents and watched two others close up, and so it is an idea that has occurred to me."[1] After his appearance on national television, he went on a national speaking tour and began meeting with party officials and fund-raisers. In early 1994, he set up an exploratory committee headed by loyal aide David Addington, but aborted the effort in January 1995 after only receiving respectful but unimpassioned interest. In the early going, he found himself a second-tier candidate behind Senator Bob Dole and Jack Kemp. By the time he ended the campaign, he was polling just 3 percent of Republicans surveyed, behind Rush Limbaugh.[2] Despite his broad experience in Congress and the executive branch, he could neither raise the money nor the political support to run a successful presidential nomination. It was the same problem his mentor Donald Rumsfeld faced in his own failed bid for the Republican presidential nomination in 1988.

In the summer of 1995, with his broad Washington and international connections, he accepted the position of president and chief executive officer of the giant multinational energy services company Halliburton. When appearing at a Dallas news conference in August to announce his appointment, Cheney sounded as if he were leaving his political life behind once and for all. "When I made the decision earlier this year not to run for president, not to seek the White House, that really was a decision to wrap up my political career and move on to other things," he said.[3] His tenure at the company involved modest success, despite a merger he oversaw with Dresser Industries that cost Halliburton hundreds of millions of dollars due to asbestos liabilities. Now in the private sector, Cheney's natural inclinations for anonymity and secrecy enjoyed greater latitude. "There's a fair amount of secrecy in the business, just to keep competitors from getting an edge on you," recalled Allen Mesch, a Texas energy consultant. "But that kind of thing can be a style thing with him—the closed door meeting. And the higher up you go in the company, the more paranoid you become about real and perceived threats." At Halliburton, Cheney was neither a chief strategist nor involved in the day-to-day operations. His chief role was "more of a door opener, leveraging his variety of international contacts."[4]

Yet, Cheney never fully left politics behind. After Clinton won a second presidential term in 1996, leading conservatives created a new organization to win back the White House. The Congressional Policy Advisory Board sought to provide a forum where notable experts and intellectuals and congressional Republican leaders could exchange ideas. The board assembled officials from former Republican administrations dating to the Nixon era, as well as the heads of leading conservative think tanks, and congressional Republicans. Beginning in early 1998, the board's activities continued until 2001 when the GOP regained the Oval Office. The quarterly meetings held in the Rayburn House Office Building not only fostered and honed ideas for possible new legislation, but also developed lines of attack on the Clinton Administration in preparation for the next presidential contest. Cheney joined the foreign policy discussions along with his mentor Donald Rumsfeld and former aide Paul Wolfowitz, all of whom would find senior positions in the George W. Bush Administration. They were joined by other former senior officials, including former Secretary of Defense Caspar Weinberger and former Secretary of State George Shultz. If nothing else, these meetings on Capitol Hill once again reunited Cheney, Rumsfeld, and Wolfowitz, who worked closely with congressional Republican leaders and think tank intellectuals.

Rumsfeld proved to be the most active member among the foreign policy group. After failing to win the 1988 Republican presidential nomination, he left government to earn a fortune as chief executive officer of a cable and communications firm. Now, independently wealthy and retired from corporate life, he devoted his attention to the organization. At the same time, Paul Wolfowitz, Cheney's former Pentagon policy chief, had become one of the leading conservative thinkers on international affairs. His ideas not only would play an influential role in the congressional policy group, but also in the run-up to the 2003 invasion of Iraq. After leaving the first Bush administration, Wolfowitz was named dean of the prestigious Johns Hopkins School of International Studies. Despite his academic pursuits, he stayed grounded in public policy matters, writing numerous articles and op-ed pieces, and testifying before Congress on tough international issues.[5] But Iraq consumed his passion. By the time he joined the congressional policy board, his views on Saddam Hussein and his senior leadership had considerably hardened. After the Gulf War, he argued that the United States may have missed an opportunity to eliminate Saddam Hussein, while explaining the reasons why he was left in power. As late as 1997, Wolfowitz wrote an essay in defense of the Bush Administration's decision not to invade Iraq, arguing that it would have led to a "more or less a permanent occupation of a country that could not govern itself" and where "the rule of a foreign occupier would increasingly be resented." In that same essay, however, he warned that the policy of containment was proving ineffective and that the coalition against Iraq would unravel as the major powers would lift sanctions for oil and trade. Saddam Hussein would once again have the resources to reconstitute his programs of weapons of mass destruction, intimidate and destabilize the regimes of the gulf, and upset the Arab-Israeli peace process.

Wolfowitz concluded that a new Iraqi regime posed the best solution, but stopped short of calling for U.S. military action.[6]

By the end of 1997, however, Wolfowitz went further, calling for the outright use of American military power to wipe out Saddam Hussein's tyranny. In a coauthored article entitled "Overthrow Him" in the *Weekly Standard*, Wolfowitz and Zalmay Khalilizad claimed that military force was not enough by itself. It "must be part of an overall political strategy that set its goal not merely the containment of Saddam but the liberation of Iraq from his tyranny."[7] Thereafter, Wolfowitz fervently publicized his views on ousting Saddam in op-ed pieces, opinion magazines, and before Congress. He called for supporting opposition leaders, indicting Saddam Hussein as a war criminal, and creating a protected zone in southern Iraq similar to the liberated zone established in the north in 1991. But just as Wolfowitz was pushing a harder line against Saddam Hussein, the international coalition that James Baker assembled against Iraq in the 1991 Gulf War seemed to be unraveling. In response to this alarming development, Wolfowitz argued that America's European and Middle East allies would dutifully follow its lead once the United States took strong action—a claim that not only proved false, if not naïve, in the run-up to the 2003 American invasion of Iraq, but also helped to set the United States on a course of unilateralism without the support of the 1991 coalition.[8]

BACK IN ACTION

When Cheney accepted the job at Halliburton, he left Washington for Dallas to run the giant international oil services firm, putting him only a short drive away from George W. Bush's governor's mansion in Austin. The former Pentagon chief had forged close ties with President Bush, the governor's father, during the Persian Gulf War. When Governor Bush began exploring a run for the Republican presidential nomination, he invited Cheney to Austin on several occasions to discuss politics, including foreign policy. Cheney proved a convenient and knowledgeable advisor. As Bush geared up his campaign, he invited Cheney and other experts to his Austin mansion to discuss national security issues. Cheney suggested that his former Pentagon aide Paul Wolfowitz join the group, which also included the likes of Condoleezza Rice, Richard Armitage, and Dov Zakheim. The foreign policy team soon expanded to include Donald Rumsfeld and Richard Perle, prominent neoconservatives who along with Wolfowitz believed in an aggressive moralism in foreign affairs—the notion that the world could be refashioned in America's image or at least bent to its interests.

After the Texas governor defeated John McCain, the maverick Arizona senator, for the nomination, he asked Cheney to head up his vice presidential search committee. Cheney accepted the assignment after Bush told him that among the most important qualities of a vice president was someone who could help him govern. He recruited his close advisors David Addington and David Gribben, his old high school friend from Wyoming who had worked for Cheney in Congress, the Pentagon, and Halliburton, to help with the search process. As Bush began fully mobilizing his campaign, the press speculated about who his running mate would be. At an Austin rally in July 2000, in an unprecedented situation, Bush announced that the man leading his vice presidential search team—former Defense Secretary Dick Cheney—would be his vice presidential running mate. Gesturing toward Cheney before a crowd of onlookers and a national television audience, Bush said, "I'm proud to call him my friend, and honored to call him my running mate." The announcement came after three months of vetting a list of potential candidates that at various times had included former Missouri Senator John Danforth, Senators Chuck Hagel of Nebraska and Fred Thompson of Tennessee, Governors Frank Keating of Oklahoma, George Pataki of New York, and Tom Ridge of Pennsylvania, as well as Colin Powell, who made it clear he wanted the State Department.[9]

While Cheney provided Bush with the advice and counsel of a veteran Washington insider with broad defense and foreign policy credentials, the question involved whether he would help the GOP nominee get to the White House. Unlike more traditional vice presidential running mates, he neither added geographically to the ticket with Wyoming's paltry three electoral votes, nor united the party ideologically. But he brought a gravitas and weight to the ticket with his knowledge of national politics and policy, while weathering Democratic attacks during the presidential race. In his first television appearance, on *Larry King Live*, as Bush's running mate, Cheney gave the first inkling of how saw his role as vice president. "In recent administrations," he said, "the vice president's role has taken on new meaning and new significance, but that's because the job of the man on top is big enough that there's plenty of work to go around. And recent presidents have been willing to share that."[10]

He may not have given Bush much of a boost at the polls, but he soon proved valuable during the disputed 2000 presidential election. While lawyers fought over one of the most bitterly controversial elections in American history, with the presidential election in the balance, Cheney was already planning the transition and staffing a prospective Bush Administration. Again he recruited trusted loyalists Addington and Gribben onto his transition team. On November 24, the U.S. Supreme Court agreed to hear *Bush v. Gore* involving the disputed Florida recount. A harshly divided high court issued a 5-4 ruling in favor of Bush on December 12. The ruling sanctified earlier tallies that had given the state of Florida, a razor-thin Electoral College majority, to Bush. Following the Court's ruling, Al Gore conceded the election to Bush, halting the recounts in Florida. Although Bush won the Electoral College majority by just two votes, he lost the popular vote, becoming the fourth president in American history to do so. For the second time in history of the Republic, the eldest son of a U.S. president assumed the Oval Office previously entrusted to his father. The distinction long was unique to John Quincy Adams, who became the sixth president twenty-four years after his father and namesake retired as the nation's second chief executive.

CHENEY AS VICE PRESIDENT: PRE-9/11

After Cheney took the oath of office, former Vice President Dan Quayle visited Cheney to offer advice about his old job. Quayle learned just how much the vice presidency had changed. He recalled the conversation in a 2007 interview with the *Washington Post*. "I said, 'Dick, you know, you're going to be doing a lot of this international traveling, you're going to be doing all this political fundraising ... you'll be going to funerals,'" Quayle said. "I mean, this is what vice presidents do. We've all done it.'" Cheney replied that he had a different understanding with the president, a special arrangement.[11]

When the new Bush Administration prepared to take office, Cheney scoffed at a list of portfolios that resembled Quayle's Council of Competitiveness or Gore's National Partnership for Reinventing Government. "The vice president didn't particularly warm to that," recalled White House Chief of Staff Joshua B. Bolten, who was then the Bush team's policy director and who had helped to compile a list of responsibilities that he thought might be appropriate. Instead, Cheney arranged an improbable portfolio that would define his office in a new and wholly novel light—in short, an imperial vice presidency. As Bolten later recounted, Cheney preferred, and Bush approved, a mandate that gave him access to "every table and every meeting, making his voice heard in whatever areas the vice president feels he wants to be active in." Cheney wasted little time in using this mandate to work his will. While other recent vice presidents won standing invitations at the president's cabinet and National Security Council meetings, Cheney's presence in the administration involved another dimension. He not only exerted his influence in the president's absence, but also at the Cabinet and sub-Cabinet levels where his predecessors were rarely seen. Cheney's portfolio involved the core issues of most concern to every recent president—economic issues, intelligence and national security, energy, and the White House's legislative agenda. But Cheney's influence also stemmed from his early role leading the transition and exerting control over nominations and appointments in the new administration.[12]

After winning the presidential election via the Supreme Court, Cheney formally took the transition in hand for the incoming Republican administration. He moved quickly to populate numerous Cabinet departments with many of his closest allies. They found positions as chief and deputy chief of the Office of Management and Budget, deputy national security advisor, undersecretary of state, and assistant or deputy assistant secretary in numerous Cabinet departments. Cheney placed other loyalists in less senior but nevertheless significant posts. He wasted little time in becoming the quiet force behind the new president. Previous vice presidents like Al Gore also had named political allies to influential positions, but the scope of Cheney's appointments involved a far greater scale of influence. Until George W. Bush, no president had been willing to yield such vast domains of his powers to the vice president. Unlike the elder Bush, a highly experienced veteran of the executive branch who chose an obscure and callow vice president in Dan Quayle, his unseasoned son selected a hardened Washington insider as vice president in Cheney, a man used to occupying positions of power and exerting authority, including firing generals. It was the inverted image of his father's presidency. As events would prove, the new president's inexperience and proclivity to delegate would allow Cheney to elevate the vice presidency to unprecedented levels.

Within days of the December 16, 2000, Supreme Court decision, Bush began announcing his top Cabinet appointments. He named Colin Powell as his secretary of state, Condoleezza Rice as national security advisor, and Rumsfeld as secretary of defense, a position he held a quarter of a century earlier in the Ford administration. In briefly complimenting each of the members of his foreign policy team, he ironically seemed to foreshadow the conflicts to come within his administration. "General Powell's a strong figure, and Dick Cheney's no shrinking violet, but neither is Don Rumsfeld, nor Condi Rice," Bush said. "I view the four as being able to complement one another."[13] That Cheney was included in this group already signaled his remarkable presence within the administration. From almost the beginning, Powell's presence stirred anxiety among conservatives in the Republican Party and in the administration. He had opposed American military intervention in the Gulf and the Balkans, favoring force through sanctions. He had become the most powerful chairman of the Joint Chiefs of Staff in American history. And in both Panama and the Gulf conflicts, he had achieved celebrity status, overshadowing the less charismatic Cheney.

Bush announced Powell's appointment at a press conference at his ranch at Crawford, Texas, just days after winning the election. After Bush spoke, with Cheney standing alongside the president-elect, Powell took the podium, dominating the event as reporters directed their questions almost entirely his way. His remarks covered the sweep of foreign policy and defense issues. His impressive and wide-ranging performance outshone the president. "The general's remarks were broader and more expansive than the incoming president's, and when it came time for questions, it was General Powell who answered them," reported the *New York Times*. The general "sounded as if he were speaking not just as the next secretary of state but as the next secretary of defense too."[14] In the first Gulf War, Cheney had snapped at Powell: "Don't be . . . the secretary of defense. Just do military options." Now, conservatives worried whether he would not just run foreign policy, but the Pentagon as well. The conservative *Weekly Standard* head-lined an article "The Long Arm of Colin Powell: Will the Next Secretary of State Also Run the Pentagon?"[15]

But such a scenario was unlikely given that Rumsfeld was a hardened vet-eran of the executive branch, including as former secretary of defense, and a consummate bureaucratic infighter. Further, as Cheney's former mentor and long-time friend, the two would act to limit Powell's authority over the administration's foreign policy. Cheney influenced the selection of Rumsfeld nomination. His reach also extended to the appointment of others who served under him at the Pentagon in the first Bush administration. Wolfowitz became the new deputy secretary of defense; Stephen Hadley, another Wolfo-witz aide, was appointed the White House's deputy national security advisor; and Scooter Libby, another Wolfowitz aide, was named Cheney's chief of staff. Cheney also maneuvered Libby into serving as the president's special assistant, thus integrating his chief of staff into the White House staff. The administration also named Zalmay Khalilizad to the National Security Coun-cil to lead policy regarding Afghanistan and Iraq. By influencing these and other appointments, Cheney outmaneuvered the more popular Powell among the Republican foreign policy elite. At the same time, Cheney's ascendancy and his alliance with Rumsfeld, Wolfowitz, and others positioned them to dominate foreign policy at the expense of Powell. Against Powell's reluctance born of experience to commit American armed forces overseas, Cheney's alli-ance aimed to emphasize a foreign policy based more on American military power. The differing orientations inevitably would create fractious relations between the Pentagon and State Department.

Because the president-elect neither had experience in foreign affairs, nor in matters of major bureaucratic battles, Cheney became the dominate influ-ence throughout much of the administration's two terms in office. He fur-ther strengthened his hand by assembling his own national security and foreign policy staff, paralleling that of the president's National Security

Council. The vice president's staffers, moreover, fully participated with White House staff on all major foreign policy discussions. This arrangement was not completely unheard of. President Carter also had integrated the staffs of the president and vice president into a working team, but Vice President Mondale never contemplated assembling an entire shadow national security staff. Cheney's arrangement enhanced his role in international affairs far beyond that of any previous vice president. His grip on national security extended to his staffers having access to all e-mail traffic between the president and his NSC staff. In brief, Cheney shaped the organization of the White House to his distinct advantage, not only outmaneuvering Powell's State Department, but also the president's own Texas inner circle. The vice presidency had long been ridiculed as a graveyard of political ambition.[16] Cheney would transform it into a fulcrum of extraordinary power.

Cheney entered the vice presidency as a firm believer in executive supremacy. He had spent much of his career as a close witness to or involved in the various crises that plagued the presidency in the later half of the twentieth century. He entered the Nixon Administration amid the growing controversy surrounding the Vietnam War, but briefly left public life only to witness the destruction of Nixon's presidency over Watergate. He served in the Ford White House when Congress imposed new rules and laws on government eavesdropping after a wave of intelligence scandals engulfed the administration. These restrictions, he believed, encroached on the president's inherent constitutional powers as commander-in-chief. He denounced the War Powers Act of 1973 as a direct and dangerous violation of the president's constitutional authority because it prescribed congressional authorization for a declaration of war. As a six-term congressman under a Democratic majority, he quietly chafed under the tutelage of the majority party and opposed most of his colleagues regarding the investigation of the Iran-Contra affair. His career had been shaped mostly by being on the losing side on issues involving congressional efforts to rein in presidential unilateralism. As secretary of defense, he advised the president to go to war in the Gulf without congressional support.

Now in his rise to the vice presidency, his central agenda involved restoring what he believed to be the lost powers of the presidency. In important respects, it was a peculiar position to take. The presidency, often with the help of the courts, had already thrown off many of the old congressional constraints imposed on it following Vietnam and Watergate. Despite early fears that the freedom of information law would divulge the nation's secrets to foreign spies, the courts had shown a pattern of deferring to the executive branch when it came to classifying information. The Supreme Court had negated one-House legislative vetoes in 1983. Constraints on the FBI and

CIA had been loosened as far back as the Reagan Administration. The independent counsel statute had expired in 1999. And the War Powers Resolution's 60-day restriction on committing military forces in foreign lands had eroded into irrelevancy. The presidency had already retaken much of the terrain lost in the 1970s. But in Cheney's view, the world involved brutal realities that required a strong and unrestrained presidency and the projection of power abroad.

Cheney's aim to strengthen presidential power found adherents among the administration's White House lawyers. Bradford Berenson, named a member of the White House's new legal team, later recalled that well "before 9/11, it was a central part of the administration's overall institutional agenda to strengthen the presidency as a whole." Although for decades the vice president watched and even fought congressional efforts to contain presidential power, others expressed more immediate concerns about the possible consequences of the Clinton-era scandals on the Bush presidency. The Republican-led Congress had launched several scandal investigations against Clinton, subpoenaing administration attorneys as well as a wide range of White House information, including e-mails. Although Clinton mounted a vigorous legal defense, he lost several critical decisions in the federal courts, undercutting presidential privilege. After immediately taking office, the White House's new legal team wanted to reverse the damage that a Republican Congress had inflicted on the presidency. "In January 2001, the Clinton scandals and the resulting impeachment were very much on everyone's mind," said Berenson. "Nobody at that point was thinking about terrorism or the national security side of the house."[17] But it was Cheney and his counsel, David Addington, who set the agenda and led the charge for enlarging presidential power.

In January 2002, Cheney publicly assumed responsibility for the administration's quest to expand presidential authority. In an interview with ABC's *This Week*, the vice president spoke of the restraints imposed on the presidency following the Nixon years, calling them "unwise compromises" that "weaken[ed] the presidency and vice presidency." He said that in his more than three decades of public life in Washington, he had "repeatedly seen an erosion of the powers and the ability of the president to do his job."[18] Other senior officials followed Cheney's lead. In May, the *New York Times* quoted another senior administration official as saying that there was "recognition that within the administration that presidential authority has been eroded over the years beyond the proper constitutional separation of powers." Further, Alberto R. Gonzales, then White House counsel, emphasized that the framers of the Constitution intended that there "be a strong presidency in order to carry out certain functions" and that Bush felt obligated to "leave the office in better shape than when he came in."[19]

SECRECY

One of the administration's first battles to extend executive power came soon after Bush and Cheney were sworn into office. After scarcely more than a week in office, the president faced a domestic energy crisis in California with its rolling power outages, shortages, and utility bankruptcies. Rather than heeding the pleas of California politicians to intervene in the nation's most populous and financially powerful state, the president confronted the energy crisis circuitously by forming the National Energy Policy Development Group to address the nation's energy needs. On January 29, 2001, the president issued a memorandum establishing the energy task force within the executive branch to write a new national energy policy. Bush assigned Cheney to chair the group. "I can't think of a better man to run it than the vice president," he said. For about five months, the vice president oversaw an energy task force that solicited input mostly from representatives of the energy industry. In late May, the task force issued a final report and then went out of business. But the vice president's stealthy deliberations attracted a blast of unwanted scrutiny from congressional Democrats and environmental and consumer groups, alleging that the process had been hijacked by corporate interests who were big campaign donors to Republican coffers.

At the request of ranking House Democrats, the General Accountability Office (GAO), the investigative office of Congress, asked for information regarding who the task force met with. At the same time, two public interest groups, Judicial Watch, a conservative watchdog outfit, and the Sierra Club, the liberal environmental group, requested all the working papers and communications produced by the task force. The vice president rebuffed the requests, citing executive confidentiality. At first glance, the controversy seemed nothing more than typical Washington trench warfare. The task force's consultations with energy representatives were widely known and completely expected. There was nothing improper about these contacts, but Cheney moved to transform these pedestrian controversies into major constitutional tests of presidential power.

In the GAO's case, the standoff ignited an unprecedented and escalating battle of interpretations of its statutory authority to demand information from, and even sue, the White House. The vice president seized upon the GAO's request, which accorded with numerous past investigations of executive branch activities, for a much larger purpose—to eviscerate the agency's statutory powers on behalf of Congress to investigate the White House. Early in the dispute, David Walker, the GAO's comptroller general, accused the vice president and his lawyers of having launched a "broad-based frontal assault on our statutory authority." He expressed concern that the case had been wholly transformed into a defense of the GAO's very reason for being. Walker had already tried to reach an accommodation with the vice president, even scaling back requests for deliberative information, including meeting minutes and notes and information presented by nongovernment participants.[20] But efforts at negotiations with the vice president and his lawyer, David Addington, proved futile.

Confronted by Cheney's intransigence, in February 2002, Walker reluctantly filed an unprecedented lawsuit against the administration in federal district court.[21] The suit constituted the first time in the agency's history that it went to court to defend its statutory authority to conduct investigations of the executive branch. Carter Phillips, the outside attorney representing the GAO, argued that if the administration won the case, it "would be extremely damaging or fatal to the GAO's ability to investigate the executive branch." Paul Clement, the principal deputy solicitor general representing Cheney, countered that the GAO not only was overstepping its authority by demanding information on executive deliberations, but seeking a revolution in the separation of powers. If the vice president were ordered to release the information, he warned, there would be no end to similar lawsuits filed by the GAO against the executive branch. On December 9, 2002, Judge John Bates of the U.S. federal district court, an appointee of President George W. Bush and with many friends in the administration, threw out the case against the vice president. According to Bates, the case established neither a personal injury to Walker nor an institutional injury to Congress sufficient to merit standing.[22]

The implications of the Bates ruling, if left to stand, were potentially serious, even precedent setting. Without the power to bring legal action to enforce compliance with requests for information, critics charged, there would be little incentive for the executive or agencies to comply. Fearing the worst, open-government advocates urged Walker to appeal the ruling. But after Republicans won majorities in both houses in the November 2002 elections, Walker came under pressure to drop the suit. He reluctantly did so after looking at the chances of winning the case on appeal. Walker was facing a situation in which he had already suffered a court defeat at the hands of a Republican judge with ties to the Bush-Cheney Administration, was under political pressure from a Republican-controlled Congress not to appeal the Bates ruling, and was looking at the prospect of ultimately arguing the case before a conservative Supreme Court. Given these odds, Walker and his attorney seemed to conclude it would be best to make a strategic retreat and reserve the GAO's fight over its statutory authority for another day.

As Cheney battled the GAO, the vice president also invited lawsuits filed by the Sierra Club and Judicial Watch, which were seeking much the same information on the workings of the energy task force. The case that began with a pedestrian discovery request in two consolidated civil suits went to the U.S. Supreme Court. The suit against the vice president resembled the GAO's, involving separation of powers issues and whether Cheney could keep information about his energy task force's meetings secret. Both groups claimed that the task force violated the 1972 Federal Advisory Committee Act (FACA), requiring that its activities and records be open to the public if nonfederal individuals participated. Under the statute, presidential and other federal advisory groups that involve nongovernmental participants must hold their meetings in public, take minutes of the meetings, and allow for differing views to be represented. The law also allows for public access to minutes and other records, reports, and transcripts, but exempted access to classified information. Committees composed entirely of federal officials and employees were exempt from the statute, however.[23] The plaintiffs argued that energy industry representatives and lobbyists who were major donors and political allies of the administration were so integral to the task force's deliberations that they comprised de facto members of the group, a charge that Cheney denied. The vice president claimed that the task force was exempt from the law's requirements because it involved exclusively senior Bush Administration officials. He argued that requests for information intruded into the heart of executive deliberations and that for the courts to make even a preliminary disclosure would violate the constitutional separation of powers between the executive and judicial branches.

The act was passed in 1972 with the best of intentions for promoting open government, but in the end, executive confidentiality trumped open government in the courts, handing the Bush-Cheney Administration another important victory in building a higher wall of confidentiality around the White House. The public interest groups had won their case at the district and appellate court levels, ordering Cheney and others to turn over nonprivileged documents to determine whether the task force and its subgroups were covered by the federal open meetings statute. Cheney's lawyers contended that even for the courts to require discovery to determine the constitutional issues would violate presidential prerogatives. On June 24, 2004, the majority of the Supreme Court's justices agreed with the vice president that private deliberations among the president, vice president, and their close advisors must be given special consideration.[24] The Court sent the case back to the appeals court with instructions to give more deference to the administration's separation of powers objections. On May 10, 2005, the same federal appeals court that previously ordered Cheney to turn over information on his energy task force threw out the lawsuit against the vice president. The court found that compelling the White House to produce documents about internal policy deliberations would violate the president's constitutional powers. Critics denounced the ruling for giving the White House sweeping authority to set up policy groups, provide access to influential outsiders who have a stake in the outcome of policy decisions, and carry on such proceedings behind closed doors.[25] The vice president succeeded in negating another congressional statute that aimed to promote open government in order to extend executive confidentiality.

PRESIDENTIAL RECORDS ACT

Early in Bush's first term of office and before the 9/11 attacks, his administration took aim at another post-Watergate, open-government statute. In 1978, a bipartisan Congress passed the Presidential Records Act (PRA) to declare public ownership over the records of the president and vice president after they left office. The law stemmed from the constitutional struggle over access to Nixon's presidential tapes and records after he resigned under threat of impeachment. In 1974, when Nixon moved to claim ownership of his presidential materials, Congress passed an emergency law, seizing them for the continuing Watergate investigations and trials and preserving them for posterity. The former president sued to reclaim ownership, but lost his case before the Supreme Court in 1977. One year later, Congress passed the PRA, which overturned two centuries of tradition governing private ownership of presidential papers. The law allowed citizens to review all materials, including confidential communications with advisors, twelve years after a president leaves office. The act also assured that the most sensitive records related to national security, foreign relations, financial and trade secrets, and personal privacy were exempt from disclosure.

When the National Archives gave notice under the law that it would be releasing 68,000 pages of Reagan's previously privileged documents on January 20, 2001, twelve years after he left office, Alberto Gonzales stepped in to stop their availability. The release of the records was put on hold while the administration reviewed its options about what to do about the PRA. Then, on November 1, 2001, Bush issued an executive order that all but rewrote the act to reverse what it viewed as an unacceptable infringement on executive powers. By doing so, the White House reversed, if not nullified, one of the key post-Watergate reform acts to make government more open and accountable. It comported with the vice president's agenda to roll back the "unwise decisions" that were made after Watergate, Vietnam, and the intelligence scandals of the 1970s.[26]

The order was just as notable for the privileges it granted to the vice president as to the president himself. In violation of the 1978 act, the Bush order authorized former presidents and vice presidents, their designated representatives, or surviving family members and heirs to withhold materials in seeming perpetuity by asserting executive privilege, no matter how arbitrary the claim. Beyond radically extending executive privilege to former presidents and vice presidents—private citizens—outside the confines of the law, both sitting presidents and vice presidents were given authority to indefinitely postpone public release just by withholding their permission. The order also required that a "specific need" be demonstrated to gain access to records, placed the burden on the person requesting materials to bring a lawsuit in order to challenge a denial of access, and stripped the U.S. archivist of his affirmative responsibilities under the PRA to carry out the systematic and timely release of presidential and vice presidential records to the public. Congress passed the act to further the public's right to know, but the presidential order inverted this presumption to a strict "need to control" basis.

Scholars and other critics assailed the White House for trying to withhold documents that might be embarrassing or incriminating not only to the president's father, George H.W. Bush, but also to other administration officials who served under Reagan. What critics missed, however, was how the order gave equal status to the vice president, inventing a distinct executive privilege for Cheney and other holders of that office. Under the order, a former vice president or his personal representatives, even heirs, could block the public disclosure of his records indefinitely in violation of the intent of the 1978 law.

As public interest groups challenged the decree in the courts, Congress twice tried but failed to strike it down. After the Democrats won a slim majority in both houses in the November 2006 elections, Congress made a third attempt to override Bush's executive order and restore the Presidential Records Act. Against White House threats of a veto, both the House and Senate passed the measure in 2007, but it became hostage to floor maneuverings of a few Senate Republicans. As politics played out on the Senate floor, a federal district court struck down part of the president's executive order on the presidential records law. The lawsuit against Bush's presidential order had been brought by Public Citizen on behalf of several academic and public interest organizations. The lawsuit claimed that Bush's executive order was not only unlawful but that it was causing researchers lengthy delays in obtaining access to the records of former Presidents Reagan and Bush because of the unlimited time the order permitted for privilege reviews by the officeholders and their representatives. The court concluded that these significant delays violated the PRA's public access mandate and were not, as the government argued, required by the Constitution. The court did not rule on other aspects of Bush's executive order, finding them "unripe," as no former president or vice president had yet asserted a unilateral veto granted under the decree. Public Citizen declared the court victory a "rejection of the government's unfounded constitutional theories of executive privilege," but the presidential order still remained in place.[27]

CLASSIFICATION AUTHORITY

Cheney's obsession with secrecy also carried over to his classification authority. On March 25, 2003, President Bush signed a little-known decree that gave what one critic said was the "greatest expansion of vice presidential power in U.S. history." The presidential order gave Cheney the same authority to classify intelligence beyond public and congressional reach as the president. The order marked another example of Cheney's sweeping executive authority in the White House, a sign of his veritable copresidency. "By controlling classification," said Sidney Blumenthal, a former senior advisor to President Clinton, "the vice president can control intelligence, and through that, foreign policy." The order amended a 1995 executive order signed by Clinton that provided for the automatic declassification of federal agency records after twenty-five years. It granted the government more discretion in keeping information classified indefinitely, especially if it fell within a broad new definition of "national security." Bush's order facilitated the government's ability both to reclassify documents that had already been declassified and to classify what was characterized as "sensitive" material. It further allowed the CIA to override declassification rulings from an interagency panel.[28]

The order required all agencies and "any other entity within the executive branch" to report on their classification activities to the Information Security Oversight Office (ISOO), an obscure unit within the National Archives charged with making sure the executive branch protects classified information. The ISOO was run by J. William Leonard, the federal government's chief classification authority. Since becoming director of the ISOO in 2002, Leonard developed a reputation for integrity as an official spokesman for a credible classification policy and an outspoken critic of classification policies. In 2006, he noted that few, if any, would deny that too much government information was being classified. "The integrity of the security classification program is essential to our nation's continued well-being," he said. These sentiments led him into a highly publicized clash with the vice president's office, which decided in 2003 to stop complying with ISOO's inspection and reporting requirements. The vice president's office claimed that it was exempt from classification oversight procedures under Bush's presidential order on grounds that it was not an "entity within the executive branch" because Cheney also served as president of the Senate. In 2006, Leonard twice urged Addington to reconsider the vice president's noncompliance, but was ignored. In January 2007, Leonard appealed to Attorney General Gonzales requesting his interpretation as to whether the vice president's office was subject to reporting on its classification activities.[29]

Although the dispute centered on a relatively obscure process, it underscored the wider struggle over Cheney's mania for secrecy. Since becoming vice president, he had drawn an iron curtain around the workings of his office, cloaking an array of information such as the participation of industry executives who helped write the administration's national energy policy, details about privately funded travel, the names and size of his staff, even ordering the Secret Service to destroy his visitor logs. While Leonard's appeal to the Attorney General languished in the Justice Office, Cheney responded by trying to abolish the ISOO and to amend the presidential order to include a provision exempting the vice president's office from oversight; both recommendations, however, were rejected by an interagency group. Not long after, Leonard abruptly resigned his position, inviting speculation that his imbroglio with Cheney's office and the vice president's public humiliation played a role in his departure.[30]

Eight

The Terrorist Attacks: Transformation of the Vice Presidency

Cheney's crucible was the September 11, 2001, terrorist attacks in New York and Washington. The attacks originated in Afghanistan, Osama bin Laden's safe haven and where the hijackers received their training in suicide missions at al Qaeda terror camps. September 11 involved the catastrophic failure predicted by CIA director George Tenet three years before. It comprised a systematic failure of many of the key institutions of the American government, including the White House, the National Security Council, the FBI, the Federal Aviation Administration, the Immigration and Naturalization Service, and the Congressional Intelligence Committees. Beyond constituting a failure of policy and diplomacy, wrote Tim Weiner in *Legacy of Ashes*, it "was a failure to know the enemy. It was the Pearl Harbor that the CIA had been created to prevent."[1]

Shortly after Bush took office in January 2001, James Monnier Simon Jr., the assistant director of Central Intelligence, warned that the CIA lacked the capability to gather and analyze intelligence, leaving the nation at risk. The agency was in trouble, he warned. The United States was faced with a growing, "almost dizzying disparity between its diminished capabilities and the burgeoning requirements of national security," Simon said. "The disconnect between what we are planning for and the likelihood of what the United States will face has never been so stark." Although the CIA was in a shambles, the president gave the agency the barest of support in his first nine months in office, while providing the Pentagon an immediate 7 percent budget increase. The decision rested primarily with Rumsfeld's Pentagon, where the intelligence community had no voice. Both Rumsfeld and Cheney, who exerted enormous power over the administration's national security policies, had long distrusted the capabilities of the CIA.[2]

Even so, Tenet met with the president, Cheney, and National Security Advisor Condoleezza Rice at the White House nearly every morning at eight o'clock. At these early morning briefings, Tenet's warnings about bin Laden's intentions to strike America went mostly unheeded. Tenet also sounded the alarm about al Qaeda during the Clinton years, sending a memo to the entire intelligence community saying that he wanted no effort spared in the war with bin Laden. He further pressed Clinton's closest advisors to authorize a military strike on an al Qaeda base in Afghanistan. Tenet now sounded the same warnings to the new administration with little success. National Security Advisor Rice saw little urgency in reports that al Qaeda aimed to strike in the United States. Moreover, the president's national security concerns were focused elsewhere, including unraveling much of the global arrangements forged under the previous administration. The White House remained mostly aloof to the warning signals as the CIA increasingly received a deafening volume of fragmentary and uncorroborated information about a pending terrorist attack. By the spring and summer of 2001, warnings were arriving from everywhere—Saudi Arabia, the Gulf States, Jordan, Israel, and Europe. The administration's big sleep ended on September 4 when Bush's lead national security team met for the first time on the problem of bin Laden. On the same day, Richard Clarke, a national security staffer and counterterrorism expert, sent an urgent e-mail to National Security Advisor Rice to move the CIA to take immediate action. The intelligence agency was a "hollow shell of words without deeds." He warned that, unless something was done, hundreds could be killed.[3]

On the morning of September 11, 2001, in the bunker beneath the White House, Cheney watched CNN as New York's Twin Towers burned against a cerulean sky. Thousands would die that day, surpassing Clarke's prophetic warnings. Among others evacuated to the Presidential Emergency Operations Center were a few senior White House aides, including National Security Advisor Rice; her deputy, Stephen J. Hadley; Cheney's chief of staff, Scooter Libby; deputy White House chief of staff, Josh Bolten; counselor Mary Matalin; Bush's communications director, Karen Hughes; and Cheney's wife, Lynne. Cheney expressed little emotion beyond closing his eyes for a brief moment as they watched the south tower of the World Trade Center collapse. Within minutes, Cheney took control, dominating the events of that day. If anyone had the government experience to respond in times of national emergency, it was Cheney. He served as chief of staff under President Ford, gaining an understanding of the machinery of the White House. In Congress, he was on the House Intelligence Committee, mastering an understanding of the operations of the intelligence agencies. During the 1980s, he participated in a highly classified program to maintain the continuity of government in case of nuclear attack. Further, as secretary of defense, he oversaw the U.S. armed forces and waged two successful wars.

At the time of the attacks, the president and his wife were reading to second graders in the Emma E. Booker Elementary School in Sarasota, Florida. By phone, the vice president convinced the president not to return to Washington, directing Air Force One to a secure site at Offutt Air Force Base in Nebraska. In another phone conversation with the president that no government witnesses or telephone logs could corroborate, the vice president ordered U.S. warplanes to shoot down any threatening incoming aircraft. Cheney asserted that the president authorized his shoot-down order. The claim would later be challenged by the 9/11 commission, raising questions about whether his unconditional shoot-down order without the president's knowledge was unconstitutional and violated the military chain of command, which prescribes no role for the vice president. The vice president tried to quash the creation of the commission, but the administration relented under intense public pressure. Even so, the White House proved uncooperative with the commission's investigation, refusing to turn over documents and to help investigators arrange interviews. In a stunning finding, the commission's investigators—after carefully examining detailed records of communications and phone logs on the day of 9/11—concluded that Cheney's account of the shoot-down order was false. The decision to issue the shoot-down order had not been made by Bush, but by the vice president alone. Cheney and Addington were livid by the suggestion that the vice president had given an unconditional shoot-down order without the president's knowledge or authorization. Just days before the public release of the commission's final report, Cheney demanded that the sections indicating his unilateral action be struck from the record. No changes were made, however.[4]

With the country at war, Cheney became the animating force behind Bush's "war on terror." In the vice president's view, the terrorist attacks created the immediate imperative to give the president unrestrained authority to defend the nation. This outlook would define the central philosophy and legacy of the Bush presidency at home and abroad. Cheney and his formidable general counsel David Addington would aggressively drive sweeping legal changes through the White House, the Justice Department, and the Pentagon. Their expansive interpretation of presidential power would define the administration's policies on a range of issues under the banner of the "unitary executive"—imprisoning suspected terrorists beyond sovereign law, rendering terrorism suspects to secret prisons in foreign lands, employing harsh interrogation measures, boosting police powers at home, enabling the

National Security Agency to conduct domestic surveillance operations without warrants, and ignoring or overriding hundreds of congressional provisions through presidential signing statements.

Cheney wasted little time in beginning his legal revolution. On the morning of September 11, the vice president summoned Addington to the White House bunker. Addington was headed to his Virginia home after being evacuated from the Eisenhower Executive Office Building next to the White House. As he approached the Arlington Memorial Bridge, he received a call telling him that the vice president needed him. In the bunker, Cheney and Addington began outlining the powers the president would need to fight the war on terror. Before the day ended, they had involved Timothy E. Flanigan, deputy White House counsel, and John C. Yoo, deputy chief of the Office of Legal Counsel at the Justice Department. White House counsel Alberto Gonzales would later joined Cheney's core legal group.

Yoo, a former Berkley law professor and former clerk to Justice Clarence Thomas, became the theorist in efforts to liberate the commander in chief from laws that constrained the presidency. For years, Yoo was a member of the Federalist Society, an association of conservative intellectuals who viewed international law with skepticism. "Addington, Flanigan, and Gonzales were really a triumvirate," recalled Bradford Berenson, former associate White House counsel, adding that Yoo "was a supporting player." Addington with his imposing physical and intellectual presence dominated the group; he was the force in the meetings. With his national security background, he offered legal certitude at a time of political and legal confusion. His legal background stood out in an administration in which neither the president, vice president, nor the national security advisor was a lawyer. Neither Attorney General John Ashcroft nor Gonzales, a former Texas judge, could even approach Addington's understanding of national security law. Moreover, Ashcroft's strained relations with the White House excluded him from Cheney's inner circle that initiated the most radical legal strategies on the war on terror. Gonzales's influence stemmed from his long-term relationship with the president, but "he was an empty suit," said one administration lawyer. "He was weak. And he doesn't know shit about the Geneva Conventions."[5]

Five days after the attacks, Cheney expressed the new mindset, arguing on *Meet the Press* that the government needed to go to the "dark side." He said, "A lot of what needs to be done here will have to be done quietly, without discussion, using sources and methods that are available to our intelligence agencies, if we're going to be successful. That's the world these folks operate in. And so it's going to be vital for us to use any means at our disposal, basically, to achieve our objective."[6] The vice president's remarks mirrored the recollections of a former State Department lawyer after 9/11:

"The Twin Towers were still smoldering. The atmosphere was intense. The tone at the top was aggressive—and understandably so. The Commander-in-Chief had used the words 'dead or alive' and vowed to bring the terrorists to justice or bring justice to them. There was fury."[7]

With advice from Yoo, Flanigan wrote the authorization for military force in Afghanistan, approved by Congress on September 18. As congressional members worked through the initial draft, Flanigan and other White House representatives tried to push through broader language that would endorse the president's authority to use military force to "deter and preempt any future acts of terrorism or aggression against the United States."[8] This wording was so broad that it would have given the president sole discretion to wage war against any nation or entity, whether or not it had any association with 9/11. Congress denied the request, limiting the resolution to Afghanistan and the war against al Qaeda. The final document authorized the president to "use all the necessary and appropriate force against those nations, organizations, or persons he determines planned, authorized, committed, or aided the terrorist attacks of September 11, 2001 . . . in order to prevent any future acts of international terrorism against the United States."[9] Yoo and Flanigan attempted to draft the authorization in the broadest possible terms because "this war was so different, you can't predict what might come up," Yoo recalled.[10]

But Cheney and his legal team knew what would come next. They swiftly moved to authorize the National Security Agency (NSA) to intercept—without judicial warrants—communications to and from the United States. The program was banned under the 1978 Foreign Intelligence Surveillance Act, one of the many post-Watergate reforms that Cheney believed had badly eroded the powers of the presidency. Cheney aimed to override the law. "The president of the United States needs to have his constitutional powers unimpaired, if you will, in terms of conducting national security policy," Cheney would later say in justifying the domestic spying program. "I believe in a strong, robust executive authority. And I think the world we live in demands it." It was Cheney who conceived of the NSA operation, who exerted the political muscle behind it, and who cloaked it in secrecy.

After 9/11, the intelligence community expressed grave concerns of a strong and continuing threat to the homeland, a second wave of attacks. In Cheney's view, the president required unfettered power to counter the threats. Within days of the attacks, the NSA began ramping up its surveillance technologies, with the help of U.S. telecoms, to intercept and sift through vast amounts of communications going into and out of Afghanistan in the hunt for al Qaeda. Unlike such foreign operations, the Federal Intelligence Surveillance Act (FISA) required the NSA to obtain a warrant any time it sought to monitor communications inside the United States. In these cases, the law required the agency to establish "probable cause" that the target of electronic surveillance was a foreign power or an agent of a foreign power.[11] But there was no telling whether other al Qaeda sleeper cells were in the country ready to strike again. From the perspective of Cheney's legal team, the nation was at war and FISA's legal constraints posed a national security threat. The NSA offered vast and new far-reaching surveillance capabilities, but the agency faced the traditional constraints of the court system. "Blindly following FISA's framework," wrote Yoo, "will hamper efforts to take advantage of what is known as 'data mining'"—the ability to detect patterns of activity that could reveal al Qaeda's network before they launched another attack.[12] Addington also saw little use for the FISA system, telling colleagues, "We're one bomb away from getting rid of that obnoxious court."[13]

As with many of the administration's counter-terrorism initiatives, Cheney became the impetus for using the vast capabilities of the NSA to engage in domestic surveillance. Weeks after the 9/11 attacks, he asked CIA director George Tenet what more the NSA could do. The question signaled the vice president's wish to use the agency's full capabilities in the war on terror. Tenet posed the same question to General Michael Hayden, the Air Force general and director of the NSA. "Not within my current authorities," Hayden responded. Tenet then invited Hayden to talk to the administration about what role the agency could play. At a high-level meeting, Hayden proposed a plan of wiretapping suspected terrorists inside the United States without court orders.[14]

Hayden saw opportunity in using the agency's technological prowess in the United States. Advances in technology involving acoustic, engineering, and statistical theory, combined with the efficient use of computing power, offered new capabilities to monitor communications from the vast stream of global voice and data traffic that passed through U.S. networks. With a growing fraction of the world's telecommunications traversing through junctions on U.S. territory, the administration had both the incentive and capability for a new and highly effective kind of espionage. But the plan violated FISA. The law prevented the government from tapping into access points on U.S. soil without a warrant to monitor the contents of communications to or from individuals in the United States. The surveillance was soon justified, in secret, as "incident to" the authority Congress had granted to go to war in Afghanistan. Yoo authored a secret memorandum justifying the new presidential powers to bypass the law and carry out warrantless domestic surveillance, completing it on September 25, 2001. Like the administration's other secret legal opinions, Yoo aimed to give the president unbridled power at the expense of the checks and balances embedded in the Constitution that limited executive power. It was an extraordinary move, evading Congress, the courts, and key administration officials who were likely to object. President Bush authorized Hayden's plan on October 4, 2001. "I could *not* not do this," Hayden said.[15] Once again, the NSA began to spy on American soil.

Congress had passed the FISA law as one of its cornerstone post-Watergate reforms to check unfettered executive power and restore the democratic balance of powers. Created in 1952, the NSA initially faced few legal constraints on its powers to spy on Americans. Then came the massive revelations in the 1970s of the intelligence gathering abuses of the Johnson and Nixon presidencies, when the NSA, CIA, and FBI spied on the administration's political enemies and civil rights and anti-Vietnam war demonstrators. Johnson and Nixon justified their domestic spying operations as necessary to protect national security from activists who might be communist agents. When the Church committee investigated and revealed the sensational misdeeds of the intelligence agencies in 1975, Senator Frank Church warned of the dire threat to Americans' fundamental civil liberties and privacy rights. Congress heeded the warning and passed the warrant law to assure that a special court would review and authorize electronic surveillance on U.S. soil. By doing so, the legislative branch sought to protect the basic constitutional rights of American citizens and to guarantee that executive branch officials would never again abuse their power over the nation's intelligence agencies. Carter signed the law in 1978, and until 2001 every president had complied with its provisions.

The Bush-Cheney Administration debated whether to ask Congress to amend FISA to permit Hayden's proposed warrantless domestic surveillance program, an idea that was rejected. In December 2005, Gonzales later explained the administration's reasoning for not asking Congress to amend the law after the secret operation went public: "We have had discussions with Congress in the past—certain members of Congress—as to whether or not FISA could be amended to allow us to adequately deal with this kind of threat, and we were advised that that would be difficult, if not impossible."[16] But Congress had already agreed to amend the warrant law when the USA Patriot Act was passed on October 26, 2001. Among the Patriot Act's provisions expanding police search and seizure powers included one that extended retroactive warrants under FISA from twenty-four to seventy-two hours in emergency cases.

Rather than consult Congress, which had already proved willing to amend the law, Yoo drafted another secret opinion entitled "Authority for Use of Military Force to Combat Terrorist Activities within the United States." The opinion argued that the United States was a battlefield and that Congress could not restrict the president in combating the enemy on U.S.

soil. Congress could neither limit the president's use of the military to gather "battlefield intelligence" within America's borders, nor could it regulate the means by which the president did so, including requiring him to get court orders. In an interview with author and journalist Charlie Savage, Yoo explained his reasoning. "Our legal system had been built on the idea that the home front could operate under normal rules of the criminal justice system, and that wars are things that happen abroad," he said. "Nine-eleven showed that a clean line doesn't exist as strongly as it used to. The NSA wiretapping is a good example of that. The commander in chief's authority to prevent attacks on the United States has to follow the terrorists. If the terrorists come into the United States and are sending communications into and out of the country, then the president's authority should be able to follow them."[17] In another interview, Yoo said there was a law greater than FISA, which was the Constitution, and "part of the Constitution is the president's commander-in-chief power. Congress can't take away the president's power in running war." Yoo's argument in this and other matters was essentially that there was no limit on a president's wartime powers.[18]

Concurring with Yoo's arguments, Cheney and Addington also pushed for the NSA to get involved in intercepting purely domestic telephone calls and e-mails without court warrants in the hunt for terrorists. The idea of intercepting domestic communications met opposition from lawyers and officials at the intelligence agency. The agency had been badly scarred by the surveillance scandals of the 1970s and ever since had exercised its powerful technology with considerable caution to stay within the parameters of the law. Trained in the agency's rules against domestic spying and resistant to approving any surveillance without court orders, they argued that any wiretapping should be limited to communications into and out of the country— a view that ultimately prevailed. Even with this limitation, the program marked a decisive break with the provisions of FISA, which required court approval for all eavesdropping on U.S. soil. General Hayden, who aimed to stay within the agreed-upon parameters, accepted the argument that as commander in chief, the president owned the constitutional authority to order surveillance on communications to and from the United States without court approval, a position vigorously contested by critics across the political spectrum after the classified program became public. Unlike Cheney and Addington, who believed that surveillance on solely domestic communications should be done in the hunt for terrorists in the United States, Hayden was particularly concerned about ensuring that at least one end of each conversation be outside the United States.[19]

The secret eavesdropping program signaled the start of dissolving any legal distinctions between the U.S. homeland and foreign territory. The world over was a battlefield. On October 7, three days after the president secretly authorized domestic spying, the United States went to war in Afghanistan. Before the attacks, the CIA's capacity to run paramilitary operations had withered to a skeleton force. But in just a few weeks after 9/11, the agency mobilized a cadre of paramilitary commandos to go into Afghanistan, gather intelligence, and hand out millions of dollars to gain the loyalties of tribal leaders against the ruling Taliban. Small teams of Special Forces slipped behind enemy lines to target massive air power at the enemy. By the third week of November, American forces and their Afghan allies toppled the Taliban's political leadership, capturing about 7,000 al Qaeda and Taliban prisoners. The Americans paved the way for a new government in Kabul, but tens of thousands of Taliban loyalists fled and melted away into the countryside to fight again.

MILITARY COMMISSIONS

Almost immediately after the United States launched the war in Afghanistan, the question arose about what to do with captured al Qaeda and Taliban fighters. By late October 2001, Cheney and his allies were becoming frustrated with an interagency panel led by Pierre-Richard Prosper, ambassador-at-large for war crimes. The panel resulted from a meeting among a group of lawyers from across the administration to address how to prosecute terrorists if they were captured. The meeting, which occurred in Gonzales's office just over a week after 9/11, also involved deputy White House counsel Tim Flanigan, National Security Council lawyer John Bellinger, Pentagon general counsel Jim Haynes, Addington, and Prosper. The meeting produced an agreement that Prosper would lead an interagency working group to devise policies for prosecuting terrorists. Prosper assembled a team of experienced specialists from across the government, including military lawyers and Justice Department prosecutors. The panel extended invitations to Cheney's staff to participate, but received no response.

The working group debated several options—prosecuting terrorists in federal criminal courts, using court-martial procedures, or establishing military commissions similar to those held for the Nazis under the Roosevelt Administration. Each option posed difficulties. Lawyers at the White House saw the federal criminal courts as a minefield. Much of the evidence would involve classified intelligence and be too sketchy to meet the exacting standards of evidence. There also would be emphasis on protecting defendants' rights. And then there was the issue of whether it would be safe to prosecute terrorists in a federal courtroom on American soil. The court-martial process could take place anywhere, even outside the United States, but the standards of evidence and defendants' rights would resemble those of the criminal courts. Instituting a new system of military commissions would provide greater flexibility, but some lawyers argued that it might require congressional authorization. Further, although military commissions had no statutory rules of their own, in past American wars when such tribunals had been used to carry out battlefield justice, they had mostly heeded to prevailing standards of military justice. While advocates for the commissions argued for lower standards of proof and applying the death penalty more liberally, others viewed the issues as more complicated. Terrorism had never been clearly defined as a war crime under international law. Creating tribunals could require the writing of new law, which would be more problematic than prosecuting terrorists in the criminal courts.[20]

Amid the fevered atmosphere following 9/11 and the fear of an imminent second wave of attacks, the vice president brushed aside the interminable discussions and took charge. He relied on his small group of White House allies to work in secrecy to devise a new system of justice for the new war they had declared on terrorism. Entire agencies and most of the government's experts in military and international law were left out of the process. Flanigan secretly drafted a presidential order, without informing Prosper, allowing Bush to invoke his wartime powers to set up a system of military commissions on his own. This approach not only would provide greater latitude than the criminal courts in the admission of evidence, but also would centralize the process wholly in the executive branch. Flanigan worked closely with his aide, Berenson, and Addington throughout October and early November in drafting the order. Their efforts received critical backing on November 6 when Patrick Philbin, an attorney in the Justice Department, authored a thirty-five-page confidential memo justifying the president's authority to unilaterally set up military commissions. An old colleague of Yoo's from their undergraduate days at Yale and Harvard law school, Philbin also worked in the Office of Legal Counsel (OLC) as a deputy assistant attorney. In the 1990s, before arriving at the Justice Department, he had worked for a corporate law firm on behalf of telecommunications firms, but he had no expertise in the laws of war.[21]

And yet, at the behest of Yoo, he drafted a critical legal memo, arguing that the president, under his full wartime powers, had inherent constitutional authority to establish military commissions as he saw fit and without congressional authorization. Philbin argued that the September 11 attacks were clearly sufficient to set loose the laws of war. The document also declared that the White House could observe international law selectively, a point that would later ignite intense debate within the administration. Prosecuting terrorists under the laws of war "does not mean that terrorists will

receive the protections of the Geneva Conventions or the rights that laws of
war accord to lawful combatants." In important respects, the Philbin memo
rolled back the laws of war to 1942 when Roosevelt set up military commissions to try Nazi saboteurs captured inside the United States. When the
prisoners challenged the president's power to prosecute them in military
commissions, the Supreme Court upheld Roosevelt's action, leading to their
executions. Since that case, both international and American military law
had evolved dramatically. In 1949, the United States became a signatory to
the Geneva Conventions, providing prisoners of war the right to a fair trial.
And in 1952, Congress adopted the Uniform Code of Military Justice, a set
of laws that assured that future military commissions would use the same
standards of evidence and defendants' rights that American troops received
in courts-martial. Nevertheless, Philbin's memo stated that the 1942 ruling
had established a "clear constitutional analysis" that fundamental due process rights did not apply to military commissions. Under this reasoning, the
Pentagon could detain foreign suspects indefinitely. Further, the implications
of his memo were clear: neither international law nor a congressional act
could limit the president's wartime powers.[22]

Roosevelt also had set up his military commission without explicit congressional approval. Moreover, he had authorized the military to create its
own procedural rules and established himself—instead of a military judge—
as the final reviewing authority for the case. Addington seized on Roosevelt's
example as a guiding precedent, despite important differences. Roosevelt's
actions involved enemy saboteurs in a traditional war among nations. But
Bush would be assuming similar powers, long discarded, to confront a network of stateless enemies in a seemingly indefinite conflict. With Philbin's
memo in hand, Addington and Flanigan drafted the order. With his long
experience in national security law, Addington was particularly influential in
shaping the presidential order.

The secret order involved the kind of policy surprise that Cheney had
always counseled against, insisting that unvetted decisions often lead to presidential blunders. In 1980, Cheney had advised then incoming presidential
chief of staff James Baker to be an honest broker and not to use the process
to impose his personal views on the president. He told Baker, based on his
own personal experience as Ford's chief of staff, to ensure that proposals
were vetted by others and to avoid policy surprises, which could hurt the
president politically. In 1999, he emphasized the same point at a conference
of White House historians. "The process of moving paper in and out of the
Oval Office, who gets involved in the meetings, who does the president listen to, who gets a chance to talk to him before he makes a decision is absolutely critical," he said. "It has to be managed in such a way that it has

integrity."[23] But two years later at a November 13, 2001, private luncheon with Bush, Cheney offered the president a tightly guarded and far-reaching order that almost none of his top advisors had seen. Neither Colin Powell's State Department with its cadre of leading experts on the laws of war, nor Condoleezza Rice and her staff at the National Security Council knew of the vice president's backroom maneuvering. The writing of the order had been considered so urgent and secret that Cheney had advocated the withholding of the draft order from both Rice and Powell. Nor had anyone even considered consulting Congress, least of all the vice president.

Equally important, the order gave the Justice Department no role in selecting which terrorists would be prosecuted in the military commissions. When learning of the order, an angry Attorney General John Ashcroft confronted the vice president at the White House over Veterans Day weekend, on November 10. At a broad conference table in the Roosevelt Room, Ashcroft emphasized that he was the president's chief law enforcement officer with responsibility for the FBI and terrorism prosecutions nationwide. Ashcroft demanded a voice in the tribunal process and became furious at learning that Yoo, his subordinate, had taken part in a strategy to deny jurisdiction to the federal courts. But Ashcroft's blunt talk failed to move Cheney. Three days later the vice president delivered the order for military commissions to Bush for his review. After his regular luncheon with the president, Cheney swiftly executed its formal authorization through trusted channels, leaving few fingerprints. Addington and Flanigan knew of his role, but when the order passed to Berenson, associate White House counsel, his trail vanished. Berenson had little knowledge of its origins. Berenson delivered the order to deputy staff secretary Stuart W. Bowen with urgent instructions to prepare it immediately for signature and bypass the normal procedures of distribution to the president's top advisors. Within the hour the president had signed the three-page presidential order creating military commissions to try terrorists. Powell, Rice, and Prosper only learned of the new policy from the media that evening.[24]

Bush signed the order without ceremony or comment, but its historical significance was far reaching. The president had only played a modest role in the debate, agreeing that military commissions should be an option. Now with presidential authorization, the Pentagon could detain and prosecute any foreign suspect deemed to have "engaged in, aided or abetted, or conspired to commit terrorism." The Bush document recalled the Roosevelt order in promising free and fair tribunals, but provided few protections. As Tim Gold of the *New York Times* reported, it offered "no promise of public trials, no right to remain silent, no presumption of innocence." Like Roosevelt's commission, proving guilt beyond a reasonable doubt was not necessary and a death sentence could be meted out even with a divided ruling. But there was one important and dramatic difference. Roosevelt's order only applied to eight Nazi saboteurs. Bush's order would apply and grant few rights to potentially untold numbers in a war that had no foreseeable end.[25]

It was a dramatic move, igniting immediate and widespread criticism at home and abroad. Congressional critics and civil libertarians accused the administration of aiming to impose a new criminal justice system and extend executive power. Critics alleged that the administration would define the crimes, set the rules for trials, and select the judges, juries, and appellate panels. The process would be rigged in favor of presidential power at the expense of the rights of the accused. Among other lawmakers, Patrick Leahy, the Democratic senator from Vermont, asserted that the administration's policy required congressional approval. He argued that any military commissions that might be created include the defendant's presumption of innocence and appellate review by the Supreme Court. Bush's order also drew criticism from abroad. Spanish authorities declared that they would not extradite terrorist suspects to the United States if they would be prosecuted in the tribunals. Senators called Rumsfeld and Ashcroft to testify, but the administration sent lower-level officials. Congressional opposition to the tribunal plan, however, eroded amid the public's strong support for the president's antiterrorism measures.

CHENEY'S NEXT STEP

On November 14, 2001, the day after the president signed the commissions order, Cheney told the U.S. Chamber of Commerce that terrorists "don't deserve to be treated as a prisoner of war." It was a statement that indicated another dramatic leap in his legal and executive power revolution. Although the president had signed the order authorizing the creation of military commissions, the rules governing the prosecution of terrorists and what rights they would have still had to be drafted. The vice president explained that the tribunals would involve "a procedure whereby [the president] will make the decision in each case in terms of whether or not a particular suspect, individual, who's come into our custody is transferred, if you will, from the traditional sort of criminal procedural branch of our government through the courts." The basic proposition, he said, "is that somebody who comes into the United States of America illegally, who conducts a terrorist operation killing thousands of innocent Americans, men, women, and children, is not a lawful combatant. . . . They don't deserve the same guarantees and safeguards that would be used for an American citizen going through the normal judicial process." Cheney said they would have a fair trial, but it would be "under the procedures of a military tribunal and the rules and regulations to be established in connection with that."[26]

The vice president's remarks that terrorists "don't deserve to be treated as prisoners of war" essentially meant that the Geneva Conventions would not apply to al Qaeda or Taliban fighters captured on the battlefield, a policy that the president had yet to sanctify. The issue set off a fierce brawl inside the administration before Bush authorized Cheney's policy. Since 1949, the Geneva Conventions had provided fundamental protections for the treatment of civilians and combatants in times of armed conflict. The protections differed with the status of the combatants captured by opposing armies, but the United States had always heeded the prevailing international view that even war criminals warranted certain rights. At a news briefing, Rumsfeld expounded on Cheney's position, dismissing the relevancy of the Conventions. Those who were captured on the battlefield in Afghanistan, he said, constituted "unlawful combatants" and had no rights under Geneva.

Rumsfeld assumed responsibility for drafting the rules governing how the tribunals would be conducted. Initially, Cheney's small circle including Addington and others proposed a harsh system that would involve convicting defendants with a low standard of proof, prohibiting the hiring of civilian defense attorneys and allowing the imposition of the death penalty even when members of the tribunal were divided. Many of the Pentagon's own uniformed lawyers fought these and other draconian measures that strayed from the Uniform Code of Military Justice. Since its inception, the Code had assumed due process standards similar to those of the federal courts; it was a source of pride for senior military lawyers. They might support using tribunals to prosecute terrorists, but they believed that the system should assure basic defendant rights. Even though senior uniformed lawyers participated in drafting the rules, they nevertheless felt frozen out, bypassed in a process that should have been delegated to them. Attorney General Ashcroft and others in the Justice Department also pushed for changing the proposed rules that would not be seen as extreme. Rumsfeld ultimately struck a compromise. He granted the presumption of innocence, required that guilt be proved beyond a reasonable doubt for convictions, allowed defendants to hire civilian lawyers, and required a unanimous ruling for the death penalty. The commission rules involved legally questionable procedures, however, including allowing the admission of secret evidence obtained through coercive interrogations. Rumsfeld signed off on the rules in March 2002, but the special commissions still had no authorization from Congress. Over the next several years, an unfolding drama surrounding these issues would earn the administration international condemnation and become entangled in the Supreme Court.[27]

GUANTANAMO BAY, CUBA

From the beginning, the administration sought to deny prisoners the right to appeal the legality of their detentions in federal court. The decision proved critical as officials began searching where to detain hundreds of prisoners captured on the battlefield in Afghanistan. Because holding the prisoners on American soil would subject them to the reach of federal courts and pose security risks, the administration searched for a location outside the United States. After considering such locations as an American military base in Germany and islands in the South Pacific, on December 27, 2001, Rumsfeld announced at a press conference the administration's intention of imprisoning detainees at Guantanamo Bay, Cuba. Guantanamo had a history of problems, however, stemming from when the United States tried to hold Haitian and Cuban refugees on the base a decade earlier. The policy ignited long-drawn-out litigation after the federal government sought to bar the entry of AIDS-infected refugees into the country. Nevertheless, Rumsfeld said the base was the "least worst place we could have selected."[28] One day later, Philbin and Yoo wrote a secret memorandum to the Pentagon stating that a strong claim could be made that prisoners detained at Guantanamo would be beyond the reach of the federal judiciary. Further, the base had the advantage of being outside the jurisdiction of any other nation's court system. Its unique status derived from the United States having signed a permanent lease with the Cuban government before Fidel Castro seized power. Of all places on the globe, Guantanamo presented the best location to set up a military prison free from American law, but under the absolute control of the Pentagon and the U.S. president. The memo sounded a warning, however, that although Guantanamo stood outside U.S. sovereign territory, an argument could be made that it existed within the jurisdiction of a federal court. It was a point that would later return to haunt the administration.

INTERROGATIONS

Soon after the first detainees began arriving at Guantanamo Bay on January 11, 2002, several CIA officials arrived at the Situation Room to discuss a sensitive matter with White House counsel Alberto Gonzales. Gonzales possessed little experience on the issue, but David Addington, who had considerable national security knowledge, sat close by. John Yoo recalled that the meeting signified the first time that top White House officials discussed the issue of interrogations. According to Yoo, who represented the Justice Department at the meeting, the CIA officials voiced concern about running into "real difficulties getting actionable intelligence from detainees," if the interrogators heeded the restrictions of the Geneva Conventions. From this moment, reported the *Washington Post* based on dozens of interviews with knowledgeable current and former officials, "Cheney turned his attention to the practical business of crushing the captive's will to resist." The vice president and his aides led the way in "shattering limits on coercion of prisoners in U.S. custody, commissioning and defending legal opinions" that the Bush Administration later "portrayed as the initiatives of lower-ranking officials." Cheney and his allies invented a distinction between prohibited "torture" and acceptable use of "cruel, inhuman, and degrading" interrogations. It essentially was a distinction without a difference.[29]

The issue of the Geneva Conventions and whether the administration would apply the long-standing treaty to al Qaeda and Taliban fighters ignited intense debate within the administration. On January 18, 2002, Bush decided that the conventions would not apply in the conflicts with al Qaeda and the Taliban, but Powell asked the president to reconsider at a meeting of senior national security officials several days later. The debate involved the administration's most senior national security officials. Yoo, only a deputy in the OLC, claimed that Afghanistan was a "failed state." The Taliban did not constitute a legitimate army, he said, but a militant terrorist group. In early January, he and another Justice Department lawyer drafted another secret memo, asserting that the president as commander in chief could declare that those captured in Afghanistan would not be covered by the Geneva Conventions. Adopted following World War II, the 1949 treaties had established fundamental protocols for the humane treatment of prisoners of war and anyone else captured during wartime. They prohibited protected persons from being subjected to violence; outrages upon personal dignity; torture, and cruel, humiliating, or degrading treatment; and criminal proceedings devoid of judicial guarantees that are "recognized as indispensable by civilized peoples." The Conventions also granted protected individuals the right to an individual hearing to determine the nature of their status.[30]

American presidents and members of Congress had long respected the treaties ever since they were signed by President Harry Truman in 1949 and ratified by the Senate in 1955. Decades later in 1996, a Republican Congress passed the War Crimes Act, embedding the protections of the Conventions in federal law. The act made it a criminal offense to commit certain violations of the laws of war when such offenses were committed by or against U.S. nationals or armed service members. Among other things, the law prohibited certain violations of the Geneva Conventions regarding the minimum standards for the treatment of detainees in armed conflicts.[31]

Powell and the State Department fought for upholding the Conventions, but lost the argument. In a January 11, 2002, memo to Yoo, the State

Department's legal advisor, William Taft IV, argued that Yoo's analysis was critically flawed. Taft's forty-page memo said that Yoo's contention that the president could ignore the conventions was "untenable," "incorrect," and "confused." Taft disputed Yoo's assertion that Afghanistan existed outside the Conventions because it was a failed state. He wrote that the American position before, during, and after the Taliban's authoritarian rule was that it was a state. He further cautioned that ignoring the Conventions not only would deny American soldiers the protections of the Conventions, but would subject the president to accusations of a "grave breach" by other nations and prosecution for war crimes. Others argued that the Geneva Conventions covered fighters in everything from world wars to local rebellions. Taft urged Yoo and Gonzales to warn the president that he would be seen as a war criminal throughout world.[32] Although Powell agreed that the Conventions may not apply to al Qaeda and Taliban fighters, he believed that each detainee warranted a status review under Geneva rules. He believed that few, if any, would qualify as POWs because they neither wore uniforms nor followed a lawful chain of command.[33]

But Cheney's allies viewed the Conventions as outdated and an impermissible encroachment on the president's wartime powers. According to Yoo, "Importing customary international law notions concerning armed conflict would represent a direct infringement on the President's discretion as Commander in Chief and Chief Executive to determine how best to conduct the nation's military affairs."[34] Addington supported Yoo's opinion, and ghost-authored a separate January 25, 2002, memo for the president's consideration under Gonzales's signature. The memo, written shortly after the meeting with the CIA delegation, pioneered the new agenda on interrogations. It argued that Geneva's strict limitations on questioning of enemy prisoners hindered efforts "to quickly obtain information on captured terrorists." The memo indicated the vice president's aim to push or obliterate the boundaries of impermissible treatment in conducting interrogations. It also took aim at Powell. While characterizing the Conventions as "quaint," it attacked Powell as a defender of "obsolete" rules and privileges created for another time.

The question became, How much coercion could be used to make the enemy talk? Addington expressed concern that future prosecutors might bring charges against interrogators or Bush Administration officials. The Geneva Conventions prohibited the use of "violence," "torture," "cruel treatment," or "humiliating and degrading treatment." The Convention Against Torture, ratified by the Senate in 1994, included similar language, banning the use of "torture and other cruel, inhumane, or degrading treatment or punishment" of prisoners. The treaty declared its prohibition to be absolute: "No exceptional circumstances whatsoever, whether a state of war or a threat of war, internal political instability or any other public emergency, may be invoked as justification of torture." And the War Crimes Act of 1996 made any grave breach of the Geneva restrictions a criminal offense. Addington tried to navigate around these strictures. He wrote that the possibility of future criminal liability could be thwarted by a broad presidential directive for humane treatment that also included exceptions under the president's unrestricted executive authority. It would be a carefully crafted and ambiguous directive. It would provide for the humane treatment of detainees "to the extent appropriate and consistent with military necessity" and in a manner that accorded with the principles of the Geneva Conventions. The language gave the president all the latitude he needed. Two weeks later on February 7, 2002, Bush signed a written directive adopting Addington's formula to the letter. The directive involved a crucial distinction, referring only to military interrogators, not to CIA officials.[35]

The Geneva debates furthered a power shift within the administration, temporarily boosting Yoo's stature, while diminishing the influence of Powell and lawyers at the State Department. While at the Office of Legal Counsel, Yoo seemed keenly attuned to sensitive legal issues involving foreign affairs, defense, and intelligence. His broad views of presidential power were shared by Addington, the vice president's advisor and counselor. Their close alliance provoked John Ashcroft, then attorney general, to call him "Dr. Yes" for his eagerness to serve the White House's legal justifications.[36] In previous administrations, the OLC served as the final arbiter on issues that had already been deliberated by the legal staffs of other agencies. In the Bush-Cheney Administration, however, the OLC often had the first and final say. In February 2002, the Cheney-Addington faction began excluding the State Department from further discussions on interrogations— discussions that involved treaties that State officials had a right to know about. Taft was tagged as ideologically suspect and unfit for fighting terrorism. At times, the infighting sank to rank pettiness. On arranging trips for administration lawyers to visit Guantanamo, invitations would sometimes be extended last to the State Department and National Security Council, hoping their lawyers would be unable to make the trip on short notice.

Bush's declaration that the United States would not heed the Geneva Conventions ignited world-wide condemnation as a violation of international law. Cheney swept aside the criticisms, saying on *Fox News* in late January that the Guantanamo detainees were the "worst of a very bad lot." They were very dangerous, he said, "devoted to killing millions of Americans, innocent Americans. ... And they need to be detained, treated very cautiously, so that our people are not at risk."[37] At the same time, while en route to tour Guantanamo, Rumsfeld told reporters that the prisoners were "among the most dangerous, best-trained, vicious killers on the face of the earth."[38] As it turned out, however, most of the detainees were lowly combatants who proved to be of little use for intelligence purposes.

RENDITION

Nearly one month later on March 13, 2002, another secret memo emanated from the OLC, largely drafted by Yoo. The memo was sent to the Pentagon's legal counsel, William J. Haynes, under the signature of Assistant Attorney General Jay Bybee. The opinion said that the president had the authority to transfer captives in the war on terror to foreign governments for interrogation, a policy known as "rendition." The policy of rendering terrorist suspects to other countries known for torture began in late summer 1995 when Clinton signed an Executive Finding, declaring bin Laden and al Qaeda enemies of the state. The finding directed the intelligence agencies to eliminate al Qaeda as a threat to U.S. national security. "It was begun in desperation," said Michael Scheuer, a former CIA counterterrorism expert who helped create the rendition program. At the time, Scheuer was director of the CIA's Islamic-militant unit, whose mission was to dismantle terrorist operations, including bin Laden's al Qaeda network. The CIA's first use of covert rendition as a systematic tactic began on September 22, 1995, with the capture of terrorist Abu Talal al-Qasimi in Croatia. He was later transferred to and executed in Egypt, a strategic ally whose secret police was known for its brutality. But in 1998, the largest pre-9/11 CIA rendition occurred when five suspects were abducted and transferred to Egypt. All were brutally tortured and two were hanged without trial. The practice allowed the CIA to evade American courts where transparency and standards of evidence could compromise sensitive intelligence sources and the cooperation of foreign governments. Nevertheless, Sheuer claimed that "there was a legal process" behind the early renditions. All captive suspects, he said, had been convicted in absentia. The CIA's legal counsel reviewed and signed off on every proposal. According to Scheuer, the system prevented innocent people from being snared in the program. "Langley would never let us proceed unless there was substance," he said. The covert program was pursued out of expedience—"not out of thinking it was the best policy."[39]

The covert rendition program before and after 9/11 violated the Convention Against Torture, signed by President Reagan in 1988 and ratified by the Senate in 1994.[40] The international treaty forbade governments from forcibly abducting and transferring prisoners to other countries where there were substantial grounds that they might face torture. The policy also seemingly transgressed the Geneva Conventions, which required the prompt registration of detainees so that the treatment of soldiers and civilians captured in war could be monitored. Further, in 1998, Congress passed legislation declaring that it was "the policy of the United States not to expel, extradite, or otherwise effect the involuntary return of any person to a country in which there are substantial grounds for believing the person would be in danger of being subjected to torture, regardless of whether the person is physically present in the United States."[41] But the March 13, 2002, memo declared the supremacy of the president's wartime powers as commander in chief over any restrictions imposed by statutes or treaties. After 9/11 and with cover of this legal memo, the number of renditions expanded dramatically. The CIA executed transfers of suspects to such countries as Egypt, Morocco, Syria, and Jordan, all known to torture suspects.

HOW EXTREME

But the question persisted, how extreme could interrogations be? The new legal framework was crafted to give the president room for maneuver. It was designed to push the legal limits of the justification for torture of al Qaeda suspects and to define the administration's war on terror outside U.S. and international law. In late March of 2002, the question of extreme interrogation became urgent after the CIA captured Abu Zubaida, believed to be a top al Qaeda operative. The CIA wanted to know what the legal limits were for coercive interrogations. At a time when many counterterrorist officials viewed another attack as imminent, and with information on al Qaeda scarce, the capture of Zubaida was seen as a potentially vital breakthrough. Zubaida's detention precipitated a series of meetings in the White House Situation Room among senior Bush officials who virtually choreographed some of the interrogation sessions. The group involved not only Cheney, but also National Security Advisor Condoleezza Rice, Defense Secretary Donald Rumsfeld, Secretary of State Colin Powell, CIA director George Tenet, and Attorney General John Ashcroft. The grim discussions troubled Ashcroft, who agreed with the general policy of using aggressive methods and had repeatedly advised that they were legal. But he argued that senior White House officials should not be involved in the tough details of interrogations. At one meeting, Ashcroft asked, "Why are we talking about this in the White House? History will not judge this kindly." As the national security advisor, Rice chaired the meetings. The CIA briefed the White House group on its plans to use a range of aggressive techniques, including head slapping, deprivation of sleep, or simulated drowning, receiving explicit approval.[42]

Yoo later authorized such techniques in a controversial August 1, 2002, classified opinion. Under the signature of Assistant Attorney General Jay S. Bybee, the opinion claimed that U.S. law against torture "prohibits only the worst forms of cruel, inhuman or degrading treatment," permitting many other forms of cruel interrogation methods. The fifty-page opinion declared that it was admissible to inflict pain up to a level just short of that "associated with serious physical injury so severe that death, organ failure, or permanent damage resulting in loss of significant bodily function will likely result." Anything less was conceivably permitted. The memo's qualifying language stated that it was "difficult to take a specific act out of context and conclude that the act in isolation would constitute torture." It named seven techniques that courts have considered torture, involving severe beatings with truncheons and clubs, threats of imminent death, burning with cigarettes, electric shocks to genitalia, rape or sexual assault, and forcing a prisoner to watch the torture of another person. "While we cannot say with certainty that acts falling short of these seven would not constitute torture," the memo advised, ". . . we believe that interrogation techniques would have to be similar to these in their extreme nature and in the type of harm caused to violate law." If a government official were to cross the line into torturing a suspect, the memo said, "he would be doing so in order to prevent further attacks on the United States by the Al Qaeda terrorist network." The memo argued that "necessity and self-defense could provide justification that would eliminate any criminal liability."[43]

The memo became known as the so-called "Golden Shield" for CIA agents who worried about their liability if the tough interrogations became public. Even after the memo was issued, the meetings in the White House to discuss individual interrogations continued. In an effort to protect his agents, Tenet routinely sought verification that the interrogation plans were legal. CIA agents in the field were sending cables into the agency's headquarters asking for approval for specific methods, worried about overstepping their boundaries.[44]

The White House repudiated the memo two years later when it surfaced in the news media. Administration officials dismissed it as a theoretical piece authored by Yoo, a law professor at the University of Berkeley who was serving a stint at the OLC. But Yoo was not the sole author of the "Torture Memo," as it became known. Yoo later said that Addington, Gonzales, and deputy White House counsel Tim Flanigan also participated in drafting the lengthy opinion. Addington, the vice president's lawyer, originated the memo's most radical claim that the president could authorize any interrogation methods, even those that ventured into torture. As commander in chief, the president could act outside U.S. law and international treaties that prohibited torture. Congress could "no more regulate the President's ability to detain and interrogate enemy combatants than it may regulate his ability to direct troop movements on the battlefield," the memo said.[45]

On the same day, August 1, 2002, Yoo signed off on a second secret opinion that authorized a long list of interrogation methods proposed by the CIA. Among the approved techniques was waterboarding, a method that simulates near-drowning. Since at least 1901, the United States had prosecuted as a war crime those who used the technique. The opinion did not approve everything on the CIA's wish list, however; it banned threatening to bury a prisoner alive. In an interview with the *Washington Post*, Yoo said that he verbally cautioned the presidents' lawyers, as well as Cheney and Rumsfeld, about allowing military interrogators to use techniques that were meant for the CIA. Yoo believed that the military might overuse the methods or exceed the stipulated limits. "I always thought that only the CIA should do this," he said, "but people at the White House and DOD felt differently." The adoption of these techniques by the U.S. military later proved disastrous with the revelations of the abuses at Guantanamo Bay and Abu Ghraib, igniting worldwide condemnation.[46]

The legal reasoning of the torture memo influenced a March 2003 report by Pentagon lawyers reviewing interrogation rules governing the military prison at Guantanamo Bay. The assessment came after Secretary of Defense Rumsfeld asked the lawyers to examine the logistical, policy, and legal issues regarding interrogation techniques. Like the 2002 memo, the Pentagon sought to explore the legal limits of interrogating suspects. The Pentagon conducted its own review of the limits of torture in consultation with the Justice Department. The assessment undertaken by a working group comprising officials from the military services, the Justice Department, the Joint Chiefs of Staff, and the intelligence community sought to design a legal scheme for "exceptional interrogations." In devising these legalities for the treatment of al Qaeda and Taliban prisoners, the working group's report cited the Justice Department's 2002 position that domestic and international laws banning torture could be overridden by the president's wartime powers.

The Justice Department's legal analysis had stunned some of the military lawyers in drafting the new guidelines. Yoo's torture memo was unprecedented and took the United States into uncharted legal territory. For more than 30 years, military lawyers had taught the Geneva Conventions. "Once you start telling people it's okay to break the law, there's no telling where they might stop," said one senior military attorney. But the Pentagon's report, prepared under the direction of General Counsel William J. Haynes II, declared that "in order to respect the President's inherent constitutional authority to manage a military campaign . . . [the ban of torture] must be construed as inapplicable to interrogations undertaken pursuant to his Commander-in-Chief authority." The Pentagon's report made a distinction between the applicability of the antitorture law at Guantanamo and other jurisdictions outside the United States, such as Iraq and Afghanistan. While the 1994 law did "not apply to the conduct of U.S. personnel" at Guantanamo Bay, it did cover detainees in Iraq and Afghanistan.[47]

National Security Advisor Condoleezza Rice and Secretary of State Colin Powell learned of the torture memo two years after it was drafted, from a story in the *Washington Post* on June 8, 2004. The revelation led Rice and Powell to confront Gonzales in his office. Rice dressed down the president's counsel for keeping them out of the loop. She warned him that if there were any more secret opinions on international and national security law, they would take the matter to the president. As they emerged from the attorney general's office, Powell quipped that Rice had put Gonzales through the wringer in "full Nurse Ratched mode," alluding to the frigid head nurse in the psychiatric hospital in the 1975 film *One Flew over the Cuckoo's Nest.*[48] But their anger was perhaps misdirected, if not indicative of their impotence. After all, it was not the president's lawyer, but the vice president who had cut Powell and Rice out of the loop. And it was Cheney's allies who had crafted the secret memos to advance the vice president's legal and executive power revolution to fight the war on terror.

Nine

Iraq

In the days immediately following the terrorist attacks, tensions erupted among the administration's top officials over how America should respond. Although there was no question that the United States would take military action, the question involved what the nature and scope of it would be. Some officials led by Paul Wolfowitz, the deputy secretary of defense, and Scooter Libby, the vice president's chief of staff, pressed for early and broad military action not only against al Qaeda in Afghanistan, but also against Iraq. These officials argued that 9/11 created the opportunity to topple Saddam Hussein, a goal long advocated by Wolfowitz and other conservatives who believed that abruptly ending the ground campaign in the 1991 Gulf War, leaving Saddam Hussein in power, had been a grave mistake. Even before 9/11, the Bush Administration was working to undermine Saddam Hussein, with Wolfowitz seeking support for new international sanctions and examining a range of military options to eliminate the perceived danger he posed to Israel and the West in his quest to acquire weapons of mass destruction. As it turned out, however, this view proved false, leading the administration into uncharted territory.[1]

In meetings, Wolfowitz argued for a campaign that would end state support for terrorism. "It's not going to stop if a few criminals are taken care of," he said. Although no evidence existed of Iraqi involvement in the attacks, Wolfowitz claimed that the networks of terrorism in the Middle East were all interwoven. If Saddam were removed, it would deal a major blow to terrorism in the region. Rumsfeld helped his deputy raise the issue of Iraq in meetings, but wondered if it was the right time to attack.

Secretary of State Powell urged caution, arguing that the administration should take time to prepare the diplomatic groundwork for American military action in Afghanistan, saying that it was imperative to consult with allies and build the case to justify military action under international law. Powell counseled Bush against striking Iraq, because it would alienate America's coalition partners, which were all behind the United States. He advised focusing on Afghanistan. The question was, if the United States was not going after Iraq prior to 9/11, what would justify action afterward when no apparent link existed between the Iraqi regime and the terrorist attacks? It was important not to lose focus or wreck the coalition.[2]

Cheney initially joined Powell in opposing action on Iraq. So did CIA director George Tenet and Andy Card, the president's chief of staff. The vice president believed that it would take too much time to build an international coalition. He suggested it was not a good time to topple the Iraqi regime. The United States would lose momentum. Still, the vice president expressed deep concern about Saddam Hussein, stating that he would not rule out going after Iraq at a later point. Bush also initially sided with Powell, choosing to strike first at al Qaeda and the Taliban in Afghanistan. The media portrayed Wolfowitz, the most aggressive proponent of going to war with Iraq, as having lost the argument.[3] But the administration never stated it would not go to war in Iraq, only that it would focus first on Afghanistan. The White House left plenty of leeway for a broader campaign beyond al Qaeda and Afghanistan. As with many aspects of the administration's response to 9/11, Cheney pointed the way to the policy on Iraq. In an appearance on the Sunday news program *Meet the Press* just days after the terrorist attacks, Cheney said that the administration would unleash "the full wrath of the United States" on any nation that supported terrorism. These words seemed to echo Wolfowitz's own proposal for a major campaign to end state support for terrorism. When asked about military action against Iraq, Cheney said the focus was on Osama bin Laden "at the moment . . . at this stage."[4]

Following 9/11, the idea that the Bush-Cheney Administration would abandon its parochial approach to the world gained momentum. The administration had discarded at least six international agreements negotiated by President Clinton, including accords banning germ warfare and controlling global warming. But many anticipated that the war on terror would require the administration to engage the global community just as it did during World War II and the Cold War. In addition, America responded to Iraq's invasion of Kuwait by assembling an international coalition, seemingly providing a model for how the administration should formulate its response to the terrorist attacks. "Now that the Bush administration sees that it needs the rest of the world, it will have to temper its unilateral instincts on many issues," predicted C. Fred Bergsten, head of the Institute for International Economics in Washington.[5] But Bergsten was mistaken.

At the time, the White House drew the sympathy of most of the world. America received a flood of support from European countries. In France, *Le Monde*, the French daily newspaper, long suspicious of the United States, declared in a banner headline, "We are all Americans." In an unprecedented move, NATO declared that the terrorist attack on the United States could be considered an attack on the entire nineteen-nation alliance. "An attack on one is an attack on all," said NATO secretary general George Robertson in Brussels, where NATO ambassadors decided for the first time in the alliance's fifty-two-year history to invoke Article Five—the North Atlantic Treaty's mutual defense clause. Article Five of the NATO pact was signed in April 1949 to confront the threat of the former Soviet Union. It committed the alliance to assist any member who came under attack. The NATO resolution carried important symbolic importance, designed to show that Washington's European allies stood with America at a time of great national crisis. The United States also won support from the United Nations, with the Security Council and the General Assembly, sitting in separate sessions, unanimously condemning the attacks. The two bodies called on the international community to work together to bring the perpetrators and sponsors of the attacks to justice.[6]

The administration appeared eager for the support of an international coalition to wage war in Afghanistan. But military leaders and CIA officials, in their effort to mount a swift and unorthodox campaign halfway around the world—using airpower, CIA paramilitary teams, and special operations forces—saw the prospect of coordinating their response with the Europeans as more of a hindrance. Initially, at least, America's unilateralism in response to 9/11 stemmed from the military's inability to decide how to use the offers of assistance from its allies. As one author noted, America's unilateral approach to Afghanistan "did not originate with the Bush administration. It grew directly out of the military realities of the 1990s: the operational difficulties between U.S. and allied forces in the Balkans and the overall disparity in military power between America and Europe."[7] The 9/11 attacks also opened up a wider chasm between America and Europe, thrusting the United States into a new age of confronting terrorism, putting the United States on a war footing and transforming the nation's view of the realities of the world. However horrified at the 9/11 attacks, Europe still remained a place of relative tranquility until later terrorist outrages struck Britain and the continent.

While Europe remained moored to the multilateral approach of the Cold War, the 9/11 attacks accelerated the administration's rethinking of ideas of national security and foreign policy. The nature of security threats had changed from totalitarian regimes like the Soviet Union to asymmetrical warfare involving rogue regimes or non-state terrorist groups that could kill thousands with unconventional means. In December 2001, the administration abandoned the ABM treaty, a hallmark of the Cold War security arrangement, in favor of missile defense. The Pentagon also proposed the development of new, smaller nuclear weapons that could not only be used against the major nuclear powers of Russia and China, but also against such rogue regimes as Iraq, North Korea, Iran, Syria, and Lybia.[8] The Cold War orientation of nuclear deterrence had shifted to one of willingness to wage limited nuclear warfare in the Third World. In a speech in January 2002, Rumsfeld said that the "terrorists who struck us on Sept. 11 were clearly not deterred from doing so by the massive U.S. nuclear arsenal." He explained that "defending against terrorism and other emerging 21st-century threats requires that we take the war to the enemy."[9] The new concepts of national security and the willingness to use military force only seemed to confirm Cheney's long-standing view that the world was a dangerous place.

But it was Iraq that belied the consensus view that 9/11 would unavoidably force the administration to abandon its unilateral approach to world affairs. Even before the last battle on December 16, 2001, against al Qaeda holdouts at Tora Bora, high in the mountains in Eastern Afghanistan, the administration was already considering action against Iraq unbeknownst to its allies. Planning began the day after Kabul fell in November 2001. As Cheney indicated early on, Afghanistan involved stage one in the war on terror, and with the Taliban defeated, the administration turned to the question of Iraq.[10] Osama bin Laden and some of his aides had escaped the American attack at Tora Bora, leaving the effort against al Qaeda best suited for an underground intelligence war. In the continuing debate over Iraq, one of the central questions involved whether Saddam Hussein could be linked to al Qaeda. Although there was no intelligence suggesting any association, the hawks within the administration expended considerable time and energy searching for possible connections that would justify going after the Iraqi regime. In a very real sense, however, the debate went beyond Iraq to remaking the map of the Middle East, ridding the region of nation states that armed, trained, and sheltered shadowy terrorist groups.[11]

After swiftly defeating the Taliban and al Qaeda in Afghanistan, America's global war on terrorism seemed to stall as national security officials struggled to create an overall vision and set a new direction. It was not long before the Pentagon ramped up its war planning against Iraq at the U.S. military headquarters for the Middle East beginning in February 2002. By August of that year, the military had flushed out a complete plan of attack that was ready to be shown to the president. In the intervening time, Bush began preparing the nation for the war against Iraq. In January 2002, just two months after the fall of Kabul, the president gave his State of the Union address, declaring the existence of an "axis of evil" involving Iraq, Iran, and North Korea, nations that were seeking to develop weapons of mass destruction. "By seeking weapons of mass destruction, these regimes pose a grave and growing danger," Bush said. "I will not stand by while peril draws closer and closer." The president declared that America would not allow "the world's most dangerous regimes to threaten us with the world's most destructive weapons."[12]

After hearing the speech, Ike Skelton, the senior Democrat on the House Armed Services Committee, walked back across Capitol Hill into his office, turned to his staff and said, "That was a declaration of war."[13] Skelton's remarks confirmed what David Frum, one of Bush's speechwriters, later admitted. The speech was directed mainly at Iraq.[14] For the vice president, Wolfowitz, and others in the administration, Iraq, Iran, and North Korea, in the aftermath of Afghanistan, represented the sources of global terror. If the administration's war on terror did not have direction immediately after Afghanistan, it now had one. The hunt for bin Laden and al Qaeda became secondary to the effort to stop rogue states from developing weapons of mass destruction that could be used against the United States. The speech marked the beginning of a drumbeat to war, involving statements and speeches claiming that Iraq posed a gathering and imminent danger.

Bush's "axis of evil" speech stunned many governments overseas. America's European allies maintained ties with Iran, and in Asia, Japan, and South Korea were struggling with how to deal with the reclusive regime in North Korea. The administration gave no warning to its allies about the president's remarks, representing a stark expression of unilateralism in its war on terror. The speech started the United States down the road of alienating its allies and destroying the coalition. The president's remarks came under heavy criticism in Europe. While French Foreign Minister Hubert Vedrine called the speech "simplistic," the German Foreign Minister Joschka Fischer declared that "alliance partners are not satellites." The British Conservative Party leader, Christopher Patten, criticized Washington by quoting Winston Churchill: "In working with allies, it sometimes happens that they develop opinions of their own." In response, conservatives in and out of the administration denounced the Europeans for misunderstanding the dangers of weapons of mass destruction and marginalizing themselves into near irrelevance by failing to bolster their defense budgets. Europe was little more than an "axis of petulance," said neoconservative columnist Charles Krauthammer. "The ostensible complaint is American primitivism. The real problem is their irrelevance." Colin Powell ridiculed the French foreign minister for "getting the vapors." It was an ironic quip coming from the secretary of state, who anticipated just days after 9/11 that any campaign against Iraq would "wreck" the coalition.[15]

WE'RE TAKING HIM OUT

"Fuck Saddam, we're taking him out," Bush declared in March 2002, as he interrupted a meeting Condoleezza Rice was having with three senators.[16] Cheney, Rumsfeld, and their senior aides contended that Arab leaders might publicly protest but secretly celebrate Saddam Hussein's downfall, as long as the military campaign was decisive. The warnings of setting Arab populations aflame were exaggerated, they argued, comparing them to the false warnings before the first Gulf War.[17] In June 2002, the president took the next step against Iraq in a key speech at West Point, where he unveiled his doctrine of preemption, the core of the administration's new national security strategy. The president said that the United States reserved the right to attack preemptively before there was a clear and imminent threat to the country. "We must take the battle to the enemy, disrupt his plans and confront the worst threats before they emerge," the president said.[18] It was no accident that he gave the speech at West Point, the most hallowed Army institution in the country, as a message to the military to prepare for war in Iraq. Three months later, the administration formulated its comprehensive national security policy, the first since the 9/11 attacks. The new policy, issued in a thirty-one-page document, laid out the administration's vision of its relations with the world. The policy of preemption involved only part of the new strategy. It also emphasized unchallengeable American military superiority and promoting democratic values overseas. The new national security policy tied together a moralistic foreign policy with unprecedented military power. The strategy declared that there was only "a single sustainable model for national success: freedom, democracy and free enterprise." America would seek a "balance of power that favors human freedom," it said, and stressed the importance of cooperation with other major powers. At its center, however, was the notion that the United States must maintain its overwhelming status as a superpower in the world and be ready to defend itself from hostile forces.[19]

The administration's new national security policy was largely drafted by Condoleezza Rice's National Security Council. Although the strategy incorporated many of the ideas of the vice president and others, neither his office nor Rumsfeld's Pentagon had been closely involved in this endeavor, focusing instead on overthrowing Saddam Hussein. With the new doctrine of preemption in place, Cheney, Rumsfeld, Wolfowitz, and others were ready to push for regime change in Iraq, a rogue nation with a history of seeking to develop nuclear weapons, ousting UN weapons inspectors, waging war on other nations, using chemical weapons on its own people, and repressing fundamental human freedoms.[20]

"Simply stated, there is no doubt that Saddam Hussein now has weapons of mass destruction," Cheney declared in a speech to the Veterans of Foreign Wars on August 26, 2002. "There is no doubt he is amassing them to use against our friends, against our allies, and against us." The vice president's remarks inaugurated the administration's public campaign to attack Iraq. Cheney publicly aimed some of his remarks at Powell, who had been arguing that the United States should not move unilaterally against Iraq, but in coalition with allies. In the administration's internal debate, Powell recommended slowing the rush to war. He favored a more deliberate approach, beginning with trying to get the UN weapons inspectors back inside Iraq. Cheney disagreed. He said it was time not to seek any new authorization, but to advise the United Nations to move against Iraq for failing to comply with past Security Council resolutions. Others echoed Powell's views, including former senior officials in the first Bush Administration who had secured UN support and assembled the broad international coalition that expelled Iraqi forces from Kuwait in 1991. Former national security advisor Brent Scowcroft and former secretaries of state James Baker and Lawrence Eagleburger issued warnings against any immediate war with Iraq. The three former officials separately called on the administration to slow the pace of events and seek UN support against Saddam Hussein. "We should try our best not to have to go it alone, and the president should reject the advice of those who counsel doing so," said Baker. Like Powell, Scowcroft recommended that the administration get the UN to return weapons inspectors to Iraq. If Saddam Hussein "doesn't agree to it," he said on a Sunday news program, "that gives you the *casus belli* that we really don't have right now." Further, in an op-ed piece in the *Wall Street Journal*, Scowcroft argued for diplomacy, dismissing Cheney's assertion that Saddam Hussein was tied to the 9/11 al Qaeda attacks on America. Scowcroft warned that overthrowing the Iraqi regime "would not be a cakewalk. On the contrary, it would be very expensive—with serious consequences for the U.S. and the global economy—and could well be bloody."[21]

In his speech to the veterans, the vice president publicly dismissed this advice. "Saddam has perfected the art of cheat and retreat, and is very skilled in the art of denial and deception," he said. Any return of inspectors, Cheney claimed, "would provide no assurance whatsoever of his compliance with UN resolutions." He warned that with weapons of mass destruction,

Saddam Hussein could be "expected to seek domination of the entire Middle East, taking control of a great portion of the world's energy supplies." In dismissing Scowcroft's claim that moving against Iraq would inflame tensions in the Middle East, Cheney argued instead that "extremists in the region would have to rethink their strategy of jihad. Moderates throughout the regions would take heart."[22]

Cheney's remarks signified a dramatic departure from his stance on invading Iraq when he was secretary of defense in the first Bush Administration. In an August 1992 speech at the Discovery Institute in Seattle, he explained the numerous reasons why it would have been a grave mistake to march on Baghdad after ousting Iraqi forces from Kuwait in 1991. He warned that U.S. troops would have become bogged down in urban warfare and a prolonged occupation. Overthrowing Saddam Hussein would be one thing, but he asked what kind of government would take its place, noting the country's hostile sectarian divisions. He believed that U.S. troops would have suffered significant additional casualties, that the country would have come apart, and that the United States would have lost the support of the Arab coalition.[23]

The vice president's remarks were prescient, but he concluded that the conditions on the ground had significantly changed in the intervening decade. In the course of the 1991 Gulf War, the allies severely degraded Iraq's armed forces. Saddam Hussein lost fully two-thirds of his army, half of his air force, and most of his weapons of mass destruction. He no longer posed a threat to his neighbors, Cheney believed. But the calculus had changed in the decade since the first Gulf War. Cheney was convinced that Saddam Hussein now possessed significant quantities of chemical and biological agents and was busy reconstituting his nuclear weapons program, even if the intelligence did not verify his conclusions. The Iraqi dictator posed an ever-menacing threat to both the region and to U.S. interests, if not to the American homeland itself after 9/11. "Many of us are convinced that Saddam will acquire nuclear weapons fairly soon," he had said to the VFW. Against this reality, he stated that "many of those who now argue that we should act only if he gets a nuclear weapon would then turn around and say that we cannot act because he has a nuclear weapon. At bottom, that argument counsels a course of inaction that itself could have devastating consequences for many countries, including our own."[24] According to the vice president, the crisis was upon America. It was of the utmost urgency to act now and disarm Iraq before it went nuclear.

On September 12, weeks after Cheney's VFW speech, Bush sounded a different alarm when taking the case to the international community. Our "greatest fear," he said, "is that terrorists will find a shortcut to their mad ambitions when an outlaw regime supplies them with the technologies to kill on a massive scale. In one place—in one regime—we find all these dangers, in their most lethal and aggressive forms. . . ." He warned that "Saddam Hussein's regime was a grave and gathering danger."[25] The president declared, however, that he would take the Iraq issue to the UN's Security Council for passage of a new resolution regarding its alleged weapons of mass destruction. Iraq should "disclose and remove or destroy all such weapons if it wanted peace," Bush said. He never mentioned reviving weapons inspections in Iraq, a step that Cheney denounced the previous month as "dangerous" and providing "false comfort."[26]

At first glance, it appeared that Powell and Scowcroft won the debate against Cheney, convincing the president to slow the pace of events and seek the support of the UN and international community. But no one, not even Powell or Scowcroft, argued against going to war with Iraq. Instead, the question involved how, when, and with what international support to confront the growing threat emanating from Iraq. Cheney pushed to bypass the step of going to the United Nations, but the administration calculated that the president would lose little by doing so. Within the administration, senior officials deemed it unlikely that Saddam Hussein would comply with any new resolution governing weapons of mass destruction, strengthening the administration's hand both domestically and in the international arena.

With the president's speech to the UN General Assembly, the administration shifted its argument from Iraq possessing and threatening to use weapons of mass destruction to being a likely supplier of these weapons to al Qaeda to carry out even far greater outrages than 9/11. If Iraq had no current ties to al Qaeda, it would in the future. There was perhaps additional context to this fear. The Pakistani government had earlier arrested and questioned three scientists involved in the country's nuclear weapons program for their visits to Afghanistan and their association with the Taliban.[27] Letters containing deadly anthrax spores had been put in the U.S. mail, killing five and infecting twenty others. It was easy to fathom what would happen if a determined and ruthless enemy like al Qaeda got their hands on weapons of mass destruction. Instead of thousands, hundreds of thousands could be killed.[28] Bush's remarks to the General Assembly internationalized the debate in foreign capitals, leading to an ever-widening split with U.S. allies.

In many respects, Cheney drove the events leading up to the invasion of Iraq on March 20, 2003. Within the administration, he became the strongest proponent for toppling Saddam Hussein from power. He took the most consistently dire view of the terrorist threat. Bush may have been the "decider," but more than any other advisor, Cheney made the case to the president that war against Iraq was an urgent necessity. He persistently warned that Saddam Hussein was amassing weapons of mass destruction and was reconstituting his nuclear weapons program and repeatedly suggested that Baghdad had ties to al Qaeda. He sharply refused to rule out suggestions that Iraq was somehow behind the 9/11 attacks and may have even been involved in the 1993 terrorist bombing at the World Trade Center. The CIA, FBI, and a later congressional investigation into the 9/11 attacks dismissed these conspiracy theories. He spoke of a report indicating a meeting between 9/11 hijacker Muhammad Atta and an Iraqi intelligence official in Prague in April 2001, even though the report had been widely discredited by U.S. intelligence officials. According to the vice president, Iraq served as "the geographical base of the terrorists who have had us under assault for many years, but most especially on 9/11." The extremity of the statement prompted the president to issue a public correction: no evidence existed, he confessed, linking Iraq to the 9/11 attacks.

He was not content, however, with airing his views to other senior White House advisors. Over the course of 2002, the vice president and his senior aide, Scooter Libby, began to gather intelligence anywhere they could find it. Along with Libby, he paid multiple visits to the CIA and Defense Intelligence Agency, questioning analysts studying Iraq's weapons programs and possible links to al Qaeda. Later with his staff, he would try to connect the dots. It was an extraordinary hands-on role for any U.S. vice president to assume. The size of his staff was equally unusual—about sixty people, far larger than the size of his vice presidential predecessor, Al Gore. Intelligence analysts reportedly felt pressured by Cheney's visits to make their assessments fit the administration's policy objectives on Iraq. The analysts felt the continual drumbeat, not only from Cheney and Libby, but also from Paul Wolfowitz, the deputy defense secretary, Douglas Feith, undersecretary for policy at the Pentagon, even from CIA director George Tenet, to find evidence or write reports supporting the administration's urgent case for war against Iraq. Cheney also was anxious about the threat of germ warfare and had Libby call the Pentagon repeatedly to ask what the military was doing to protect the nation against a bioterrorism attack from crop-dusters. In July 2002, Cheney made an unannounced and unpublicized visit to the Centers for Disease Control and Prevention in Atlanta. He sought to probe public health experts about their efforts to guard against bioterrorism.[29] The vice president had little confidence in the CIA, especially after the first Gulf War. The bombing had missed an enormous nuclear weapons development facility, and it was discovered that Saddam Hussein was much further along in the development of weapons of mass destruction than originally thought. The CIA's assessment had missed the facts on the ground; they could scarcely be trusted to get it right this time.

Driving Cheney's actions after 9/11 seemed to be a Hobbesian view of human nature. He long believed the world was a brutish place. If anything, 9/11 did not revolutionize his views, only intensified them. The national-security state had to be strengthened, ever vigilant, even ready to take preemptive action. Bolstering the national-security state could only be done through expanding presidential powers. Whatever critics said about the vice president, few disagreed that he was genuinely convinced about the imminent and menacing threat emanating from Iraq. The vice president tended to embrace the worst-case scenario, the dark prognosis, while ignoring more nuanced and complicated analyses. He was all the more powerful with the aid of his large and assertive staff that constituted nothing short of a parallel government, the power center, on the road to war. His drumbeat of statements aimed to convince a hesitant public of the urgency of the crisis. On September 8, 2002, Cheney insisted that intelligence assessments regarding Iraq's nuclear program were known "with absolute certainty." Less than two weeks later, on September 20, he declared that Saddam Hussein's nuclear weapons program was known through "irrefutable evidence." On March 16, 2003, on the eve of war, after inspectors working for the International Atomic and Energy Agency (IAEA) reported finding "no evidence or plausible indication of the revival of a nuclear weapons program in Iraq," the vice president stated, "[w]e believe [Saddam Hussein] has, in fact, reconstituted nuclear weapons." As later investigations into the events leading up to the war reported, none of the vice president's assertions about the threat posed by Saddam Hussein were supported by the intelligence at the time or afterward.[30]

In October 2002, the CIA produced the most flawed national intelligence estimate in its long history on Iraq's weapons of mass destruction. Special national intelligence estimates were supposed to constitute the best judgment of the American intelligence community, produced and directed by the CIA. The estimate, titled "Iraq's Continuing Programs for Weapons of Mass Destruction," was commissioned at the request of the Senate Intelligence Committee. With the administration bent on going to war, members of the committee wanted to review the evidence before deciding what to do. After reviewing reams of data from spy satellites, foreign intelligence agencies, and Iraq agents and defectors, the agency reported its findings in October 2002. The Iraqi threat was considerable, it said. Not only did Baghdad have chemical and biological weapons, but Saddam Hussein was ramping up his missile technology, amassing deadly stockpiles, and reviving his nuclear weapons program. "If Baghdad acquires sufficient fissile material from abroad," said the estimate, "it could make a nuclear weapon within several months." Most worrisome, Iraq could carry out chemical and biological attacks on American soil.

While the agency confirmed everything the president and vice president had been saying, it based its estimate on exceedingly flawed information and untrustworthy human intelligence sources. Part of the problem lay in CIA director George Tenet's desperation to please his superiors, leading to a highly flawed special national intelligence estimate. The CIA's conclusion about the existence of weapons of mass destruction stemmed from the aftermath of the 1991 Gulf War. Following Saddam Hussein's defeat, UN weapons inspectors spent seven years combing Iraq for weapons of mass destruction. He destroyed his weapons of mass destruction sometime in the mid-1990s according to the dictates of the United Nations, fearing international economic sanctions more than another U.S. military attack. But he kept his weapons production facilities, while lying about it, leading the inspectors and U.S. intelligence officials to distrust his every word and move. In 1998, in a spectacular move, the CIA and NSA managed to tap Iraqi telecommunications in Baghdad, but the agency learned nothing about the existence of weapons of mass destruction in Iraq. That spring, weapons inspectors discovered what they believed to be traces of VX nerve gas in Iraqi missiles, an allegation that Iraq denied. The allegation further fueled mutual distrust between the Iraqis and the weapons inspectors. In December 1998, the United Nations withdrew its weapons inspectors, and the Americans resumed their bombing of the country. Iraq declared to the UN that it had destroyed its weapons of mass destruction, declarations that largely proved to be true. But Saddam sought to create the illusion of deterrence regarding his weapons, not wanting to appear defenseless before the United States, his own troops, and his timeless foes, Israel and Iran.[31]

The CIA confronted this state of affairs after 9/11. It had virtually no human intelligence and the White House, above all the vice president, wanted answers. Under enormous pressure to find these answers, the CIA relied on false information provided by Iraqi defectors, who shared a mutual interest in regime change and knew the Americans were concerned about weapons of mass destruction. "Only one thing was worse than having no sources, and that was to be seduced by sources telling lies," wrote journalist Tim Weiner. The "analysts accepted whatever supported the case for war. They swallowed secondhand and thirdhand hearsay that conformed to the president's plans. Absence of evidence was not evidence of absence for the agency. Saddam once had the weapons. The defectors said he still had them. Therefore he had them. The CIA as an institution desperately sought the White House's attention and approval. It did so by telling the president what he wanted to know"[32]—and what the vice president wanted to know.

Weiner's conclusions on the CIA's national intelligence estimate later found support from the Senate Intelligence Committee's findings in 2008.

Chaired by Senator John D. Rockefeller IV, the committee investigated whether the public statements of senior U.S. officials leading up to war were substantiated by underlying intelligence information. "During the course of its investigation," wrote Rockefeller, "the Committee uncovered that the October 2002 National Intelligence Estimate on Iraq's alleged weapons of mass destruction was based on stale, fragmentary, and speculative intelligence reports and replete with unsupported judgments. Troubling incidents were reported in which internal dissent and warnings about the veracity of intelligence on Iraq were ignored in the rush to war." The committee's report also accused administration policymakers of pressuring intelligence analysts before the war to support a nonexistent link between Iraq and al Qaeda's attacks on 9/11. The administration went beyond what the intelligence community knew or believed in falsely asserting "that Iraq and al Qaeda had an operational partnership and joint involvement in carrying out the attacks of September 11," said Rockefeller. "The President and his advisors undertook a relentless public campaign in the aftermath of the attacks to use the war against al Qaeda as a justification for overthrowing Saddam Hussein." The administration had falsely represented the two as having an operational partnership, posing a single, indistinguishable threat. The report accused the administration of misleading the American public and leading the nation to war on false premises.[33] The committee's Republican minority largely dismissed the report as nothing more than partisanship.

In the run-up to war, Cheney cited the October 2002 National Intelligence Estimate and its alarming warnings as his "gold standard." But there were plenty of warnings from the intelligence community on what the United States could be facing if it went to war. In April 2002, the Defense Intelligence Agency (DIA) produced two briefing presentations that discussed the challenges in the postcombat phase of the war plan for Iraq. The first briefing noted that the Baath Party "will attempt to return by any means necessary" and that "significant force protection threats will emerge from the Baathists, the Jihadists, and Arab nationalists who oppose any U.S. occupation of Iraq." The second DIA briefing concluded that managing rivalries would be a major challenge for the new regime and outlined the potential postwar challenges, including "preventing Kurdish separation, eradicating terrorists in the Ansar area, managing inter-ethnic/tribal violence, gaining control of the regime's geographic power base, and accounting for WMD."[34]

At the same time, the vice president evidently dismissed an August 2002 CIA report on the negative consequences in attacking Iraq. The report, titled *The Perfect Storm: Planning for Negative Consequences of Invading Iraq*, outlined worst-case scenarios if the U.S. toppled Saddam Hussein from power. The report anticipated that an attack on Iraq could produce immense complications, including anarchy and territorial breakup of Iraq, instability in key Arab states, a surge of global terrorism and deepening Islamic antipathy toward the United States, major oil supply disruptions, and severe strains in the Atlantic alliance.[35] Another agency report in August 2002 also predicted complications, noting that in the postcombat phase, "we are uncertain how rapidly Iraq ... can recover from the massive socio-economic and political damage inflicted by Saddam, especially since 1991."[36] But the vice president may have concluded that these risks were worth taking in ridding the world of Saddam Hussein and his weapons of mass destruction.

Like Cheney, the president viewed the CIA's October 2002 National Security Assessment as substantiating the dire threats emanating from Iraq. Bush presented the CIA's case to the country in his State of the Union message on January 28, 2003. "Today, the gravest danger in the war on terror, the gravest danger facing America and the world, is outlaw regimes that seek and possess nuclear, chemical, and biological weapons," the president said. "These regimes could use such weapons for blackmail, terror and mass murder. They could also give or sell those weapons to terrorist allies, who would use them without the least hesitation." America and its allies were called upon to end the terrible threats to the civilized world. All free nations had a "stake in preventing sudden and catastrophic attacks." He said Saddam Hussein possessed sufficient quantities of anthrax and botulinum toxin to kill millions and enough sarin, mustard, and VX nerve agents to kill "untold thousands," and he had mobile biological weapons labs that could produce germ warfare agents. He accused Saddam Hussein of seeking significant quantities of uranium from Africa. "Our intelligence sources tell us that he has attempted to purchase high-strength aluminum tubes suitable for nuclear weapons production."[37] The message was clear: Saddam Hussein was fully arming with weapons of mass destruction. The situation was dire; the nation needed to act. But none of it was true.

On February 5, 2003, Secretary of State Colin Powell, the most well-respected international figure in the Bush Administration, presented the American case to the world. Armed with photographs, intercepts of conversations between Iraqi military officers, and information from defectors, Powell declared, "There can be no doubt that Saddam Hussein has biological weapons and he has the ability to dispense these lethal poisons and diseases in ways that can cause massive death and destruction." In the effort to draw an explicit connection between Iraq and al Qaeda, Powell suggested that Iraq's lethal weapons could be supplied to terrorists who could use them against the United States or Europe. "Leaving Saddam Hussein in possession of weapons of mass destruction for a few more months or years is not an option, not in the post-September 11th world," he declared.

In the several days before his presentation, Powell held hours of meetings at the CIA headquarters in Langley, Virginia, poring over the evidence. He sought assurances from George Tenet that the CIA's intelligence was accurate. The CIA director looked him in the eye and told him it was rock solid. "I sat in the room looking into his eyes, as did the Secretary of State, and heard it with the firmness that only George could give it ... George Tenet assuring Colin Powell that the information he was presenting at the UN was ironclad, only to have that same individual call the Secretary on more than one occasion in the ensuing months after the presentation and tell him that central pillars of the presentation were indeed false," recalled Colonel Larry Wilkerson, Powell's top military assistant.[38]

Despite Powell's tone of urgency, few among America's allies were convinced of the necessity for military action. In Europe, polls showed that most citizens, anxious about a war with Iraq, remained unpersuaded. Envoys of France, Russia, and China—all veto-wielding members of the Security Council—argued that the evidence reinforced their view that the inspection process should be resumed and that Iraq should be pressured to cooperate. Across the country and around the world, the picture that emerged involved an administration that had tried and failed to persuade skeptics of the urgency of the Iraqi crisis. Powell tried to shake the members of the Council out of what the White House viewed as their complacency over the crisis. But European diplomats skeptical of Washington's rush to war did not consider Saddam Hussein a threat and believed he could be contained by inspections. On March 1, the Turkish parliament stunned American officials when it voted narrowly against allowing thousands of U.S. troops to use the country as a base for an attack.[39]

On March 7, IAEA general director Mohamed ElBaradei issued a report concluding there was no plausible evidence of a nuclear weapons program in Iraq. The vice president responded to the report more than a week later on March 16, just days before the American attack on Iraq. "I think ElBaradei, frankly, is wrong," said Cheney on *Meet the Press*. I think if you look at the record of the International Atomic Energy Agency on this issue, especially where Iraq is concerned, they have constantly underestimated or missed what it was Saddam Hussein was doing. I don't have any reason to believe they're any more valid at this time than they've been in the past," he stated. "We believe he has, in fact, reconstituted nuclear weapons." Like the vice president's allegations about Saddam Hussein's biological and chemical weapons efforts and Iraq's ties to al Qaeda, the charges proved groundless. There was no intelligence suggesting that Saddam Hussein had reconstituted his nuclear weapons program. Cheney predicted that American forces would be "greeted as liberators." He went on to say that Iraq was a "country that

I think, but for the rule of Saddam Hussein and his brutality and his diversion of the nation's resources and his pursuit of weapons of mass destruction,
can be one of the leading, perhaps the leading state in that part of the world
in terms of developing a modern state." He believed that the Kurds, the Sunnis, and the Shiites would likely come together to form a democracy.[40]

It was not exactly the conclusions reached by two coordinated intelligence
community assessments issued months before the war. The reports indicated
that the challenges in postwar Iraq would be far more formidable. Both
assessments were written by the National Intelligence Council in January
2003. While the assessments did not address whether U.S. forces would be
greeted as liberators, the prewar reports concluded that establishing a stable,
democratic government in postwar Iraq would be a long, difficult, and turbulent challenge. It noted that Iraq was a deeply divided society that would
likely experience violent conflict. The postwar Iraqi government would have
to walk a thin line between dismantling the worst elements of Saddam's
police, security, and intelligence forces while retaining the capability of
enforcing the peace. The new Iraqi government also would require significant outside assistance to rebuild the country's basic infrastructure.[41] In
many ways, the reports substantiated Cheney's reservations about marching
on Baghdad after the first Gulf War.

Ten

Reversals for the House of Cheney

Already by the summer and fall of 2002, some of the administration's leading lawyers warned that the president's broad claims of wartime powers, crafted by the vice president and his staff, would not hold up in court. One of these lawyers was Theodore Olson, the Justice Department's solicitor general, who shared Cheney's view of presidential power. Olson had more than a working or theoretical interest in these matters. His wife had been killed on September 11, 2001, when one of the hijacked planes crashed into the Pentagon. Two cases involving American citizens—Jose Padilla and Yaser Esam Hamdi—particularly concerned him. Both had been declared enemy combatants and denied access to lawyers. Olson argued that the federal courts would not approve denying American citizens the right to an attorney. On behalf of the vice president, Addington forcefully argued against granting detainees access to lawyers. The debate intensified in a meeting in Gonzales's West Wing office when associate White House counsel Bradford Berenson backed Olson's position. A former law clerk to Supreme Court Justice Anthony Kennedy, Berenson argued that the Justice would never approve sweeping presidential discretion to deny a U.S. citizen the right to be represented in court. Addington accused Berenson of being willing to surrender executive authority. But Cheney's shadow loomed over the meeting. Gonzales sided with the vice president's lawyer, ignoring the opposition of the Justice Department and his own staff. John Ashcroft later recalled that Cheney's views carried considerable weight. "He was the E. F. Hutton in the room. When he talked, everybody would listen."[1]

The courts proved to be a different arena. The vice president's strategy faltered when federal district courts ruled that Padilla and Hamdi had the right to counsel. Both were American citizens. Padilla had been arrested by the FBI in Chicago, while Hamdi, an American-born Saudi, had been captured in Afghanistan. The government claimed that the president could declare and imprison an American citizen as an "enemy combatant." The implications of this assertion were extraordinary, especially concerning Padilla, a person born and raised in America and arrested on United States soil by the police, not on the battlefield by the armed forces. If the president could declare Padilla an enemy combatant, then all Americans could be subject, under law, to arrest and imprisonment at the president's discretion without the right of habeas corpus. The administration's position recalled the English monarchs who often exerted the unfettered executive power of condemning people as enemies of the state and imprisoning them without trials or charges. After the Padilla ruling, Cheney's office insisted that Olson's deputy, Paul Clement, ask Judge Michael B. Mukasey to retract his decision on grounds that it was grossly erroneous. Clement's futile mission met a mordant response from Mukasey, who quickly rebuffed the effort, saying his court order was not a suggestion or request.

The vice president's approach went even more amiss in the Supreme Court when Padilla's and two other cases appeared for oral arguments in late April 2004. The administration had appealed the Padilla and Hamdi cases, claiming the president's exclusive authority in determining whether a prisoner was a terrorist. The courts had no jurisdiction to "second-guess the military's enemy combatant determination," the administration argued. For the courts to venture beyond such a determination would "intrude upon the Constitutional prerogative of the Commander in Chief (and military authorities acting under his control").[2]

For months, Olson and others in the Justice Department pushed for changes that would strengthen the government's position. Hamdi, an American citizen, had languished in military prison for two and half years without a hearing or a lawyer. The military had been holding Shafiq Rasul, a British citizen, even longer. Olson believed he could make something of Cheney's argument that the courts had no jurisdiction if he could show a system of due process that protected against wrongful detention. Addington, the vice president's counsel, fought this compromise, claiming that it would limit the authority of future presidents and provide grounds for further litigation. Addington's unyielding stance accomplished nothing beyond weakening the government's case. On June 28, 2004, the Supreme Court voted 8-1 in the Hamdi case that detainees must be given a lawyer and have the right to challenge their status as an enemy combatant before a neutral arbiter. The ruling upheld habeas corpus, the fundamental constitutional right to challenge one's detention, a right that may only be suspended in times of general rebellion or invasion. The same day in the Rasul case, the Court ruled 6-3 that federal law extended to Guantanamo. The judiciary, the ruling said, had the authority to decide whether foreign citizens held at the detention facility were illegally imprisoned. The rulings conveyed the message that the White House would not be allowed to prosecute the war on terrorism without judicial supervision. The pair of opinions included Justice Sandra Day O'Connor's biting comment that "a state of war is not a blank check for the President." Eleven days later, Olson resigned as solicitor general.

SURVEILLANCE

From the beginning, the vice president pressed to launch the warrantless surveillance program, including eavesdropping on purely domestic communications. But the administration's program caused mounting questions from its own senior lawyers about its legality. The eavesdropping program began with few constraints, worrying several agency officials who feared participating in an illegal operation. Concerns about the program reached a crescendo with Jack Goldsmith, a talented young law professor from the University of Chicago Law School who became head of the Justice Department's Office of Legal Counsel (OLC) in October 2003. Goldsmith replaced Jay Bybee, who left to become a federal judge that March. Bybee had signed the infamous "Torture Memo" authorizing the CIA to use harsh methods in interrogating terrorist suspects. The vice president's office and Gonzales wanted John Yoo, their main man at the Justice Department, for the job. After all, Yoo authored many of the administration's key war-power opinions, including the torture memo. He had proved an invaluable ally in helping to lay the framework for Cheney's legal revolution on behalf of unfettered presidential power. But Ashcroft and his senior aides objected, resentful over Yoo going behind the attorney general's back to give the White House a private line into the OLC. They preferred one of their own trusted lawyers for the post. The standoff ended with Goldsmith as the compromise choice. Goldsmith held sterling conservative credentials. Educated at Oxford and Yale, he worked at the Pentagon's general counsel's office after 9/11 and held broad views on presidential powers during wartime. Like Yoo, he was called a "New Sovereigntist" for his scholarly argument that international laws and treaties should not be treated as binding law by U.S. courts. Even as a strong believer in the president's wartime authority, however, he stood as a principled advocate for the law and the Constitution.

The White House may have believed that he would promote its legal agenda as the new head at the OLC, but he soon served notice of his independence. Not long after Goldsmith took the post, he began reviewing the critical legal opinions supporting the policies on the war on terror, concluding that some of them were "deeply flawed." Within six to eight weeks, "I knew that there were big problems," he recalled. The biggest problems involved the legal opinions on the National Security Agency (NSA) program and the ones on torture and interrogation. Goldsmith later described his reactions to the news program *Frontline*: "My first one was disbelief that programs of this importance could be supported by legal opinions that were this flawed. My second was the realization that I would have a very, very hard time standing by these opinions if pressed. My third was the sinking feeling, what was I going to do if I was pressed about reaffirming these opinions or something required my decision related to these programs?" The opinions that were the most flawed were also the ones that were the most secretive, Goldsmith said. "I thought that there were errors in some of the legal arguments, sometimes bad errors. I thought that there were extravagant and unnecessary claims of presidential power that were . . . wildly overbroad to the tasks at hand and had implications for other laws that I just found way too extreme."[3]

It was almost unprecedented for an administration to overturn its own OLC opinions. Goldsmith knew that questioning the legal foundations for the administration's antiterror policies would be monumentally controversial and disruptive. Goldsmith received Ashcroft's support in reviewing the legal opinions and trying to put them on firmer legal ground. The NSA program posed a leading example of the administration's taking unilateral action in secret based on flawed legal opinions. Under the 1978 surveillance law, the NSA needed to obtain a court order to eavesdrop on communications coming into or going out of the country. Claiming that getting warrants from a secret court set up under the law was too cumbersome, the administration justified evading the law by invoking a post-9/11 congressional resolution authorizing use of force against global terror. Although the White House cloaked the program in great secrecy, the program had to be reauthorized by the attorney general every forty-five days. It was Goldsmith's responsibility to advise Ashcroft on the legality of the program. When reviewing the program, Goldsmith later recalled that "it was by far the biggest and hardest and most contested and difficult challenge that I faced in government. It's where I had my greatest fights with the White House. It was where the legal analysis was the most challenging and difficult. It's where the judgment calls about whether and how to proceed were the hardest."[4]

John Yoo authored most of the controversial opinions based on his expansive theories on presidential power, including the secret one on the NSA program. The exceptional secrecy surrounding the program meant that not even Jay Bybee, Yoo's boss, had been briefed on the most sensitive operation in the government. Eric Lichtblau wrote in his book, *Bush's Law*, that

"Yoo was clearly the court of first and last resort for the White House."[5] Besides Yoo, very few people in the Justice Department knew of the program or of the legal opinions supporting it. "I don't even think the lawyers at the NSA had access to the OLC legal opinions," recalled Goldsmith. "It was so tightly held that not even the NSA, [which] was being asked to act in a way that was very unusual and contrary to its culture and traditions, not even the NSA had access to these legal opinions."[6]

Goldsmith and the Justice Department immediately ran into opposition from Addington after they began overturning some of the earlier opinions on extreme interrogation methods. Ever opposed to tying the president's hands in the war on terror, Addington warned Goldsmith on one occasion that if he ruled "that way, the blood of 100,000 people who die in the next attack will be on your hands."[7] Goldsmith did not have to hear Addington's arguments to worry that he might be putting soldiers and CIA officers in legal jeopardy or weakening the country's defenses against another terrorist attack. But he wanted to uphold the law.

When Goldsmith and other Justice Department officials examined the early legal opinions on the NSA program, they were stunned by what they found. Yoo's legal analysis failed to address the Supreme Court's most seminal ruling on presidential power—the Youngstown Steel case. In that case, the Court rebuffed President Harry S. Truman's claim of presidential power in ordering the seizure and operation of private steel mills in order to head off an impending labor strike that threatened to disrupt the Korean War effort. The steel industry challenged Truman's executive order to seize the mills, arguing that Congress, when it passed the 1947 Taft-Hartley Act, provided the exclusive framework for resolving labor disputes. In writing his influential concurring opinion in the case, Justice Robert Jackson set up a taxonomy on presidential power. That power was at its "zenith" when the president acted in concert with Congress, but was at its "lowest ebb" when he took "measures incompatible with the expressed or implied will of Congress."[8] Whereas Taft-Hartley only proscribed government seizures by implication, the 1978 surveillance law explicitly prohibited unauthorized wiretapping on American soil. More important, although Truman gave Congress and the public immediate notice of his actions, Bush moved in secret, made incomplete and classified disclosures to Congress, and tried to prevent public disclosure altogether until the operation was finally leaked to the press.[9] That Yoo would fail to even acknowledge the precedent-setting Youngstown case that addressed the very limits of presidential power in the face of congressional statute struck Goldsmith and others as sloppy and critically flawed. Even so, the opinions accorded with the vice president's imperative to extend the president's authority. Writing later in his memoir, Yoo cited previous OLC opinions in claiming that the Youngstown case "had no application to the President's conduct of foreign affairs and national security,"—an odd statement given that Truman's overreaching claims of presidential power involved similar circumstances, including taking action contrary to congressional law and in a wartime situation.[10]

To put the NSA program on firmer legal ground without dismantling it, Goldsmith sent Ashcroft a draft memorandum in November 2003 reviewing the legality of the secret operation. One month after sending his memo, Goldsmith found a critical ally in James Comey, a tall and lanky former prosecutor, who became deputy attorney general. Before arriving as Ashcroft's deputy at the Justice Department, Comey won a reputation prosecuting gun crimes in the U.S. attorney's office in Richmond, Virginia, in the late 1990s. He then was promoted in 2001 to head New York's Southern District, one of the most important prosecutor's jobs in the country. He worked as the U.S. attorney in Manhattan for only two years before receiving a call to serve as Ashcroft's deputy attorney general. In New York, Comey aggressively pursued terrorism cases, leaving civil liberties advocates doubtful that his arrival in Washington would do anything to change the administration's post-9/11 legal philosophy.[11]

But Comey was a force in his own right with a solid reputation as an honest broker and willingness to make politically unpopular decisions. Not long after becoming deputy attorney general in December 2003, he earned the enmity of the vice president's office. Amid the political uproar over the leak of CIA agent Valerie Plame's name to the media, Comey appointed Patrick Fitzgerald, a hard-charging Chicago federal prosecutor and close friend, to investigate allegations of a White House effort to disclose Plame's identity to discredit her husband, Joseph C. Wilson IV, a critic of the Iraq war. The investigation focused on Cheney's chief of staff, I. "Scooter" Libby, who was later convicted of lying about his role in disclosing Plame's name to the press. With the investigation underway, Comey soon faced another issue of far greater importance to the White House—the secret NSA program. He had no knowledge of the program until his national security aide Patrick Philbin advised him of its existence. A firm believer in the president's wartime powers, Philbin had written critical legal opinions claiming that the president had the authority as commander in chief to create military commissions unilaterally and that the federal courts had no jurisdiction over prisoners held at Guantanamo. He had drafted these early opinions while a deputy at the OLC, where he also learned of the NSA operation. But the massive surveillance operation distressed even him. And he sought to get Comey involved in giving it the kind of legal scrutiny and oversight that it warranted.[12]

Stunned that the NSA program was bypassing the Federal Intelligence Surveillance Act (FISA) court and was spying on Americans without warrants, Comey and his aides believed that the vast data-mining operation was out of control. The fierce internal battle over the legalities of the program crested in early March 2004 as the program was due to be recertified by the attorney general. A week before the deadline for recertifying the program on March 11, Comey met with Ashcroft to voice his concerns—and those of the OLC—about the illegality of certain aspects of the NSA operation. He explained the operational changes and safeguards that he thought were needed to put the administration's signature antiterror program within the law. Ashcroft listened and agreed to act on Comey's suggestions. Hours later, however, Ashcroft began having stomach pains and was rushed to George Washington University Hospital with what was diagnosed to be severe pancreatitis. He also had to undergo gall bladder surgery five days later. With Ashcroft incapacitated in the hospital, Comey became the acting attorney general with the power to sign off on the secret NSA operation. As the White House waited anxiously for his signature, matters came to a head on March 10, the day of Ashcroft's gallbladder surgery. That day, Comey met with Cheney, Addington, Gonzales, White House chief of staff Andrew Card, and other senior officials to advise that he would not be recertifying the legality of the NSA program. Although Ashcroft had signed off on the program for two years, Comey was now refusing to certify it. Cheney and the others strongly disagreed with the decision.[13]

Facing a major crisis over the legality of the program, the White House, in a dramatic move, sought to get the bedridden Ashcroft to overturn his deputy's decision. At 8:00 in the evening, Goldsmith was having dinner with his wife when he received an urgent call from the Justice Department command center to get to the hospital as quickly as possible. After double-parking at the hospital, he ran up the stairs, reaching the wing of the intensive care unit where Ashcroft was recuperating. He was joined by Comey and Patrick Philbin. On seeing the attorney general, Goldsmith was struck by his condition. "He looked terrible. . . . He had tubes going in and out of him. He looked ashen, and I actually thought he looked near death. I was taken aback by how bad he looked," Goldsmith recalled. Soon after they entered Ashcroft's room, Alberto Gonzales and Andrew Card arrived, somewhat surprised to see the others in the room. Gonzales had an envelope in his hand, and it became apparent that he aimed to ask the attorney general to authorize the operation over the heads of Goldsmith and Comey, who believed it could not be authorized by the Justice Department. Gonzales spoke briefly to Ashcroft, recounted Goldsmith, "and then, in one of the most extraordinary events I've ever seen in my life, Attorney General Ashcroft kind of lifted himself—he arose from the bed, lifted himself up and gave about a two or three minute speech or talk, addressed to Gonzales and Card in which he basically . . . showed enormous, unbelievable clarity about what the issues were and what was going on, and he explained why he also would not approve the program. He read them a bit of the riot act, and then at the end of all this he said: 'And in any event, I'm not the attorney general now; Jim Comey is.'"[14] Ashcroft stood by his deputy, refusing to recertify the vast NSA surveillance program.

The angry reaction shot beyond Cheney to the Oval Office. With his penchant for put-down nicknames, reported *Newsweek*, President Bush "had begun to refer to Comey as 'Cuomey' or 'Cuomo,' apparently after former New York governor Mario Cuomo, who was notorious for his Hamlet-like indecision over whether to seek the Democratic presidential nomination in the 1980s."[15] The day after the dramatic hospital scene, the White House went ahead with the NSA program without the Justice Department's certification. In effect, the administration was proceeding against its own lawyers at the Justice Department. Bush backed down, however, after Comey, Goldsmith, and as many as a dozen or more other top Justice Department officials, including FBI director Robert S. Mueller III, threatened to resign. The threat of mass resignations signaled a resounding vote of no-confidence in Cheney, Addington, and their allies in the White House by officials who were known for previously carrying out aggressive antiterrorism initiatives. The president ended the insurrection at the Justice Department—the biggest revolt since the Saturday Night Massacre during the Watergate scandal—by agreeing to allow the department to impose new controls on the NSA operation.

The new arrangement would involve auditing past wiretapping operations and reworking the legal opinions, basing the surveillance program on the congressional authorization to use military force against al Qaeda rather than on the president's inherent authority as commander in chief. This rationale, however, later proved a thin reed on which to hang the secret program, drawing even more skepticism from Congress. More important, several technical facets of the program were terminated, including operations that involved data mining to track communications patterns across U.S. borders. These aspects of the program were deemed by the Justice Department to be the most legally problematic. With these new restrictions—constituting a setback for the vice president's push for unfettered presidential power—the White House and the Justice Department reached an uneasy peace. But months later Cheney would strike back in blocking the promotion of Comey's aide, Patrick Philbin, for the post of deputy solicitor general. The Justice Department wanted Philbin for the job, but Cheney considered his involvement in the insurrection led by Comey and Goldsmith a betrayal.

All three—Philbin, Goldsmith, and Comey—would soon quit the administration, leaving Cheney a victor of sorts in the battle for control at the
Justice Department. Philbin left for the private sector, while Goldsmith
accepted a faculty position at Harvard. Comey stayed until the summer
of 2005 when he accepted a lucrative job as a top lawyer for an aerospace
firm. He had held on for six months after Gonzales became the new attorney
general.[16]

Even with the new controls and legal rationale in place, the secret NSA
program ignited a political firestorm when the *New York Times* revealed its
existence for the first time on December 16, 2005. Within days of the *Times*
story, the Justice Department asserted that the president possessed the constitutional authority to act outside the law and the courts to focus on international communications of Americans with suspected ties to terrorists and
that Congress had implicitly authorized that power when it voted for the
emergency Authorization to Use Military Force (AUMF) in Afghanistan on
September 18, 2001. Critics from across the political spectrum challenged
these claims of presidential power, although most congressional Republicans
supported the administration's position on national security grounds.

It was not the first time that a president made a power grab based on
implied congressional authorization. When Truman seized the steel mills, he
made similar overreaching claims. Justice Felix Frankfurter declared that it
was "one thing to draw an intention of Congress from general language and
to say that Congress would have explicitly written what is inferred, where
Congress has not addressed itself to a specific situation." But it was "quite
impossible . . . when Congress did specifically address itself to a problem, as
Congress did to that of seizure, to find in the interstices of legislation the
very grant of power which Congress consciously withheld." To discover
"authority so explicitly withheld," said Frankfurter, is "to disrespect the legislative process and the constitutional division of authority between the President and Congress."[17] After all, the 1978 surveillance law declared that it
constituted the "exclusive means" by which eavesdropping on American soil
could take place. Goldsmith may have found Yoo's early opinions on the
NSA program critically flawed for not addressing the Supreme Court's seminal ruling on the steel seizure case, but the Justice Department's reworked
rationale on the matter seemed scarcely much better.

In early February 2006, Attorney General Alberto Gonzales argued the
administration's position before the Senate Judiciary Committee, adding
that the president was the "sole organ" for the nation in foreign affairs. This
assertion referenced the 1936 Supreme Court ruling in *United States v. Curtiss-
Wrights Export Corporation*—the decision that spoke of the "exclusive power
of the president as the sole organ of the federal government in the field

expire, leading to intense negotiations over whether to revive it. One of the most controversial issues involved immunity provisions for telecommunications companies that participated in the covert surveillance program. In June 2008, Congress and the White House reached a deal on the most comprehensive overhaul of the nation's intelligence surveillance law in thirty years. A key element of the agreement gave phone companies involved in the eavesdropping program protection from lawsuits if a district court determined that they received valid requests from the government directing their participation in the operation. This standard augured poorly for more than forty lawsuits against major telecommunications carriers that provided vast troves of customer data to the NSA after the 9/11 attacks. The high likelihood that the cases would be dismissed enraged civil liberties groups, which said that a cursory review by a district court judge meant the de facto death of the lawsuits.

The agreement would expire at the end of 2012 unless Congress renewed it. The deal also expanded the government's powers to spy on terrorism suspects, including strengthening the ability of intelligence officials to eavesdrop on foreign targets. It allowed for carrying out emergency surveillance without court orders on American targets for seven days if it was determined that important national security information would otherwise be lost. But Democratic leaders won an important concession—the affirmation that the law's intelligence restrictions would serve as the "exclusive" means for the executive branch to conduct surveillance operations in terrorism and espionage cases. The language was considered key to restrain not only Bush, but future presidents, from circumventing the law. Other important provisions included requirements that the inspectors general of several agencies review the NSA's surveillance program, that the government obtain individual warrants to eavesdrop on Americans outside the United States and that the secret FISA court overseeing surveillance operations give advance authorization to the government's procedures for wiretapping operations. The deal no longer required individual court orders for wiretapping purely foreign communications— phone calls and e-mails that passed through telecommunications switches on U.S. soil. Further, the government could use broad warrants to eavesdrop on large groups of foreign targets at once.[22]

The secret surveillance program that Cheney put in motion after 9/11 had spawned heated debate in and out of the administration and created a congressional backlash, forcing the administration to backtrack and reach a deal with the legislative branch. In the end, the vice president had not suffered a total defeat, but years of bruising controversy and litigation could have been avoided had the administration initially gone to Congress to update the law. The 2008 compromise deal emphasized the law's original meaning that it constituted the "exclusive means" by which domestic surveillance could be carried out, even while expanding the government's spying powers.

TORTURE

In December 2004, the Justice Department publicly declared torture "abhorrent." The statement seemed to signal a major reversal of the administration claims of unfettered presidential authority to order coercive interrogations. But soon after Alberto Gonzales became the new attorney general in February 2005, the Justice Department issued a secret opinion endorsing the most expansive use of extreme interrogation techniques ever used by the CIA. The opinion explicitly authorized combined harsh physical and psychological methods, including head-slapping, simulated drowning, and frigid temperatures. Gonzales approved the legal memorandum over the objections of James B. Comey, the deputy attorney general, who was leaving the administration after bruising battles with Cheney's allies in the White House. Comey not only denounced the opinion for its flawed and over-reaching reasoning, but told colleagues at the department that they would be "ashamed" when the international community learned of it.

Gonzales's arrival as the new attorney general suited the vice president's expansive agenda. Compliant and largely unknowledgeable about national security affairs, he endorsed the aggressive policies of Cheney and Addington to protect the country, even though these actions drew international condemnation. On interrogation and other matters, Gonzales was quick to put the Justice Department in the service of the White House, compromising the department's cherished tradition of independence. The debate over the limits of interrogation erupted shortly after 9/11 with the vice president and his allies leading the way into uncharted territory and relying on confidential legal advice of a handful of appointees. The policies set off brawls inside the administration, pitting administration moderates against Cheney hardliners, military lawyers against Pentagon chiefs, and a few conservative lawyers at the Justice Department against the vice president's office. Throughout these debates, the CIA searched for the limits of coercive interrogation practices. In 2003, the agency's doubts proved prophetic after John Yoo left the Office of Legal Counsel and Jack Goldsmith, the new head of the OLC, began reviewing his legal opinions. Goldsmith found Yoo's work deeply flawed, throwing out the August 2002 torture memo in June 2004, infuriating Cheney and Addington. At the same time, after only a brief tenure, Goldsmith resigned his office, believing that the timing "would make it hard for the White House to reverse my decision without making it seem like I had resigned in protest."[23]

Six months later, the Justice Department declared torture to be "abhorrent both to American law and values and to international norms" on its Web site. When Bush named Gonzales as his new faithful attorney general, he assured that the Justice Department would not rebel again and would be in the loyal service of the White House. Gonzales had been his steadfast friend dating to Bush's Texas days and an ardent supporter of the president's prerogatives. On his appointment at the Justice Department, Gonzales went in search of a new chief of the OLC—the office that serves as the final arbiter on legal matters affecting the executive branch. He found a trusted appointee in Steven G. Bradbury, a former attorney at the law firm of Kirklan & Ellis where he served under the tutelage of Kenneth W. Starr, the Whitewater independent prosecutor. In June 2005, Bush nominated Bradbury to head the OLC. It was Bradbury who signed the secret opinion authorizing the combined interrogation techniques.

Comey might have been able to kill the opinion under Ashcroft, but not under Gonzales. At 6-foot-8, he was an imposing physical presence, an ardent conservative, but one who was willing to confront Addington on the limits of executive power under the law. The two clashed at one White House meeting where Comey stated that "no lawyer" would back Yoo's justification for the NSA warrantless surveillance program. Addington responded that he was a lawyer and found it sound. Comey shot back: "No good lawyer." But after the departure of Ashcroft and Goldsmith, the deputy attorney general had few allies. His opposition to the administration's policies on NSA's warrantless surveillance, interrogation, and in naming his friend Patrick J. Fitzgerald as special prosecutor in the CIA leak case leading to the conviction of I. Scooter Libby, Cheney's chief of staff, earned the enmity of the vice president and others at the White House. In a speech at the NSA's Fort Mead campus on Law Day, Comey spoke of the "agonizing collisions" of the law and the goal of protecting Americans. "We are likely to hear the words: 'If we don't do this, people will die,'" Comey said—sounding the oft-repeated refrain of Cheney and Addington. But he said that government lawyers must uphold the principles of their great institutions. "It takes far more than a sharp legal mind to say 'no' when it matters most," he said. "It takes moral character. It takes an understanding that in the long run, intelligence under the law is the only sustainable intelligence in this country."[24]

In summer 2005, Comey left the Justice Department at about the same time that Congress was considering several bills to prohibit torture by American troops. The administration had always claimed that the CIA's coercive interrogation tactics were not torture, which was outlawed by federal law and international treaty. But officials had privately decided that the agency could ignore one of the key provisions of the Convention Against Torture—the ban on "cruel, inhuman, or degrading" treatment. This understanding was about to be overturned. After revelations of the scandals at Abu Ghraib and other prisoner abuse, Republican Senator John McCain of Arizona introduced several bills to prohibit torture by U.S. forces. The amendments received the support of other powerful Republicans of the Armed Services Committee, including Senator Lindsey Graham of South Carolina and Senator John Warner of Virginia. Shot down over Vietnam in 1967, McCain spent more than five years in a North Vietnamese prison camp where he was repeatedly tortured. He believed that government-sanctioned torture would devastate America's moral and political standing and authority at home and abroad. He expressed these sentiments in a November 2005 article in *Newsweek*: "What I mourn is what we lose when by official policy or official neglect we allow, confuse or encourage our soldiers to forget that best sense of ourselves; that what is our greatest strength—that we are different and better than our enemies, that we fight for an idea, not a tribe, not a land, not a king, not a twisted interpretation of an ancient religion, but for an idea that all men are created equal and endowed by their Creator with inalienable rights."[25] On the basis of his own experiences of being tortured, he also believed—like many CIA officers—that extreme abuse achieved little more than unreliable confessions.

Cheney fought to kill McCain's amendments, arguing that they would violate the president's executive authority and leave the country vulnerable to terrorist attack. Throughout 2005, he waged an intense behind-the-scenes campaign to thwart Congress, the Pentagon, and the State Department from imposing additional limitations on the handling of terrorist suspects. During the winter of that year, when John D. Rockefeller, vice chairman of the Senate Intelligence Committee, began pushing for briefings on the CIA's interrogation practices, Cheney summoned him to the White House to urge that he halt his efforts. He also opposed the Pentagon's efforts of adding safeguards to the rules governing the treatment of military detainees, pitting him against Condoleezza Rice, who replaced Colin Powell as secretary of state in Bush's second term, and acting Deputy Secretary of Defense Gordon R. England.[26] Now, he battled McCain's attempts to ban torture and inhumane treatment of prisoners.

On October 5, 2005, McCain attached an antitorture amendment to a defense appropriation measure aimed at requiring American troops to follow interrogation standards set in the Army Field Manual, then under revision, and ban "cruel, inhuman and degrading treatment" of prisoners in U.S. custody. One of the revisions of the field manual stressed the importance of following the Geneva Conventions in the treatment of prisoners. Former

Secretary of State Colin Powell, who retired at the end of the first Bush term, joined the controversy. He had written a letter, read by McCain on the Senate floor, stating that American troops needed to hear from Congress. "The world will note that America is making a clear statement with respect to the expected future behavior of our soldiers," he wrote.[27]

But Cheney worked hard to defeat the amendment. He twice met with key legislators to lobby against the measure. On one occasion he went to Capitol Hill in July to press Senators Warner, McCain, and Graham to drop the measure. When the Senate voted 90-9 for including the provision in the $440 billion Pentagon spending bill, the White House threatened to veto the bill, arguing that the executive branch had exclusive authority over war-making policy. Upset over the Senate's passage of the amendment, Cheney made an impassioned plea to reject McCain's amendment and exempt the CIA from any interrogation limits. After Senate aides were ordered out of the Mansfield Room, just steps from the Senate chamber, the vice president said that the law would bind the president's hands and risk "thousands of lives." He dramatized the point, arguing that aggressive interrogation of detainees, such as Khalid Sheik Mohammed, could produce critical information to prevent imminent attacks. "We have to be able to do what is necessary," the vice president said. But McCain disagreed. "This is killing us around the world," he said.[28]

Cheney's impassioned appeal changed few minds. Editorial writers across the country excoriated the administration's support for extreme interrogation methods, swinging public opinion and putting pressure on the Republican-controlled Congress. On December 15, the House voted 308-122 in a resolution supporting McCain's amendment. Supporters of the measure favored clarifying the antitorture laws after the abuses at Abu Ghraib in Iraq and allegations of misconduct by U.S. troops at the detention center at Guantanamo Bay. The effort also aimed to help the United States repair its tarnished image abroad following the prisoner abuse scandals. Earlier in 2005, the Senate had included McCain's original provision in two defense bills, but the House omitted them from their versions, causing them to stall. The administration's overwhelming defeat in both houses prompted a meeting between Bush and McCain in the Oval Office. The Republican maverick and the administration had been negotiating for weeks in search of a compromise, but it became increasingly clear that McCain had the votes in Congress. In Cheney's absence, the two struck a deal. In a major reversal, Bush agreed to support the McCain amendment in exchange for the senator's endorsing language giving CIA interrogators the same legal rights guaranteed to members of the military who were accused of violating interrogation guidelines. Under the agreement, anyone accused of violating interrogation guidelines could defend themselves if a "reasonable" person could conclude they were following a lawful order.[29] Nevertheless, the law gave no immunity from civil or criminal lawsuits to those who violated the interrogation standards.[30] The administration sought to introduce protections for interrogators accused of breeching the provision. McCain stood his ground, arguing that it would undercut the ban by allowing interrogators a reason not to follow the law. On reaching agreement with McCain, Bush said it would "make clear to the world that this government does not torture and that we adhere to the international convention of torture, whether it be here at home or abroad."[31]

The agreement may have marked a public setback for the vice president, but the administration wasted little time in undercutting McCain's law and asserting executive power. As McCain's amendment gained momentum in Congress, the administration asked Bradbury at the OLC to assess whether the proposed measure would outlaw any CIA methods. Bradbury delivered what the White House wanted—a secret opinion stating that McCain's measure would not require any change in the agency's interrogation techniques. The opinion relied on a Supreme Court ruling that only conduct that "shocks the conscience" was unconstitutional. Bradbury's opinion said that not even waterboarding, in some circumstances, amounted to cruel, inhuman, or degrading treatment—especially in cases involving a suspect believed to possess vital information about a planned or imminent attack.[32] Further, although Bush signed the bill outlawing the torture of prisoners, he quietly reserved the right in a signing statement to ignore the law under his exclusive powers as commander in chief. The signing statement declared that the "executive branch shall construe [the law] in a manner consistent with the constitutional authority of the President ... as Commander in Chief." Moreover, it stated that this approach would "assist in achieving the shared objective of the Congress and the President ... of protecting the American people from further terrorist attacks."[33]

Like hundreds of others Bush issued, the signing statement was crafted by members of the vice president's legal team who routinely reviewed pieces of legislation before they reached the president's desk, searching for provisions that were seen to encroach on presidential power. David Addington, the leading architect of the signing statements, aimed to assert the president's right to ignore laws if they conflicted with the White House's expansive interpretation of executive powers under the Constitution. Among many constitutional scholars and others, the signing statements became one of the controversial hallmarks of the Bush-Cheney Administration, signaling a historical shift in the balance of powers away from the legislative branch to the executive. Although the framers of the Constitution distinguished between the powers of Congress and the presidency, declaring that Congress shall make all laws and the president shall see to it that the laws are faithfully executed, Bush exerted the right to carry out the laws only as he interpreted them.[34]

American presidents, dating to the early 1800s, had occasionally used signing statements asserting that a certain provision in a bill was unconstitutional. In response to the congressional backlash against executive power in the 1970s, President Reagan became the first to use them to reassert presidential power. Reagan's successors also used this tactic to assert executive authority, but Cheney's office radicalized the strategy to further his legal revolution. Halfway through the second term of his presidency, Bush had issued more than 800 signing statements, declaring himself and the executive branch free to disobey hundreds of laws. The implications were clear. Congress had no business regulating what the government did or how it went about doing it. These matters were only for the unitary executive to decide.[35]

The president's signing statement nullifying McCain's amendment belied his remarks at a press conference with the senator where he praised the measure and said he would accept it. One former Justice Department official noted that the "whole point of the McCain amendment was to close every loophole" [permitting torture,] but the president reopened the loophole by claiming "the constitutional authority to act in violation of the statute where it would assist in the war on terrorism."[36] Jack Goldsmith, who became head of the OLC in 2003, later recalled that the signing statement "struck me as a monumental politically imprudent thing to do. . . . If the president decided later that some application of his power was unduly restricted and unconstitutionally restricted by this law, he could at that time assert the arguments. There was nothing, no point served by the signing statement and lots of negative consequences from this in-your-face signing statement after this moment of reconciliation."[37]

Just days after the president signed McCain's amendment into law, Cheney gave a revealing interview of his convictions on the television news show *Nightline*. Based on court rulings, he said, the rule governing where the president drew the line on torture was "whether or not it shocks the conscience." He continued: "Now you can get into a debate about what shocks the conscience and what is cruel and inhuman. And to some extent, I suppose, that's in the eye of the beholder." He added that "it's important to remember that we are in a war against a group of individuals, a terrorist organization that did in fact slaughter three thousand innocent Americans on 9/11; that it's important for us to be able to have effective interrogation of these people when we capture them."[38] If nothing else, the remarks revealed an Armageddon mentality, if not a sense of vengeance. He had long made it clear that the United States was now involved in a long and dirty war with a brutish enemy eager for weapons of mass destruction and bent on committing mass outrages against the American homeland. In waging this unconventional war in the dark corners of the world, he believed terrorist suspects warranted no legal protections as enemy combatants and intelligence officials should use everything at their disposal to get intelligence to prevent further attacks. The imperative was national security; everything else was secondary, even civil liberties. The other political branches were ill suited to the new emergency and had no business interfering with the president's war powers. Their involvement would only undermine the global war on terror and risk American lives. No one could question Cheney's fervent commitment to defend the country, only the lengths to which he was willing to go.

In June 2008, the Senate Armed Services Committee held hearings that provided further evidence that top Bush Administration officials orchestrated the use of extreme interrogation techniques on detained suspected terrorists. Witnesses testified that the use of harsh methods stemmed from decisions made by senior administration officials. In April, ABC News reported that officials including Dick Cheney, Donald Rumsfeld, Condoleezza Rice, and Colin Powell convened meetings at the White House to discuss what interrogation methods could be used on prisoners suspected of terrorism. The ABC story enlarged on earlier reporting indicating that the decision to destroy video tapes of interrogations of suspects in CIA custody involved senior White House lawyers and other leading officials. These disclosures pushed the issue of criminal conduct and war crimes to the forefront among some in the United States and international community. For example, in a hearing on June 5, members of the House Judiciary Committee probing the rendition of Canadian citizen Maher Arar, a software engineer, wanted to know whether sufficient evidence existed for a criminal investigation into the conduct of administration officials. All three of the witnesses responded affirmatively, although witnesses in other hearings proved somewhat evasive and experienced lapses of memory, perhaps for fear of self-incrimination.

In the international arena, where concerns over the administration's interrogation and rendition policies were more palpable, an Italian court in Milan was trying twenty-six Americans in absentia for their involvement in abducting and rendering a radical Islamic cleric to Egypt. The Italian case perhaps augured more things to come. While prosecuting former Bush officials for war crimes was extremely unlikely in the United States, such trials overseas seemed more probable. Writing in a June 19, 2008, article in the *New Republic*, Scott Horton of Colombia University's law school said such indictments were "reasonably likely," adding that in the "past two years, I have spoken with two investigating magistrates in two different European nations, both pro-Iraq War NATO allies. Both were assembling war crimes charges against a small group of Bush Administration officials. 'You can rest assured that no charges will be brought before January 20, 2009,' one told me. And after that? It depends. We don't expect extradition. But if one of the targets lands on our territory or on the territory of one of our cooperating jurisdictions, then we'll be prepared to act."[39] Colin Powell's chief of staff, Colonel Larry Wilkerson, put it another way: "Haynes, Feith, Yoo, Bybee, Gonzales and—at the apex—Addington, should never travel outside the United States, except perhaps to Saudi Arabia and Israel. They broke the law; they violated their professional ethical code. In the future, some government may build a case necessary to prosecute them in a foreign court, or in an international court."[40]

TRIBUNALS

The vice president's legal revolution, resulting in a mountain of litigation challenging the administration's central premise that the legal status of the warrantless surveillance program, detention of suspected terrorists, exceptional interrogation, and rendering suspects to secret prisons in foreign countries, was a matter for the executive branch alone to decide and beyond the reach of federal courts and international law. Ironically, Cheney's extravagant claims of presidential power resulted in key court defeats and in the imposition of the very restrictions that he had fought to defeat. On June 29, 2006, the vice president suffered his sharpest blow yet in a landmark decision. In *Hamdan v. Rumsfeld*, a divided Supreme Court ruled 5-3 that the military commission system that was created to prosecute enemy combatants for war crimes was fatally flawed because the president had acted unilaterally without congressional authorization. Not only did the ruling declare that the administration needed congressional authority to create military tribunals to charge and prosecute terrorists, but it could not ignore the Geneva Conventions. The Pentagon's procedures for the treatment of al Qaeda prisoners had to comport with the treaty. Writing for the majority, Justice John Paul Stevens said that Geneva "is applicable here," and "requires that Hamdan be tried by a regularly constituted court affording all the judicial guarantees which are recognized as indispensable by civilized peoples." The meaning of the ruling was clear: the administration would have to start obeying the Constitution and retreat from its near lawless position of monarchal executive power. Further, the judiciary would continue to supervise the administration's war on terror.[41]

The decision constituted a seeming calamity for the vice president's agenda of expanding presidential power and his war plans against al Qaeda. Cheney and Addington maneuvered to get around the ruling, proposing a bill that would eviscerate the applicability of the Geneva Conventions, eradicate the jurisdiction of U.S. courts over foreign suspects declared as enemy combatants, and assert the president's authority to create military commissions as he saw fit. The president veered in a different direction, pressing Congress to pass a more complex bill to legalize the tribunals and authorize many of the interrogation techniques used by intelligence officials. In October 2006, in the waning weeks under Republican control, Congress acted swiftly by passing the Military Commission Act of 2006.

The measure enacted controversial changes in the system of interrogating and prosecuting terrorism suspects, setting the rules for the trials of key al Qaeda members. Surrounded by members of his Cabinet, including the vice president, and lawmakers, Bush signed the bill into law during a White House ceremony as more than 100 protestors stood outside in the rain chanting slogans denouncing the changes as a violation of fundamental constitutional rights. The new law imposed strict limits on defendants' traditional rights, including restricting their ability to examine the evidence against them, challenge their imprisonment, or exclude evidence obtained through coercive measures. The law also outlawed specific interrogation methods, while extending retroactive legal protection to military and intelligence personnel who had subjected suspects to harsh questioning. This provision allowed the CIA to continue its once secret program of detaining terrorism suspects and using exceptional interrogation methods to obtain information. The act provided that "no court, justice or judge shall have jurisdiction to hear or consider" further habeas corpus petitions from foreigners held at Guantanamo or anywhere else.[42] "This program has been one of the most successful intelligence efforts in American history," Bush had declared at the signing ceremony. "It has helped prevent attacks on our country. And the bill I sign today will ensure that we can continue using this vital tool to protect the American people for years to come."[43]

The bill was opposed by most Democrats and some Republicans. Lawyers for the detainees immediately challenged the act, chiefly on grounds that it failed to offer protections for their habeas corpus rights. In March 2007, Khalid Sheikh Mohammed, the mastermind behind 9/11, appeared before a combat status review tribunal at Guantanamo, claiming involvement in numerous terror plots. According to testimony released by the Pentagon, he declared that he "was responsible for the 9/11 operation from A to Z. . . . I decapitated with my blessed right hand the head of the American Jew, Daniel Pearl." In December 2007, the Supreme Court prepared to hear the arguments in a new round of cases. Further, after the Democrats won the 2006 midterm elections in November, new bills were introduced to rewrite the law. Still, the new law largely gave the vice president's office what it wanted in prosecuting the likes of Mohammed, passing by majorities in the House and Senate in late September 2006. The law skirted the War Crimes Act, which considered grave breeches of Geneva Conventions a criminal offense. Instead, it declared that the president, not the Supreme Court, was the ultimate authority on what standards applied in the treatment of detainees.

Even before these events, the creation of the tribunal system advocated by the vice president had been plagued with growing problems. In early 2002, the Bush administration had devised what seemed to be an uncomplicated plan—once the prisoners captured on the battlefield in Afghanistan were interrogated, the worst of them would receive swift prosecutions in the specially created military tribunals. Once the president signed off on Cheney's policy and the procedures had been worked out, it seemed that the military commissions would move smoothly and that the first trials would occur without delay. With no trials in sight one year later, some senior administration officials vocally criticized the sluggish pace of the Pentagon's new courts and the reliability of their rules. Among the most vocal was Attorney General John Ashcroft. "Timothy McVeigh was one of the worst killers in U.S. history, he said at one meeting of senior officials. But at least we had fair procedures for him."[44] The administration declared that 9/11 and the imminent threat of more attacks justified the president's assertion of extraordinary wartime powers to unilaterally set up the new system of military justice. But what first appeared straightforward became mired in problems when officials sought to apply those powers to terrorism suspects.

The vice president, Addington, and their legal allies devised the system for dangerous al Qaeda terrorists, but the majority of the detainees transferred to Guantanamo turned out to be low-level militants. The Pentagon's efforts to obtain intelligence from more valuable prisoners also ran into serious problems, impeding the prosecution of some detainees while hindering efforts to release others. Cheney's policy of secrecy and back-channel maneuvering, excluding entire agencies and other senior administration officials from the process, ignited an often fierce struggle that pitched his office and Rumsfeld's Pentagon against adversaries at the National Security Council, the State Department, and Justice Department. The vice president's secrecy and efforts to dominate policy largely backfired, fueling considerable discontent among military, foreign policy, and other officials who had been cut out of any role in shaping the post-9/11 strategy.[45]

As the later Supreme Court rulings demonstrated, Cheney's unilateral scheme for the commissions initially weakened their legal justification. When the government created military tribunals in the past, they were either authorized by Congress or took place on the battlefield, usually during declared wars. But the vice president and his allies crafted something entirely different—a commission system created unilaterally, during a time of undeclared war, and half a world away from the battlefield. Further, despite efforts to prosecute suspected terrorists held at Guantanamo, the Pentagon quickly ran into intelligence-gathering problems from a recalcitrant enemy. Rumsfeld authorized the use of more coercive interrogation methods, exploiting the White House's decision that detainees were not covered by the Geneva Conventions. He later renounced the most severe techniques, including the use of dogs to induce stress, after their disclosures gave credibility to charges of gross abuses made by former detainees.

Beyond intelligence gathering problems, many of the prisoners captured in Afghanistan proved not to be hardened terrorists. About half of the initial prisoners were deemed to be of little or no intelligence value, including some who were elderly or emotionally disturbed. The screening process for those detainees sent to Guantanamo appeared seriously flawed, but military commanders in Afghanistan and Kuwait complained that they had no other place to hold suspects who might pose a threat or be of intelligence value. The November 13, 2001, presidential order establishing the military commissions authorized the Pentagon to detain and prosecute foreigners declared by the president to be suspected terrorists. In late January 2002, the Pentagon aimed to move swiftly on the commissions, ordering its intelligence officers to complete a one-page form for each prisoner to determine their prosecution status under the president's order. But this process produced scarce evidence on most prisoners, undermining the tribunal process and leading Pentagon officials to shift the legal ground for their indefinite detentions—as "enemy combatants" in a war against the United States.

The problems with the tribunals at Guantanamo created serious divisions within the administration. Cheney maintained that the detainees posed a dangerous threat. "They may well have information about future terrorist attacks against the United States," he said. "We need that information." But foreign governments, many of them allies in the Afghan war, besieged the State Department with complaints about the open-ended detention of their citizens. FBI agents and Justice Department officials were surprised by the lack of evidence to prosecute most of the detainees. CIA officers also were raising concerns that Guantanamo could radicalize prisoners by its harsh conditions and denial of due process, fears shared by staff at the National Security Council (NSC). "There was real concern that if detainees were harshly treated and deprived of due process, they were going end up turning against the United States, if they had not already," said General John A. Gordon, a former CIA deputy director who became Bush's deputy national security advisor for counterterrorism. "We were not making any converts." Despite Cheney's efforts to freeze out the agency, the president later brought the NSC back into the process to draw up a workable strategy to handle the thousands of prisoners in Afghanistan, resulting in an interagency group to study the issue.[46]

With the vice president's support, Rumsfeld worked to stymie efforts by the NSC and officials at other agencies to modify the Guantanamo policy. In August 2002, at the council's request, the CIA produced a secret fifteen-page report that concluded many of the detainees at Guantanamo had no significant ties to al Qaeda and suggested that the facility's harsh conditions could be counterproductive. National Security Advisor Condoleezza Rice used the report in efforts to build a network of dissenters among national security officials in the administration. By the fall of 2002, questions arose in the Justice Department about the Pentagon's treatment of the detainees, the slow pace of the tribunals, and the shifting policies concerning how to prosecute suspected terrorists. The Pentagon's policies were already drawing litigation in the federal courts, including cases involving Padilla and Hamdi. At the same time, the detainee policies were creating considerable acrimony among allies, diminishing cooperation in international counterterrorism efforts. The internal struggle over the detainees' fate forced an ambivalent Rumsfeld to yield in providing information to cabinet-level officials and their deputies and to initiate changes in its detention policies. Paul Wolfowitz approved new measures in December 2002 that included revised criteria for transferring prisoners to Guantanamo, a policy of returning detainees to their home countries, and a requirement of periodically assessing whether prisoners should remain at Guantanamo.

Even with these revisions, the tribunal system stalled, mired in litigation, internal disputes, little or no evidence for prosecuting suspects, shifts in detainee policies, and complaints from disaffected allies. The vice president and his allies aggressively pushed for an expansion of presidential power that would deliver swift justice, but they created a host of problems, including further restrictions on presidential power from the Supreme Court. It was not until summer 2008 that the military commissions began moving on the first full-blown trials. Former chief military commissions prosecutor Moe Davis testified about the political pressures his office was under to begin prosecutions, particularly cases involving those implicated in the 9/11 attacks. There was a strong feeling, he said, "that if we didn't get this thing rolling before the [presidential] election it was going to implode." Among those facing trial was Khalid Sheikh Mohammed and other defendants who were transferred to Guantanamo from CIA custody in September 2006.[47]

Cheney did more than anyone to mold the legal landscape on tribunals and interrogations. The two issues merged in the case of David Hicks, an Australian citizen who unexpectedly became a terrorist threat to the United

States. Hicks stood among the thousands captured in the American war against the Taliban in Afghanistan. At every stage of his journey through the post-9/11 military labyrinth, his fate was shaped largely by the policies that the vice president set in motion and the reaction to those policies. He was transferred and imprisoned at Guantanamo Bay, arriving on opening day on an island beyond the reach of sovereign law. Interrogators questioned him under rules permitting the infliction of pain. His British lawyer filed an affidavit accusing his American captors of subjecting him to beatings, sodomy with a foreign object, sensory deprivation, disorienting drugs, and prolonged shackling in painful positions—charges that the U.S. government denied. The tribunal's rules, operating under principles advocated by the vice president, would have allowed the prosecution of the Australian with evidence obtained by cruel, inhuman, or degrading methods.

But the U.S. government had trouble figuring out what to do with him and pleaded with his home country to take him. The Australian government said that he had not violated any of its laws and would set him free, which the administration opposed. After allowing Hicks to languish at Guantanamo for nearly five years, the case became highly politicized in his home country. Australian Prime Minister John Howard came under domestic political pressure to secure his release or at least a trial. Howard demanded as much from Cheney during his February 2007 visit to Australia. After Cheney returned to the United States, the case against Hicks quickly fell apart. On March 26, the Australian pleaded guilty to providing "material support" for terrorism, but the administration conditioned its acceptance on Hicks affirming that he had never been illegally treated. The administration abruptly changed course in plea negotiations, abandoning its demand for a sentence from twenty years in prison to nine months if Hicks would admit guilt. The dramatic retreat resolved the case in time for Howard to face reelection in Australia. Negotiated without the knowledge of chief prosecutor Air Force Colonel Morris Davis, the deal involved the supervision of Susan Crawford, the convening authority over military commissions. Crawford was well known to Cheney, who had given her three different government positions when he served as secretary of defense. For administration officials, the back-pedaling on Hicks, a lowly combatant, diverted attention from its policy on detainees. The president had said in a news conference that he wanted to close Guantanamo—an action repeatedly supported by Rice and the new defense secretary, Robert M. Gates, among others—but not Cheney. The detention facility remained in operation throughout Bush's second term.[48]

Nevertheless, on June 12, 2008, the vice president's policies received another significant blow. In a historic decision on the balance between personal liberties and national security, the Supreme Court ruled 5-4 that the administration could not deny prisoners at Guantanamo Bay the right to challenge their detentions in U.S. courts. The ruling marked the Court's fourth rebuke in four years of the administration's handling of the rights of terrorism detainees. Justice Anthony Kennedy, writing for the majority, concluded that the foreign prisoners in the U.S. detention facility have "the constitutional privilege of habeas corpus. . . ." He declared that the "law and the Constitution are designed to survive, and remain in force, in extraordinary times. Liberty and security can be reconciled; and in our system they are reconciled within the framework of the law. The Framers decided that habeas corpus, a right of first importance, must be a part of that framework, a part of that law," Kennedy wrote. Further, he justified the Court's reach in this decision. "Within the Constitution's separation-of-powers," he wrote, "few exercises of judicial power are as legitimate or as necessary as the responsibility to hear challenges to the authority of the Executive to imprison a person."[49]

The close decision drew bitter dissent. Justice Antonin Scalia wrote that "America is at war with radical Islamists," adding that the decision "will almost certainly cause more Americans to be killed." Chief Justice John Roberts denounced the majority for striking down "the most generous set of procedural protections ever afforded aliens detained by this country as enemy combatants." He all but called the decision a power grab. "One cannot help but think . . . this decision is not really about the detainees, but about control of federal policy regarding enemy combatants," he wrote.[50]

The Court had ruled twice before that prisoners at Guantanamo had the right of habeas corpus in U.S. courts. In the 2004 case, *Rasul v. Bush*, the Court found that Guantanamo Bay was within U.S. jurisdiction and subject to its laws. The Court's ruling meant that detainees were entitled to some sort of due process in American courts, even though it did not specify the process. The 2006 Hamdan case involved the military commissions that Bush established at Guantanamo Bay to prosecute some of the detainees following 9/11. The Court's majority went further than the previous ruling, deciding that the president had overstepped his authority under the Constitution by creating the tribunals without congressional authorization. Moreover, it held that Common Article 3 of the Geneva Conventions applied to the Guantanamo prisoners—including the right to be heard by "a regularly constituted court affording all the judicial guarantees which are recognized as indispensable by civilized people." Both these decisions were rebukes to what the Court viewed as the administration's executive overreaching. After the 2006 decision, the administration succeeded in getting the Republican-controlled Congress to pass a law authorizing military commissions, suspending habeas corpus for foreign detainees, and stripping federal courts of any jurisdiction. The Court's 2008 decision constituted a harsh rebuke to that provision, restoring habeas corpus and limiting the reach of the executive and legislative branches to suspend the most fundamental tenet of American jurisprudence.

The majority's opinion, however, raised more questions than it answered about the scope and shape of the hearings. Among the questions were what the due process requirements would be, how the courts should handle classified information, and what the government must show to justify the continued imprisonment of detainees. Further, the administration's main reason for holding terrorism suspects without trial and beyond sovereign law vanished under the ruling, raising questions of how long Guantanamo would remain open and where detainees might be transferred on the U.S. mainland. Nonetheless, the ruling clarified one fundamental point—that all foreign prisoners held at Guantanamo could challenge their imprisonment under the writ of habeas corpus.[51] John Yoo, the former author of many of the administration's most tenuous and controversial secret legal opinions at the Office of Legal Counsel, condemned the decision in the *Wall Street Journal*. Because of his former affinity with the vice president's office, it seemed that his editorial might also reflect the views of Cheney and Addington. Yoo ridiculed the ruling for its judicial activism and "brazen power grab" and for defying "the considered judgment of the president and Congress for a third time, all to grant captured al Qaeda terrorists the exact same rights as American citizens to a day in civilian court." He laid out what he saw as the harrowing consequences of the Court's ruling: "Judicial micromanagement will now intrude into the conduct of war. Federal courts will jury-rig a process whose every rule second-guesses our soldiers and intelligence agents in the field. A judge's view on how much 'proof' is needed to find that 'suspect' is a terrorist will become the standard applied on the battlefield. Soldiers will have to gather 'evidence,' which will have to be safeguarded until a court hearing, take statements from 'witnesses,' and probably provide some kind of Miranda-style warning upon capture."[52]

Regardless of the immediate fallout of the decision, the administration's losses in the Supreme Court set precedents that were adding up, restricting presidential power. Reflecting on some of these defeats in 2007, Jack Goldsmith said that at least in the short term, "I don't think the administration has actually been stopped from doing much at all of what it's wanted to do since 9/11. In terms of what they're actually doing, the combination of congressional restrictions that have grown up and the Supreme Court restrictions to date have at best put very modest limitations on what they wanted to do. So you think that the go-it-alone strategy of pushing as hard as they could for executive prerogative, going to Congress only when necessary, has in some sense paid off, because they're still able to do what they want to do, and . . . there's been no attack since 9/11. That's likely in the White House viewed as an enormous success." But the vice president's theological convictions and willingness to push them in the courts were producing significant losses to the presidency and to the power of future presidents. "There's no doubt that Congress and the courts are more suspicious and less trustful of the president and the presidency now than they were after 9/11 and that this suspicion of the president will harm future presidencies," said Goldsmith. "I have no doubt about that."[53]

BLACK SITES

Cheney experienced another setback when the president acknowledged for the first time on September 6, 2006, the holding of senior al Qaeda detainees in secret CIA prisons overseas. Since the *Washington Post* revealed their existence in November 2005, Bush and other administration officials had kept silent on the subject.[54] The *Post*'s article and other news sources reported that the CIA had been hiding and interrogating senior al Qaeda suspects at a Soviet-era compound in Eastern Europe. The secret facility was part of a global network of covert prisons set up by the CIA nearly four years previously that included sites in such countries as Thailand, Afghanistan, and several countries in Eastern Europe. A smaller center also existed at Guantanamo Bay, Cuba. The covert global prison network became a central element in the CIA's unconventional war on terrorism after the 9/11 attacks. It relied on the cooperation of foreign intelligence services and hiding its existence from the public, foreign officials, and virtually all members of Congress charged with overseeing the CIA's intelligence operations. The CIA never acknowledged the existence of its black sites, fearing that publicity would condemn its global prison network, risk investigations at home and abroad, and open the U.S. government to legal challenges, particularly in foreign courts.

The secret prison network was conceived in the first chaotic months after 9/11 attacks with the fear of a second imminent attack. On the day of the attacks, the CIA already had a list of targets from the al Qaeda network. As American intelligence officials began investigating the plot surrounding the 9/11 attacks, more names were added to the list. The question of how to handle them quickly arose. Rather than sending out paramilitaries to infiltrate countries and assassinate designated terrorists, many at the CIA believed that al Qaeda leaders should be kept alive to provide valuable intelligence about their terrorist network. Six days after the attacks, Bush signed a broad presidential finding authorizing the CIA to disrupt terrorist activity and granting permission to kill, capture, and detain members of al Qaeda anywhere in the world. Under the September 17, 2001, finding, the agency set up its covert black-site program pursuant to its covert action authority. The program was pushed by the vice president and a small circle of White House and Justice Department lawyers. It reflected what Cheney meant when he said the government had to go to the "dark side." The covert program was set up overseas because U.S. law prohibited the government from holding people in secret prisons on American soil. The agency originally designed the program to deal with the handful of major al Qaeda leaders who were believed to be involved in the September 11, 2001, attacks and posed an imminent threat. But the CIA's paramilitary group soon began to abduct more suspects whose intelligence value and involvement in terrorism were less certain, creating a lower threshold for rendering suspects to the netherworld.

Almost from the beginning, the program ignited debate within the CIA about its legality and expediency of isolating and imprisoning even the most hardened terrorists in secret detention facilities. Some senior CIA officers argued that the system was unsustainable, was too reactive, and involved no long-term strategy about what to do with suspects consigned to the invisible universe. By late 2005, the CIA was holding about thirty major terrorism suspects under the highest level of secrecy at black sites financed and main-tained by the agency, including those in Eastern Europe and elsewhere. Other prisoners considered less important were transferred to intelligence services in Egypt, Morocco, and Jordan, countries known for torture and prisoner abuse. The CIA's black sites in Eastern European faced problems, involving posttotalitarian democracies that had accepted the rule of law and individual rights after decades of Soviet domination. Each of these countries also had moved to purge rogue operatives who had been working on behalf of others, including Russia, from their intelligence services. The CIA's covert program drew condemnation around the world as information about the black sites began to leak. The governments of Canada, Italy, France, Sweden, and the Netherlands opened up investigations into the CIA's abductions and rendering of their citizens or legal residents to its secret prisons.

Almost one year later, on September 6, 2006, Bush announced the exis-tence of the CIA's secret prisons for the first time. In a reversal for Cheney and bowing to the international outcry over the covert program, the presi-dent said the CIA prisons had been emptied of fourteen prisoners who had been transferred to Guantanamo into military custody for prosecution. Bush said the detainees, including al Qaeda leaders Khalid Sheik Mohammed, the mastermind of the 9/11 attacks, and Abu Zubaida, Osama bin Laden's deputy, would be given access to attorneys. By transferring the prisoners to Guantanamo with some international access, administration officials said that the United States and its allies would be "turning the page" on the covert detainee program.[55]

Bush's announcement, however, only fueled the investigations and judicial proceedings abroad, especially as the administration declared the right to revive the program in the future. Human rights organizations and other news accounts corroborated the *Washington Post's* November 2005 article, triggering further actions by international organizations in Europe.[56] The Council of Europe and the European Parliament moved to initiate inquiries and formal investigations. The Venice Commission, an advisory body of the Council of Europe, issued a preliminary legal opinion advising that member states respect human rights and the humane treatment of detainees.[57] In July 2006, the UN Human Rights Commission called for abolishing the secret prisons and granting detainees full legal protections. These inquiries involved mostly European rather than U.S. actions, but they nevertheless further tarnished America's image abroad.[58] In one high-profile case in Italy, prosecutors accused more than twenty Americans, allegedly CIA agents, for the abduction of an Egyptian cleric from Milan in 2003.[59]

For all his reversals, the vice president retained his most critical programs in the war on terror, including the use of secret prisons. After a private discussion with Cheney, the president agreed that the CIA's secret prisons could be used in the future, renouncing earlier statements by administration officials that the White House had shut down the practice. Beginning in the summer of 2007, the CIA secretly detained another suspected member of al Qaeda for at least six months as part of its program, authorized by the president, to use harsh interrogation methods. According to intelligence officials, the suspect, Muhammad Rahim, was the first prisoner to be held in CIA detention since the agency emptied its secret prisons in the fall of 2006. Intelligence officials described Rahim, an Afghan, as an al Qaeda planner and facilitator who also at times had served as a translator for Osama bin Laden. Reports of secret prisons also surfaced in February 2008, when the leading commander of detention operations at Guantanamo Bay confirmed for the first time the existence of a top secret prison facility on the island. Known as Camp 7, Rear Admiral Mark Buzby said the facility was for high-value al Qaeda members who had to be isolated out of concern that they would retaliate against other prisoners for talking to interrogators.[60]

Eleven

Iraq: A Failed Coalition and Its Aftermath

The inexorable march to war "wrecked" the international coalition, just as predicted. American diplomacy leading up to the invasion of Iraq proved to be an extraordinary failure. During the presidential campaign, Bush and others pledged to strengthen ties with U.S. allies. But as war approached, the debate over Iraq in the United Nations and in foreign capitals ruptured America's relations with some of its leading European allies. Powell's speech at the United Nations had done little to convince other governments overseas. Britain stood steadfast by its transatlantic ally, but America's claims of the imminent Iraqi threat were viewed with skepticism by other major European powers. If anything, they believed that U.S. intelligence pointed to the need of reviving the process of aggressive weapons inspections. France took the lead in opposing American military intervention, working in close cooperation with Germany and Russia. On February 15, 2003, French foreign minister Dominique de Villepin urged the UN Security Council to step back from the precipice of war. Let the inspections "provide an effective response to the imperative of disarming Iraq," he pleaded. Villepin challenged Powell's claim in his UN speech of links between al Qaeda and the Baghdad regime. "Given the present state of our research and intelligence in liaison with our allies," he said, "nothing allows us to establish such links." Opponents of war with Iraq also believed it would set the Middle East aflame, destabilizing governments in the region.[1] On February 17, 2003, Cheney met with the French ambassador at the dignitary's Washington residence. "Is France an ally or a foe?" the vice president wanted to know. The ambassador offered assurances that France remained an ally. "We have many reasons to conclude that you are not really a friend or an ally," Cheney replied.[2]

In September 2002, Bush said he would go to the UN to seek a new resolution on Iraq. That fall, Powell campaigned to win UN authorization for a tougher resolution on Iraq. While the United States wanted language authorizing UN members to use "all necessary means"—a euphemism for war if Saddam Hussein did not disarm—other governments, led by France and Russia, insisted on weapons inspections first before holding additional discussions about the use of force. A compromise was struck. The United States agreed to discard the "all necessary means" wording for language that if Iraq did not give up weapons of mass destruction, it would be considered in "material breech" of UN resolutions. By a vote of 15-0, the UN Security Council approved the resolution on November 8, 2002. With this and other past UN resolutions in place, including one calling on Iraq to disarm after the 1991 Gulf War, the United States believed it had all the authorization it needed to use force. In February 2003, the United States changed direction at the behest of Britain and sought approval for a second UN resolution authorizing military force. To ease opposition at home, Britain's prime minister Tony Blair gave assurances that he would seek clear authorization from the UN before going to war. As the effort bogged down, Bush personally weighed in on diplomatic activities to secure UN authority for war against Iraq.[3] In a whirlwind of telephone diplomacy, the president called the presidents of such countries as Chile, Mexico, and Angola to push a compromise proposal that U.S. and British officials believed could break the impasse. Six of the fifteen members of the UN Security Council remained undecided on whether to support the measure. But the efforts by Blair and Bush to win approval for a new UN resolution died when it met the unalterable opposition of France, which signaled that it would veto a second UN resolution on Iraq "whatever the circumstances."

Unlike the coalition assembled in 1991, the administration failed to convince governments in Europe and the Middle East of the urgency of going to war against Iraq. The administration's case for military action against Iraq, while utterly convincing to the president and vice president, failed to persuade many of its allies. The harder the United States pushed its case, the more it alienated them. The seeds for war against Saddam Hussein were planted well before 9/11. Wolfowitz and other conservative thinkers in the 1990s believed that the United States missed an opportunity in not toppling Saddam Hussein in 1991. They believed that he was rebuilding his stockpiles of weapons of mass destruction and that sooner or later his regime would have to be taken out. Cheney was not an adherent of these views at the time, but the terrorist attacks changed everything for him. For years, he warned against a terrorist attack on an American city. The al Qaeda hijackers confirmed some of his worst suspicions of American vulnerability. But worse things could happen if terrorists acquired a biological or nuclear weapon.

Following the attacks, America's allies remained largely in a pre-9/11 mindset, while the administration, led by the vice president, rushed to a war footing at home and abroad. The White House unleashed its full powers against what it perceived as a shadowy enemy bent on mass annihilation and a rogue regime willing to arm them with weapons of mass destruction. There was fear, even near panic, of a second imminent attack. It was best to take out Saddam Hussein's regime before it provided weapons of mass destruction to al Qaeda, who might use them against the United States. A network of domestic and foreign intelligence suggested the implausibility of this scenario, but the CIA had often been wrong in the past; they could not be trusted to get it right. America's allies may have failed to fully understand this crisis outlook after 9/11, but their skepticism proved to be accurate. The differences in perception between America and its allies about the imminent dangers of terrorism and the threat of Iraq had become seemingly unbridgeable. In a sense, Cheney may have been right in advising the administration not to seek UN authorization for military action against Iraq. The effort badly ruptured America's alliances with European powers and critically damaged its influence and credibility abroad. But the erosion of America's alliances and international influence would have happened anyway when the United States took near-unilateral military action against Saddam Hussein.

The administration received favorable winds in its march to war when, through historical circumstances, both houses of Congress turned Republican in the November 2002 elections. Even so, when the opposition Democrats were in control, the tough questions and hearings that may have stirred a national debate and caused the United States to think twice about invading Iraq never occurred. They thought it was politically risky to oppose the president with his soaring popularity after 9/11. The momentum for war also came from the administration's perception of a triumphant military. The armed forces had experienced repeated victories—Panama, the Gulf War, Bosnia, Haiti, Kosovo, and Afghanistan. Somalia was an aberration. But there was dissent within the Pentagon's brass over the administration's war plans on Iraq. Some believed it would be a misguided venture. There was no doubt the military could overrun Iraq, but little planning was given to replacing the regime. Few questioned the cost of the administration's war plan to oust Saddam Hussein and remake the map of the Middle East. Few questioned how long it would take or whether the military had the forces to do the job. Congress never gave the scrutiny to the approaching war that it deserved. The basic questions of this hugely ambitious project also were ignored by the administration as it went into Iraq. Public discussion was strangely absent. The framers of the Constitution had devised an ingenious adversarial system to keep the executive in check, yet it broke down. "The press, for whatever reason, didn't play as skeptical a role as it should have," said journalist Thomas Ricks. "Congress abdicated its constitutional role to skeptically examine the intentions and plans of the executive branch. And so the system didn't work. Rather than look to the sins of individuals, I would look to the collective failure of the system and all the people involved in it—not just the Bush administration, not just the U.S. military, but the Congress and the media as well. To have a real tragedy, everybody has to be a tragic actor, a player, like we all were."[4]

WAR'S AFTERMATH

On March 18, Bush addressed the nation from the White House, less than twelve hours after abandoning efforts to bring the Security Council behind his plan to force an immediate showdown against Iraq. The president gave Saddam Hussein forty-eight hours to flee into exile or face overwhelming force. The speech represented a failed end to six months of diplomacy aimed at convincing allies and the UN Security Council that only the use of force could disarm Saddam Hussein. Failing to garner the support of the UN, the Americans faced war, with only Britain providing major military support. Many other nations and a segment of domestic public opinion condemned the president for what they called his rush to war.[5]

On March 20, the Bush-Cheney Administration launched the war on Iraq. In three weeks, American and British forces seized Baghdad, incurring only light casualties. Hostilities continued throughout the rest of the country for another three weeks. Once again, America's military prowess was on display with all its modern weaponry. The dire predictions of ministers and diplomats in foreign capitals and critics at home skeptical of military action proved erroneous. Iraq did not attack Israel, the Arab street was not set aflame, regional governments were not toppled from power, and Iraqi forces did not use chemical or biological weapons against advancing American troops.

Equally wrong were the predictions and expectations of Cheney and the other proponents of war. After the combat phase of the war and the ouster of Saddam Hussein and his senior leadership, the Americans hoped to turn over the country to Iraqis as soon as possible. The vice president and others believed that Iraq possessed a civil service and civil society that would keep basic services going, while a new, more representative government assumed leadership. But the administration failed to understand how deeply embedded the Sunnis were in the Baath Party, the extent of their hold over the government, and the degree to which sectarian resentment and intertribal and interreligious factionalism had long plagued the country. These bitter divisions had only been exacerbated by Saddam Hussein's brutally repressive policies. The Iraqi army and police forces were unwilling to cooperate with the Americans. Rather then being greeted as "liberators," as the vice president predicted, the Americans had a fearful and mistrustful Iraqi population on their hands. These facts on the ground should have come as no surprise; they were predicted by plenty of prewar intelligence.

The Americans and British may have won the invasion, but the real war began just months afterward. By late summer 2003, coalition forces were facing rising armed resistance that would continue for years and claim the lives of thousands of American troops, far more than the losses sustained in the invasion. The vice president and other proponents of war also discovered that their fundamental rationale for invading Iraq proved utterly false. They had sounded the alarm of a rogue regime rearming with weapons of mass destruction, reconstituting its nuclear weapons program, and having ties with the al Qaeda network that struck America on 9/11. Iraq posed a gathering and imminent threat. They drew parallels to the great threats of the 20th century—to Hitlerism, militarism, and communism, all defeated by the will of free peoples and the might of the United States of America. "Once again we are called to defend the safety of our people and the hopes of mankind. And we accept this responsibility," declared the president in his January 2003 State of the Union address to the nation.[6] Yet, it was a mirage. After months of intensive searching throughout Iraq, American intelligence could find no evidence of wide-scale biological and chemical weapons programs. Nor could any evidence be found of an active and operational nuclear weapons program or that Saddam Hussein had accelerated efforts to develop a nuclear weapon in the years before the invasion.

In a January 2004 interview, David A. Kay, who led the government's efforts to find evidence of Iraq's illicit weapons programs, said that the CIA and other agencies failed to recognize that Iraq had all but abandoned its efforts to produce large quantities of chemical or biological weapons after the Gulf War in 1991. In the months leading up to the war, Cheney referred to "irrefutable" evidence showing Iraq to be reconstituting its nuclear weapons program. The allegation proved mistaken. Kay said that Iraq largely abandoned its quest for nuclear weapons in the 1990s, but that it did make an effort to restart its nuclear weapons program in 2000 and 2001. The effort was rudimentary at best and would have taken years to rebuild. Even so, the Iraqi dictator had become increasingly isolated and fantasy-driven, plunging Iraq into a "vortex of corruption," he said. Whatever remained of Iraq's weapons capability, he said, had become corrupted by money-raising schemes by scientists adept in the art of lying and surviving in Saddam Hussein's police state.[7]

The administration fell into an ill-conceived occupation of Iraq that ignited a deadly years-long insurgency. From the beginning, the proponents of the war inadequately prepared for the postinvasion period, underestimating the immense obstacles in replacing Saddam Hussein's regime. The United States sent in, with misplaced confidence, an American governor to oversee Iraq and its transition to representative government with disastrous consequences. The intelligence community sounded warnings of what could be expected in invading and trying to govern Iraq: anarchy, interethnic/ tribal violence, threats from Baathists who would "use any means necessary" to return to power and resist the occupation, and a surge of terrorism. These predictions came to pass. The military committed 130,000 troops to battle the rising insurgency and terrorist attacks from home-grown Jihadists and fighters from other Arab countries. The toppling of Saddam Hussein created a power vacuum from the start. The country spun out of control almost immediately with sporadic looting and the arms depots and nuclear material facilities remaining unsecured and unguarded. Iraq's ministries and institutions collapsed, undercutting the optimism in the White House and Pentagon that the civilian agencies would assume much of the burden for governing Iraq.

With its postwar planning in crisis, the military took on unanticipated occupation duties, was forced to develop new intelligence-gathering techniques, armor its Humvees, revise its tactics, and after the Abu Ghraib torture scandal, review its detention policies. After coming out of high-intensity battle, American troops found themselves among a suspicious population and in a culture they did not understand. The troops were forced to adapt in the face of a brewing insurgency and unanticipated occupation duties. L. Paul Bremer III, who replaced Jay Garner, the retired lieutenant general, as the chief civilian administrator in Iraq, plunged circumstances into deep crisis by issuing decrees disbanding the Iraqi army and banning thousands of former Baath Party members from working in the government. The decrees took U.S. commanders by surprise, creating thousands of disaffected and unemployed Sunni Arabs who fueled the insurgency.[8]

Fifteen months after Saddam Hussein was swept from power, American authorities in Baghdad, in a highly secret ceremony to foil possible terrorist attacks, turned over sovereignty to Iraqi leaders. The formal transfer of power did little to quell the chaos. American troops battled armed resistance, terrorist attacks, and murderous sectarian violence. On January 31, 2006, an internal report by the U.S. Embassy and the military command in Baghdad provided a sobering report of Iraq's political, economic, and security situation. The report came three weeks before the bombing of a revered Shiite shrine in Samarra redoubled the fury of sectarian violence. The report noted that ethnic and religious schisms had become entrenched across the country. Mass migrations from mixed Sunni-Shiite areas revealed a de facto partitioning along ethnic and sectarian lines with killings taking place in those areas where the differing groups jointly resided. Zalmay Khalilzad, the American ambassador to Iraq who in the late 1990s supported the liberation of Iraq, said the invasion had opened a "Pandora's box," warning that a civil war could engulf the entire Middle East.[9] The warning seemed plausible at the time but proved to be overstated.

In 2007, the Americans embarked on a different strategy under General David Petraeus, the new top U.S. commander in Iraq. The strategy involved adding thousands more troops, implementing a new counterinsurgency strategy, enlisting the support of thousands of Sunnis to patrol neighborhoods and fight the insurgency, and pushing the majority Shiite government to strike political compromises with other sectarian factions in Iraq. By spring 2008, these developments along with the Iraqi government's crackdown on Shiite militias were producing significant results. American casualties and sectarian killings plunged as a growing but tentative peace spread throughout the country. By midsummer, the Iraqi government and the United States began shifting focus from mainly combat to building the fragile beginnings of peace—a development almost unthinkable one year previously. The new phase focused on training the Iraqi army and police, restraining the flow of illicit weapons from Iran, supporting closer links between Baghdad and local governments, pushing for the integration of former insurgents into legitimate government jobs, and assisting in rebuilding the economy. The lull in the violence seemed to reflect a fundamental shift in the outlook for the Sunni minority, which held power under Saddam Hussein. Largely responsible for launching the insurgency in 2003, many had switched sides to cooperate with the Americans in return for money and political support. At the same time, the Shiite militias had lost their power bases in Baghdad, Basra, and other major cities as they suffered a loss of support among a Shiite population weary of war and no longer terrified of Sunni extremists. But Iraq remained badly fractured and faced tremendous problems: sectarian rivalries, power struggles within the Sunni and Shiite communities, Kurdish-Arab tensions, and corruption—conditions that could once again ignite widespread fighting.

In the final analysis, the vice president, leading the administration's case for war, misjudged whether Saddam Hussein possessed weapons of mass destruction. He was wrong about Iraqi links to al Qaeda. Before the war, the CIA assessed that Saddam Hussein viewed Islamic extremists operating inside Iraq as a threat and that Saddam Hussein and Osama bin Laden were far from being natural partners. Cheney also miscalculated what the aftermath of the invasion would look like. The descent into sectarian violence and the cost in American blood and treasure was not what Cheney expected. Rather than dealing a blow to terrorism throughout the region, the war fueled jihadist terrorist attacks throughout the world. He was wrong on nearly every account. But he remained adamant that the administration must stay the course in Iraq, not "cut and run." By 2008, the war had cost more than 4,000 American lives, almost 30,000 wounded, and more than half a trillion dollars. The war had eroded U.S. military readiness to the point that American commanders conceded that the army was at its breaking point. A General Accountability Office (GAO) report issued in June 2008 found that the United States did not have a strategy for meetings its goals in Iraq. The GAO report concluded that although violence had diminished, only about 10 percent of Iraqi units were capable of conducting operations without U.S. assistance. The Iraqi authorities passed legislation allowing lower-level Baathists to return to the parliament, but still could not reach a compromise on oil sharing and the holding of provincial elections.[10] The war had damaged America's worldwide credibility, legitimacy, and moral standing. It inflamed anti-American passions in the Middle East and South Asia, while shattering Iraqi society. By overthrowing Saddam Hussein, as brutal as he was, the war increased the influence of America's adversary and Iraq's eternal foe, Iran. It also diminished the war against al Qaeda and the Taliban in Afghanistan. Former national security advisor Zbigniew Brzesinski called the war nothing short of a "national tragedy, an economic catastrophe, a regional disaster and a global boomerang for the United States."[11]

As the Pentagon began achieving a fragile peace in Iraq, more than five years after the invasion, violence was surging in Afghanistan. The administration and the vice president had defined Iraq as the priority, giving time for Taliban and al Qaeda forces to regroup after the American-led invasion in 2001. With no exit strategy for Iraq, the swelling forces of Taliban and al Qaeda forces began posing a graver threat to American and coalition troops in Afghanistan. Violence spread to once-peaceful areas. The growing tide of militant forces also began threatening Pakistan, as its military and political leaders, caught up in their own power struggles, were failing to confront the danger. "We believe," said a *New York Times* editorial, "that the fight against Al Qaeda is the central battle for this generation, but Mr. Bush's claim that Iraq is the main front is wrong. That is Afghanistan, and the United States is in real danger of losing because Mr. Bush's failed adventure in Iraq is eating up the Pentagon's resources and attention."[12]

Tied down by two wars, the administration found itself largely impotent in confronting a more conservative and resurgent Iran, the world's foremost sponsor of terrorism. The American wars in Afghanistan and Iraq, bordering either side of Iran, freed the Shiite regime to strengthen its influence throughout the Middle East to the alarm of Sunni governments throughout the region. Iran wielded greater influence in Lebanon and Gaza through support of Hezbollah and Hamas. It strengthened ties with Syria, another regime isolated by the United States. It began making overtures to the new Shiite government in Baghdad, while funneling weapons and money to Iraq's Shiite militias in a bid to win influence and Lebanonize Iraq. More alarming, it embarked on an accelerated program of uranium enrichment, including developing suspected nuclear weapons. As it turned out, the chimera of Saddam Hussein's aggressive pursuit of weapons of mass destruction and links to terrorist networks blinded the administration to the possible greater nuclear threat from Iran.

On the home front, the administration was given enormous latitude to respond to the attacks and fortify the nation against a second wave of terrorist assaults. Cheney and his allies took the lead in pioneering a legal revolution to defend the nation. As the country moved to a war footing, his ideology of executive supremacy, long in the making, came into play. He endeavored to transform the state of emergency into a new and permanent status quo on behalf of executive power. Because the war on terror would last decades, the state of emergency should remain in place. He believed the world was a dark and deadly place and the country needed a strong and unfettered executive to meet the challenge. The war on terror involved a fight "for the future of civilization," he had said. The extra-legal measures, the disdain for Congress, the courts, and international allies, as well as the obsession with secrecy became enduring features of the administration. The efforts to roll back the "unwise decisions" of the 1970s and the lack of transparency were hallmarks of the vice president's office from the first days of the administration. The agenda of reclaiming the so-called lost powers of the presidency had already been set in motion. Cheney's extralegal policies sparked white-hot debate over the administration's war on terror. They also produced a more suspicious Congress and judiciary. The administration was forced to go back to Congress for authorization for many of its secret initiatives. At the same time, the courts extended the nation's sovereign law, including habeas corpus, to detainees at Guantanamo, striking down the administration's far-reaching claims of unilateral executive authority.

After decades of being the minority party, the Republicans won majorities in both Houses of Congress. Throughout most of the president's two terms in office, GOP leaders surrendered Congress's institutional prerogatives and historic legislative commitments, supporting the White House's policies in exchange for partisan dominance. At the same time, Democrats could scarcely muster opposition to the administration's policies for fear of being labeled weak on terrorism. The constitutional framers created Congress as the first branch of government. They designed it explicitly to check executive power. Congressional members on both sides of the aisle not only failed to ask the tough questions about the rush to war in Iraq, but also allowed the administration to pursue extreme extralegal measures that overran the laws of the land and international treaties. In 2006, the Democrats won slim majorities in the House and Senate, forcing the administration to retreat on some of its more extreme measures. By the summer of 2008, Republicans had also grown weary of the administration's disdain for congressional oversight. In response to a secret presidential order expanding the powers of the national intelligence director, for example, House Republicans on the intelligence committee walked out of a White House briefing on the directive over what they believed was the administration's pattern of disrespect for their oversight role. The administration had shut out the intelligence committee on a range of issues, including Israel's bombing of a suspected Syrian nuclear facility, changes in U.S. intelligence on Iran, and the government's warrantless wiretapping program. It remains to be seen, however, whether Congress as a whole can strengthen its oversight role over national security issues and restore the balance of powers.

Further, it remains to be seen whether Cheney's imperial vice presidency has been an aberration in the history of the office or whether it will set new patterns for his successors. From the beginning, Cheney worked his will on the executive branch. He negotiated an extraordinary portfolio that defined his office as an imperial vice presidency. His portfolio included the central issues of concern to any president—economic issues, intelligence and national security, energy, and the administration's legislative agenda. He placed numerous allies and loyalists in key posts throughout the administration, built a large parallel national security staff, and extended his reach down to the sub-Cabinet levels where his predecessors were rarely seen. After 9/11, Cheney became the quiet but animating force behind the administration's war on terror, overshadowing the secretary of state, the national security advisor, the director of the CIA, and other senior administration aides. His influence stemmed in large part from the president's inexperience and proclivity to delegate broad swaths of his powers to the more experienced vice president. It was a circumstance that could not be imagined under the presidencies of John F. Kennedy, Lyndon Johnson, or Richard Nixon. Or even under the elder Bush, who selected a callow vice president to serve as little more than a faithful and loyal aide. Under the elder Bush's administration, Cheney's tendencies for pushing the edge on executive power as secretary of defense had been held in check. A decade later, in the younger Bush's administration, Cheney won free rein to assert novel and sweeping claims of executive power. The results are yet to be fully understood.

Notes

INTRODUCTION

1. Arthur M. Schlesinger, Jr., *The Imperial Presidency* (Boston: Houghton Mifflin Company, 1973), ix–x.

2. Interview with David Gergen, "Cheney's Law," *Frontline*, http://www.pbs.org/wgbh/pages/frontline/cheneyview.html (accessed 16 September 2008).

CHAPTER 1

1. See U.S. Constitution, Article II, Section I; James Madison, *Notes on the Debates in the Federal Convention of 1787*.

2. Joseph Ellis, *Founding Brothers* (New York: Alfred A. Knopf, 2001), 166; Arthur M. Schlesinger, Jr., "On the Presidential Succession," *Political Science Quarterly* 89, no. 3 (1974): 475–506.

3. Ellis, *Founding Brothers*, 165–66, 187; J. D. Feerick, *From Failing Hands: The Story of Presidential Succession* (New York: Fordham University Press, 1965), 70.

4. Ellis, *Founding Brothers*, 165–66, 187; Feerick, *From Failing Hands*, 70.

5. Schlesinger, "On the Presidential Succession," 478.

6. Feerick, *From Failing Hands*, 52, 54.

7. C. C. Tansill, ed., *Documents Illustrative of the Formation of the Union of the American States* (Washington: Government Printing Office, 1927), 682.

8. H. C. Syrett, ed. *Alexander Hamilton, Papers*, Vol. V (New York: Colombia University Press, 1962), 248.

9. See Mark O. Hatfield, Senate Document No. 26, *Vice Presidents of the United States, 1789–1993*, U.S. Congressional Serial Set, Serial No. 14332 (Washington: Government Printing Office, 1997), xv–xvi; Schlesinger, "On the Presidential Succession," 49; Michael V. DiSalle and Lawrence G. Blochmann, *Second Choice* (New York: Hawthorn Books, 1966), 15; Jody C. Baumgartner, *The American Vice Presidency Reconsidered* (Westport, CT: Praeger, 2006), 9.

10. Hatfield, *Vice Presidents of the United States, 1789–1993*, xviii; Ellis, *Founding Brothers*, 165; Feerick, *From Failing Hands*, 70.

11. Michael Nelson, *A Heartbeat Away* (New York: Twentieth Century Fund, 1988), 30.

12. Feerick, *From Failing Hands*, 73; Schlesinger, "On the Presidential Succession," 491–92.

13. See Hatfield, *Vice Presidents of the United States*, xviii–xix, 96; DiSalle and Blochman, *Second Choice*, 25.

14. See Robert Seager II, *And Tyler Too: A Biography of John & Julia Gardiner Tyler* (Norwalk, CT: McGraw-Hill, 1963), 149; Hatfield, *Vice Presidents of the United States*, 143.

15. U.S. Constitution, 25th Amendment, Article II, section 1, passed by Congress July 6, 1965; ratified February 10, 1967.

16. Senate Document No. 26, *Vice Presidents of the United States, 1789–1993*, xix; Schlesinger, "On the Presidential Succession," 492.

17. Hatfield, *Vice Presidents of the United States*, xix.

18. Schlesinger, "On the Presidential Succession," 490.

19. Lucius Wilmerding, Jr., *The Electoral College* (Boston: Beacon Paperback, 1964), 33–34.

20. Feerick, *From Failing Hands*, 115.

21. Schlesinger, "On the Presidential Succession," 486. Also see Joel K. Goldstein, *The Modern American Vice Presidency* (Princeton, NJ: Princeton University Press, 1982), 8; Hatfield, *Vice Presidents of the United States, 1789–1993*, xx.

22. Alben Barkley, *That Reminds Me* (Garden City, NY: Doubleday, 1954), 221.

23. Alvin S. Felzenberg, "The Vice Presidency Grows Up," *Policy Review* 105, February/March (2001), 13–25.

24. Quoted in Michael Turner, *The Vice President as Policy Maker: Rockefeller in the Ford White House* (Westport, CT: Greenwood Press, 1982), xiii.

25. James MacGregor Burns, *Roosevelt: The Soldier of Freedom* (New York: Harcourt, Brace Jovanovich, 1970), 341–42; Cordell Hull, *The Memoirs of Cordell Hull*, Vol. II (New York: Macmillan, 1948), 1585–86; Goldstein, *The Modern American Vice Presidency*, 136; Merle Miller, *Plain Speaking: An Oral Biography of Harry S. Truman* (New York: Berkley Publishing Co., 1973), 187.

26. See David McCullough, *Truman* (New York: Simon & Schuster, 1992), 308.

27. Merle Miller, *Plain Speaking: An Oral Biography of Harry S. Truman*, 210.

28. Barkley, *That Reminds Me*, 221. *Congressional Quarterly*, "New Interest in the Vice Presidency," April 4, 1956, http://library.cqpress.com/cqresearcher/document.php?id=cqresrre19.

29. Dwight D. Eisenhower, *Waging Peace: The White House Years, 1956-61* (Garden City, NY: Doubleday, 1965), 316; Richard M. Nixon, *Memoirs of Richard Nixon* (New York: Grosset & Dunlap, 1978), 193–99.

30. *Congressional Quarterly*, "New Interest in the Vice Presidency," April 4, 1956.

31. Dwight D. Eisenhower, *Mandate for Change: The White House Years, 1953–56* (Garden City, NY: Doubleday, 1963), 236.

32. See Goldstein, *The Modern American Vice Presidency*, 152; Nixon makes no mention of his vice presidential assignments in his first memoir, *Six Crises* (Garden City, NY: Doubleday, 1962); Also see Nixon, *Memoirs of Richard Nixon*, 193–99.

33. Robert Dallek, *Flawed Giant: Lyndon Johnson and His Times, 1961–1973* (New York: Oxford University Press, 1998), 9–11.

34. See Theodore C. Sorensen, *Kennedy* (New York: Harper & Row, 1965), 266; Lewis J. Paper, *The Promise and the Performance: The Leadership of John F. Kennedy* (New York: Crown Publishers, 1975), 267–68.

35. George Christian, *The President Steps Down* (New York: Macmillan, 1970), 148.

36. Quoted in *Congressional Quarterly*, "Politics and the Vice President," November 11, 1970, http://library.cqpress.com/cqresearcher/document.php?id=cqresrre19.

37. Jimmy Carter, *Keeping Faith: Memoirs of a President* (New York: Bantam Books, 1982), 39–40; Paul C. Light, *Vice Presidential Power: Advice and Influence in the White House* (Baltimore, MD: Johns Hopkins University Press, 1984), 1.

38. Steven M. Gillon, "A New Framework: Walter Mondale as Vice President," in *At the President's Side: The Vice Presidency in the Twentieth Century*, ed. Timothy Walch (Columbia: University of Missouri Press, 1997), 146.

39. Nelson, *A Heartbeat Away*, 30.

40. Elaine Sciolino and Todd S. Purdum, "Al Gore, One Vice President Who is Eluding the Shadows," *New York Times*, February 19, 1995; Editorial, "Reinventing Al Gore," *New York Times*, March 21, 1999.

41. Sciolino and Purdum, "Al Gore, One Vice President Who Is Eluding the Shadows"; Editorial, "Reinventing Al Gore."

42. "Lexington: Reinventing the Vice Presidency," *The Economist* 322, 7880, (September 10, 1994).

43. Kenneth T. Walsh, "The Cheney Factor," *U.S. News & World Report*, January 15, 2006.

CHAPTER 2

1. Stephen F. Hayes, *Cheney: The Untold Story of America's Most Powerful and Controversial Vice President* (New York: HarperCollins, 2007), 52–54; "Poverty: A Losing War," *Newsweek*, November 23, 1970.

2. James Reston, "Keep an Eye on Rummy," *New York Times*, October 4, 1974.

3. Martin Tolchin, "Congressional Fellowship: Up a Golden Ladder," *New York Times*, February 3, 1984. Also see Hayes, *Cheney*, 54; Lou Dubose and Jake Bernstein, *Vice: Dick Cheney and the Hijacking of the American Presidency* (New York: Random House, 2006), 24.

4. Hayes, *Cheney*, 54.

5. "The Administration: Rumsfeld on the Rise," *Newsweek*, December 28, 1970, 17.

6. Charlie Savage, *Takeover: The Return of the Imperial Presidency and the Subversion of American Democracy* (New York: Little, Brown and Company, 2007), 22–23.

7. Quoted in Hayes, *Cheney*, 57–58.

8. Jack Rosenthal, "Advocate for the Poor," *New York Times*, August 29, 1969; Israel Shenker, "New Breed of Lawyer Serving Poor," *New York Times*, August 30, 1969.

9. Reston, "Keep an Eye on Rummy"; Savage, *Takeover*, 23–24.

10. Jack Rosenthal, "Lawyers Groups Fighting Proposed Plan to Decentralize Legal Aid to Poor," *New York Times*, September 22, 1970; Jack Rosenthal, "OEO Chief Rejects Legal Aide Changes," *New York Times*, November 13, 1970; Paul Delaney, "Antipoverty Director Is Accused of Curbing Legal Services Chief," *New York Times*, November 19, 1970.

11. "Rumsfeld on the Rise," *Newsweek*, December 28, 1970, 17; Savage, *Takeover*, 25.

12. "Legal Aid Director Ousted by Rumsfeld; Aide also Dropped," *New York Times*, November 21, 1970; Thomas P. Ronan, "Head of Legal Aid Unit for Poor Here Scores OEO Dismissals," *New York Times*, December 3, 1970; Editorial, "A Blow to Legal Services," *New York Times*, November 23, 1970; "The Administration: Rumsfeld on the Rise," *Newsweek*, December 28, 1970, 17.

13. "Rumsfeld on the Rise," 17; Savage, *Takeover*, 25.

14. "Rumsfeld on the Rise," 18.

15. Hayes, *Cheney*, 61–62.

16. Quoted in Hayes, *Cheney*, 67.

17. Linda Charlton, "Rumsfeld Chosen as Envoy to NATO," *New York Times*, December 5, 1972; Leslie H. Gelb, "Successor to Haig," *New York Times*, September 25, 1974; Dubose and Bernstein, *Vice*, 25; Savage, *Takeover*, 25; Hayes, *Cheney*, 68–69.

18. Henry A. Kissinger, *Years of Upheaval* (Boston and Toronto: Little, Brown and Company, 1982), 105.

19. Kissinger, *Years of Upheaval*, 114.

20. War Powers Act of 1973, Public Law 93-148, 93rd Cong., H.J. Res. 542; James Reston, "Unbalanced Government," *New York Times*, May 16, 1971; Arthur Schlesinger, "Fallacies of the War-Powers Bill," *New York Times*, January 5, 1972; Richard L. Madden, "House and Senate Override Veto by Nixon on Curb of War Powers," *New York Times*, November 8, 1973; Kissinger, *Years of Upheaval*, 510.

21. Bob Woodward, "Cheney Upholds Power of the President," *Washington Post*, January 20, 2005.

22. Quotation in Lincoln Capland, "Who Cares About Executive Supremacy?" *American Scholar* (Winter 2008); *United States v. Nixon*, 418 U.S. (1974).

23. Reston, "Keep an Eye on Rummy"; Dubose and Bernstein, *Vice*, 25-26; Savage, *Takeover*, 26; Hayes, *Cheney*, 70.

24. Hayes, *Cheney*, 76.

25. Interview with David Gergen, "Cheney's Law," *Frontline*, http://www.pbs.org/wgbh/pages/frontline/cheney/themes/cheneyview.html (accessed 16 September 2008); Philip Shabecoff, "Rumsfeld Likely to Replace Haig," *New York Times*, Septmber 24, 1974; Gelb, "Successor to Haig."

26. Interview with David Gergen, "Cheney's Law."

27. John Herbers, "Ford Acts to Curb Own Powers in a More Informal Presidency," *New York Times*, August 17, 1974.

28. Quoted in Andrew Rudalevige, *The New Imperial Presidency* (Ann Arbor: University of Michigan Press, 2005), 60.

29. See Congressional Budget and Impoundment Control Act of 1974; "Dispute on Nixon's Powers," *New York Times*, October 1, 1972; Marjorie Hunter, "House Acts to Cut President's Right to Impound Funds," *New York Times*, November 25, 1973; John Herbers, "Ford Acts to Curb Own Powers in a More Informal Presidency." Also see Louis Fisher, *Congressional Abdication on War and Spending* (College Station: Texas A&M Press, 2000); Allen J. Matusow, *Nixon's Economy: Booms, Busts, Dollars, and Votes* (Lawrence: University Press of Kansas, 1998); James P. Pfiffner, *The President, Budget, and Congress: Impoundment and the 1974 Budget Act* (Boulder, CO: Westview Press, 1979).

30. See Rudalevige, *The New Imperial Presidency*, 60–64; Congressional Budget and Impoundment Control Act of 1974; "Dispute on Nixon's Powers," *New York Times*, October 1, 1972; Marjorie Hunter, "House Acts to Cut President's Right to Impound Funds"; John Herbers, "Ford Acts to Curb Own Powers in a More Informal Presidency."

31. John Herbers, "Ford Acts to Curb Own Powers in a More Informal Presidency."

32. See Schlesinger, *The Imperial Presidency*, ix–x.

33. Editorial, "President and Congress," *New York Times*, October 21, 1974.

34. See text of agreement between Richard M. Nixon and Arthur F. Sampson reprinted in Congressional Record, 93rd Cong., 2nd Sess., 1974, 120, Pt. 25, 33965. Also see Cong. Record, 93rd Cong., 2nd Sess., 1974, Pt. 25, 32290, 32465, 32501, 33848, 33850–51, 33855, 33857, 33860; James Naughton, "Senate Bids Ford Undo Nixon Pact and Retains Tapes," *New York Times*, October 5, 1974; Mary McCarthy, "Postscript to Nixon," *New York Review of Books*, October 17, 1974, 10–13; I. F. Stone, "The Fix," *New York Review of Books*, October 3, 1974, 6–8; "Nixon's Crisis—And Ford's," *Newsweek*, September 23, 1974; Stanley I. Kutler, *The Wars of Watergate: The Last Crisis of Richard Nixon* (New York: Alfred A. Knopf, 1990), 563; Stanley I. Kutler, *Abuse of Power: The Nixon Tapes* (New York: The Free Press, 1997), xiv; Dubose and Bernstein, *Vice*, 28–29.

35. See text of agreement between Richard M. Nixon and Arthur F. Sampson reprinted in Congressional Record, 93rd Cong., 2nd Sess., 1974, 120, Pt. 25, 33965. Also see Cong. Record, 93rd Cong., 2nd Sess., 1974, Pt. 25, 32290, 32465, 32501, 33848, 33850-51, 33855, 33857, 33860; Naughton, "Senate Bids Ford Undo Nixon Pact and Retains Tapes"; McCarthy, "Postscript to Nixon," 10–13; Stone, "The Fix," 6–8; "Nixon's Crisis—And Ford's," *Newsweek*, September 23, 1974; Kutler, *The Wars of Watergate: The Last Crisis of Richard Nixon*, 563; Kutler, *Abuse of Power: The Nixon Tapes*, xiv; Dubose and Bernstein, *Vice*, 28–29.

36. "The Election: Bitter Harvest," *Newsweek*, November 4, 1974.

37. "The Big Sweep: What Now?" *Newsweek*, November 18, 1974.

38. See FOIA, 5 U.S.C. Section 552 (b). The statute's nine exemptions include 1) classified information; 2) internal agency personnel rules and practices; 3) information specifically exempted from disclosure by statute; 4) private commercial and trade

secret information; 5) interagency or intraagency privilege communications; 6) personnel, medical, or similar files, the disclosure of which would constitute a clearly unwarranted invasion of personnel privacy; 7) information compiled for law enforcement purposes; 8) information relating to reports for or by an agency involved in regulating financial institutions; and 9) geological information concerning oil wells.

39. Office of the White House Press Secretary, *Statement by the President Upon Signing S. 1160*, July 4, 1966; "Bill Moyers on the Freedom of Information Act," NOW, April 5, 2002, http://www.pbs.org/now/commentary/moyers4.html (accessed 16 September 2008).

40. See Marjorie Hunter, "Public Access to Data Said to Lag," *New York Times*, September 22, 1972; David K. Shipler, "Antisecrecy Bills Offered in House," *New York Times*, February 24, 1973; Robert Reinhold, "Experts Ask Congress to Ease Flow of Information to Public," *New York Times*, November 20, 1973.

41. Richard L. Madden, "By 383, House Votes Bill to Strengthen Public Access to Government Information," *New York Times*, May 15, 1974; Richard L. Madden, "Senate Votes to Ease Access to Federal Documents," *New York Times*, May 31, 1974.

42. Madden, "Senate Votes to Ease Access to Federal Documents."

43. Savage, *Takeover*, 27.

44. Martin Arnold, "Congress, the Press, and Federal Agencies Are Taking Sides for Battle over Government's Right to Secrecy," *New York Times*, November 15, 1974; James M. Naughten, "House Overrides Two Ford Vetoes by Huge Margin," *New York Times*, November 21, 1974.

45. Seymour Hersh, "Huge CIA Operation Reported in U.S. Against Antiwar Forces, Other Dissidents in Nixon Years," *New York Times*, December 22, 1974.

46. Tim Weiner, "Files on Illegal Spying Show CIA Skeletons from Cold War," *New York Times*, June 27, 2007; Alex Johnson, "CIA Opens the Book on a Shady Past," available at http://www.msnbc.msn.com/id/19438161/, June 26, 2007 (accessed 16 September 2008); Tim Weiner, *Legacy of Ashes: The History of the CIA* (New York: Doubleday, 2007), 336–39.

47. Quotation in Savage, *Takeover*, 28; Hayes, *Cheney*, 84–85; Weiner, *Legacy of Ashes*, 337; "A New CIA Furor," *Newsweek*, January 6, 1975.

48. Quotations in Weiner, *Legacy of Ashes*, 338.

49. See "Text of Report by Colby in Response to Charges of Domestic Spying by CIA," *New York Times*, January 16, 1974.

50. James R. Gaines, Anthony Marino, and Stephan Lesher, "Investigation: The FBI's Turn," *Newsweek*, February 17, 1975.

51. *Final Report of the Select Committee to Study Governmental Operations with Respect to Intelligence Activities*, U.S. Senate, April 1976 [hereafter Church Report]; Kissinger, *Years of Upheaval*, 495.

52. Weiner, *Legacy of Ashes*, 346.

53. Savage, *Takeover*, 30.

54. Weiner, *Legacy of Ashes*, 346–47.

55. Tom Wicker, "Mr. Ford Reaches Both Ways," *New York Times*, November 4, 1975; Philip Shabecoff, "Mutual Decision: Vice President's Letter Gives No

Reason for His Withdrawal," *New York Times*, November 4, 1975; James Reston, "Mr. Ford's Machismo," *New York Times*, November 5, 1975; "Shotgun Separation," *New York Times*, November 9, 1975; Weiner, *Legacy of Ashes*, 346–47.

56. U.S. Senate, Church Report, April 1976. Also see *Legislative Oversight of Intelligence Activities: The U.S. Experience: Report*. Washington, D.C.: U.S. Government Printing Office, 1994; Brad Roberts, *U.S. Foreign Policy After the Cold War* (Cambridge, MA: MIT Press, 1992); Frank J. Smist, Jr., "Seeking a Piece of the Action: Congress and Its Intelligence Investigation of 1975–1976," in *Gerald R. Ford and the Politics of Post-Watergate America*, Vol. 2, ed. Bernard J. Firestone and Alexej Ugrinksi (Westport, CT: Greenwood, 1993), 463.

57. Weiner, *Legacy of Ashes*, 351.

58. Savage, *Takeover*, 30.

59. Quoted in Dubose and Bernstein, *Vice*, 37; also see Savage, *Takeover*, 37.

60. See "Text of Ford's Plan on Intelligence Units and Excerpts from His Executive Order," *New York Times*, February 19, 1976.

61. Church Report. Also see "Frank Church: Idaho's Man," Idaho Oral History Project, Boise State University, http://idahooratory.boisestate.edu/churchbio2.htm (accessed 16 September 2008); Savage, *Takeover*, 29.

62. Quoted in Weiner, *Legacy of Ashes*, 348.

63. "Ford's Rescue Operation," *Newsweek*, May 26, 1975; Ron Nessen, *It Sure Looks Different from the Inside* (Chicago: Playbook Press, 1978), 123–24; Philip Shabecoff, "Ford is Backed: Senate Unit Endorses His Right to Order Military Action," *New York Times*, May 15, 1975; Sydney H. Schanberg, "Mayaguez Captain Tells Story of Rescue," *New York Times*, May 18, 1975; Philip Shabecoff, "U.S. Now Reports 15 Dead in Recapture of Mayaguez," *New York Times*, May 21, 1975; Philip Shabecoff, "23 Dead in Copter Crash Related to the Mayaguez," *New York Times*, May 22, 1975; "Ford's Rescue Operation," *Newsweek*, May 26, 1975.

64. Seymour Hersh, "Submarines of U.S. Stage Spy Missions Inside Soviet Waters," *New York Times*, May 25, 1975.

65. Dubose and Bernstein, *Vice*, 34–35.

66. Alan Theoharis, *Spying on Americans: Political Surveillance from Hoover to the Houston Plan* (Philadelphia: Temple University Press, 1978), 148; also see James Kirkpatrick Davis, *Spying on America: The FBI's Domestic Counterintelligence Program* (Westport, CT: Praeger, 1992); Ward Churchill and Jim Vander Wal, *The COINTELPRO Papers: Documents from the FBI's Secret Wars against Domestic Dissent* (Boston: South End Press, 1990), 125, 213–16; Dubose and Bernstein, *Vice*, 36.

CHAPTER 3

1. See Nessen, *It Sure Looks Different from the Inside*, 133; John J. Casserly, *The Ford White House: The Diary of a Speechwriter* (Boulder: Colorado Associated University Press, 1977), 126–27.

2. Quotation in Hayes, *Cheney*, 92–93. Also Nessen, *It Sure Looks Different from the Inside*, 133; Casserly, *The Ford White House: The Diary of a Speechwriter*, 126–27.

3. Charles Mohr, "New Chief Assistant," *New York Times*, November 5, 1975.

4. Philip Shabecoff, "Rumsfeld Likely to Replace Haig," *New York Times*, September 24, 1974; Leslie H. Gelb, "Successor to Haig," *New York Times*, September 25, 1974.

5. Interview with David Gergen, "Cheney's Law," *Frontline*, http://www.pbs.org/wgbh/pages/frontline/cheney/themes/cheneyview.html (accessed 16 September 2008); Shabecoff, "Rumsfeld Likely to Replace Haig"; Gelb, "Successor to Haig"; Gerald R. Ford, *A Time to Heal* (New York: Harper & Row, 1979), 132.

6. Interview with David Gergen, "Cheney's Law"; Shabecoff, "Rumsfeld Likely to Replace Haig"; Interview with James Cannon, quoted in Dubose and Bernstein, *Vice*, 27.

7. Nessen, *It Sure Looks Different from the Inside*, 161.

8. Dubose and Bernstein, *Vice*, 39.

9. Frank Lynn, "Rockefeller Seen in Tune with Ford on Vital Issues," *New York Times*, August 21, 1974; Linda Charlton, "Rockefeller's Future," *New York Times*, September 14, 1974.

10. Charlton, "Rockefeller's Future."

11. Samuel Kernell and Samuel L. Popkin, "Tales from the Top: Eight Former Chiefs of Staff Reflect," *Washington Monthly*, March 1987.

12. Jude Wanniski, "The Vice President Who Might Have Been," *Wall Street Journal*, August 12, 1976; Joseph Lelyveld, "Rockefeller Has Made Something of His New Job," *New York Times*, September 28, 1975.

13. Wanniski, *Wall Street Journal*, August 12, 1976.

14. Cannon, *Time and Chance*, 407; Ford, *A Time to Heal*, 327–28; Yanek Mieczzkowski, *Gerald Ford and the Challenges of the 1970s*, (Lexington: University of Kentucky Press, 2005), 311.

15. See Robert T. Hartmann, *Palace Politics: An Inside Account of the Ford Years* (New York: McGraw-Hill, 1980), 35; John Osborne, "Nice Guy with Villains," *New York Times*, August 10, 1980.

16. Lou Cannon, *Governor Reagan: His Rise to Power* (New York: Public Affairs, 2003).

17. Nessen, *It Sure Looks Different from the Inside*, 249.

18. Philip Shabecoff, "Ford's Primary Losses Divide White House Staff as Factions Trade Charges of Laxity," *New York Times*, May 24, 1976.

19. Quoted in John Nichols, *The Rise and Rise of Richard B. Cheney* (New York: The New Press, 2004), 67.

20. See Shabecoff, "Ford's Primary Losses Divide White House Staff as Factions Trade Charges of Laxity."

21. Nessen, *It Sure Looks Different From the Inside*, 162.

22. Quoted in Dubose and Bernstein, *Vice*, 41.

23. Quoted in Hayes, *Cheney*, 120.

24. Hartmann, *Palace Politics: An Inside Account of the Ford Years*, 283.

25. Quoted in Dubose and Bernstein, *Vice*, 32.

26. John Herbers, "On Record, Jordan's Job Has Proved Thankless," *New York Times*, July 29, 1979.

27. 5 USC 55 2b.

28. See Public Law 92-463; Jay S. Bybee, "Advising the President: Separations of Powers and the Federal Advisory Committee Act," *Yale Law Journal* 104 (October 1994), 51–128.

29. Levi guidelines quoted in Athan G. Theoharis, "FBI Surveillance: Past and Present," *Cornell Law Review* 69 (April 1984), 889.

30. Executive Order 12036, January 24, 1978; Rudalevige, *The New Imperial Presidency*, 112; Geoffrey R. Stone, "The Reagan Amendment, the First Amendment, and FBI Domestic Security Investigations," in *Freedom at Risk*, ed. Richard O. Curry, (Philadelphia: Temple University Press, 1988), 277.

31. See Public Law 95-511, codified at 50 U.S.C., 1801-1862; In Re: Seal Case 02-001, U.S. Foreign Intelligence Surveillance Court of Review (November 18, 2002), 3–5; George Lardner, Jr., "Carter Signs Bill Limiting Foreign Intelligence Surveillance," *Washington Post*, October 26, 1978.

32. See Public Law 97-409; Rudalevige, *The New Imperial Presidency*, 134.

33. See Hearings on S.2803 and S.2978 Before the Subcommittee on Separation of Powers of the Senate Committee on the Judiciary, 93rd Cong., 2nd Sess (1974); Katy J. Harriger, *The Special Prosecutor in American Politics*, 2nd rev. ed (Lawrence: University Press of Kansas, 2000), 234–35; Robert J. Spitzer, "The Independent Counsel and the Post-Clinton Presidency," in *Presidency and the Law*, ed. Adler and Genovese, 89–94; Jack Maskell, *Independent Counsel Provisions: An Overview of the Operation of the Law*, Congressional Research Service Report 98-283A (March 20, 1998); Rudalevige, *The New Imperial Presidency*, 136–37.

34. See Presidential Records Act of 1978, 44 U.S.C. secs. 2201–7 for terms and conditions of law.

35. Statement by Deputy Attorney General Larry A. Hammond, *Hearing before the Senate Committee on Governmental Affairs on S. 3494*, 95th Cong., 2d sess (1978), 14.

36. James L. Sundquist, *The Decline and Resurgence of Congress* (Washington, DC: Brookings Institution Press, 1981), 332; Paul C. Light, *Monitoring Government: Inspectors General and the Search for Accountability* (Washington, DC: Brookings Institution, 1993); Rudalevige, *The New Imperial Presidency*, 114–15; Public Law 95-452.

37. See Congressional Research Service and Ellen C. Collier, *The Loss of the Legislative Veto* (Washington, DC: Government Printing Office, 1983); William West and Joseph Cooper, "The Congressional Veto and Legislative Rulemaking," *Political Science Quarterly*, 98, no. 2 (1983), 285–304; Jakob Schissler, "The Impact of the War Powers Resolution on Crisis Decision Making," in *The Reagan Administration: A Reconstruction of American Strength?* ed. Helga Haftendorn and Jakob Schissler (Berlin and New York: Walter de Gruyter, 1988), 218–19; Rudalevige, *The New Imperial Presidency*, 115; Sundquist, *The Decline and Resurgence of Congress*, 344–45; Barbara Hinkson Craig, *The Legislative Veto: Congressional Control of Regulation* (Boulder, CO: Westview, 1983), 18–20.

38. U.S. Cong., Senate, 96th Cong., Senate Report No. 96-570 (1980), 5–8.

39. Rudalevige, *The New Imperial Presidency*, 124–25; Loch K. Johnson, *The Making of International Agreements: Congress Confronts the Executive* (New York: New York University Press, 1984), 137–44; Public Law 92-403 (1 U.S. Code 112b) amended by Public Law 95-426; Savage, *Takeover*, 33–34.

40. Kenneth Bredmeier, "Goldwater, Other Lawmakers File Suit over Repeal of Taiwan Defense Pact," *Washington Post*, December 23, 1978; Savage, *Takeover*, 42.

41. Don Baonafede, Daniel Rapoport, and Joel Havemann, "The President versus Congress: The Score Since Watergate," *National Journal*, May 29, 1976, 738.

42. Rudalevige, *The New Imperial Presidency*, 138; Gordon S. Jones and John A. Marini, eds., *The Imperial Congress: Crisis in the Separation of Powers* (New York: Pharos Books, 1988), I.

CHAPTER 4

1. Hayes, *Cheney*, 138.

2. Weiner, *Legacy of Ashes*, 374.

3. Institute for the Study of Diplomacy, Edmund A. Walsh School of Foreign Service, Georgetown University, "The Soviet Invasion of Afghanistan in 1979: Failure of Intelligence or of the Policy Process?" Working Group Report, no. 111, September 26, 2005.

4. See CNN Cold War—Historical Documents: U.S memos on Afghanistan, Memo from Zbigniew Brzezinski to President Jimmy Carter, December 26, 1979, available at http://www.cnn.com/SPECIALS/cold.war/episodes/20/documents/brez.carter.

5. "Interview with Representative Dick Cheney," *Pinedale Roundup*, April 17, 1980. Also cited in Hayes, *Cheney*, 146.

6. "Interview with Representative Dick Cheney," *Pinedale Roundup*.

7. See Peter Goldman, "The Republican Landslide," *Newsweek*, November 17, 1980; Anthony Lewis, "Abroad at Home: The Tidal Wave," *New York Times*, November 6, 1980.

8. Howell Raines, "Hostages Hailed at White House; Reagan Vows 'Swift Retribution' for Any New Attack on Diplomats," *New York Times*, January 28, 1981.

9. Hayes, *Cheney*, 156.

10. David Haberstam, *War in a Time of Peace* (New York and London: Simon & Schuster, 2002), 67–68.

11. Dubose and Bernstein, *Vice*, 48–49.

12. Peter Goldman, "Mr. Reagan Goes to Washington," *Newsweek*, November 24, 1980.

13. Savage, *Takeover*, 42–43.

14. Joseph Hogan, "Back to the 1970s: The Context of the Reagan Presidency," in *The Reagan Years: The Record in Presidential Leadership*, ed. Joseph Hogan (Manchester and New York: Manchester University Press, 1990), 15–16.

15. Savage, *Takeover*, 44.

16. Transcript, "Revitalizing America: What Are the Possibilities?" American Enterprise Institute, Forum 49, December 9, 1980.

17. Ibid.

18. Quotation in Rudalevige, *The New Imperial Presidency*, 168. Also see Louis Fisher, *Recess Appointments of Federal Judges*, Report RL31112, Congressional Research Service, September 5, 2001; Myron Struck, "Reagan's Recess Hiring Elicits Resentment," *Washington Post*, July 11, 1984; Richard P. Nathan, *The Administrative Presidency* (New York: Macmillan, 1983), 75.

19. Alexis Simendinger, "The Paper Wars," *National Journal*, July 25, 1998; Kenneth R. Mayer, *With the Stroke of a Pen: Executive Orders and Presidential Power* (Princeton, NJ: Princeton University Press, 2001), 78–88; William G. Howell, *Power without Persuasion: The Politics of Direct Presidential Action* (Princeton, NJ: Princeton University Press, 2003), 80–88; Rudalevige, *The New Imperial Presidency*, 170–72.

20. See *Hearings before the Subcommittee on Government Information, Justice, and Agriculture of the Committee on Government Operations*, H.R., April 29, 1986; W. Andrew Jack, "Note: Executive Orders 12,291 and 12,498; Usurpation of Legislative Power or Blueprint for Legislative Reform?" *George Washington University Law Review* 54 (May 1986), 521; Mayer, *With the Stroke of a Pen*, 125–34.

21. Christopher S. Kelley, "Rethinking Presidential Power—The Unitary Executive and the George W. Bush Presidency," Paper prepared for the 63rd Annual Meeting of the Midwest Political Science Association, April 7–10, 2005, Chicago, Illinois.

22. Rudalevige, *The New Imperial Presidency*, 175–76.

23. See "A Memorandum for the Executive Departments and Agencies Concerning the Law Enforcement Amendments to the Freedom of Information Act," 5 U.S.C. Sec. 552, Enacted as the Freedom of Information Reform Act of 1986, Sections 1801–1804 of the Anti-Drug Abuse Act of 1986, 100 stat. 3207-48, October 27, 1986, available at http://www.usdoj.gov/04foia/86agmemo.htm (accessed 16 September 2008). Also see Howell Raines, "Reagan Order Tightens the Rules on Disclosing Secret Information," *New York Times*, April 3, 1982; Richard Hallor, "Pentagon to Give Polygraph Tests to Personnel to Fight Disclosures," *New York Times*, December 10, 1982; Stuart Taylor, Jr., "Administration Seeks a Stronger Lock on Classified Files," *New York Times*, March 24, 1985; Linda Greenhouse, "Justices Grant CIA Wide Discretion on Secrecy," *New York Times*, April 17, 1985; Linda Greenhouse, "Agencies Get New Power to Withhold Investigative Reports," *New York Times*, October 29, 1986.

24. See U.S. House Subcommittee on Government Information, Justice, and Agriculture of the Committee on Government Operations, *Statement on Behalf of the Office of General Counsel to the Clerk of the House of Representatives*, 99th Cong., 2nd sess. (April 29, 1986), 3; Seymour Hersh, "A Reporter at Large: Nixon's Last Cover-up," *New Yorker*, December 14, 1992, 86; Stanley I. Kutler, "Presidential Materials: Nixon's Ghost at Justice," *Wall Street Journal*, April 1, 1986. Also see *Public Citizen v. Burke*, 843 F.2d 1473 (D.C.C.1988).

25. Weiner, *Legacy of Ashes*, 377.

26. U.S. Constitution, Article II, Sec.1.

27. U.S. Constitution, Article II, Sec. 3.

28. Savage, *Takeover*, 47–48; Jess Bravin, "Judge Alito's View of the Presidency: Expansive Powers," *Wall Street Journal*, January 10, 2006; John W. Dean, "New

Developments in the U.S. Attorney Controversy," FindLaw, available at http://writ.news.findlaw.com/dean/20070323.html (accessed 16 September 2008); Christopher S. Kelley, "Rethinking Presidential Power—The Unitary Executive and the George W. Bush Presidency," Paper prepared for the 63rd Annual Meeting of the Midwest Political Science Association, April 7–10, Chicago, Illinois.

29. Hayes, *Cheney*, 163.

30. Richard Rhodes, *Arsenals of Folly: The Making of the Nuclear Arms Race* (New York: Alfred A. Knopf, 2007), 114–15.

31. Rhodes, *Arsenals of Folly*, 129.

32. Rhodes, *Arsenals of Folly*, 130–32.

33. Rhodes, *Arsenals of Folly*, 147–48.

34. See Strategic-Air-Command.com at http://www.strategic-air-command.com/missiles/Peacekeeper/Peacek (accessed 16 September 2008); Kenneth Kitts, *Presidential Commissions and National Security* (Boulder, CO: Lynne Rienner Publishers, 2006).

35. See Lou Cannon, *President Reagan: The Role of a Lifetime* (New York: Public Affairs), 279–80; see Strategic-Air-Command.com at http://www.strategic-air-command.com/missiles/Peacekeeper/Peacek (accessed 16 September 2008); Kitts, *Presidential Commissions and National Security*.

36. "Breaking the Defense Deadlock," *Time*, October 1, 1984.

37. See John Perry Barlow, "Sympathy for the Devil," reprinted in *Washington Monthly*, November 9, 2003; http://www.washingtonmonthly.com/archives (accessed 16 September 2008).

38. See Union of Concerned Scientists, "Space-Based Missile Defense: A Report by the Union of Concerned Scientists," Cambridge, MA, March 1984; Edward Reiss, *The Strategic Defense Initiative* (New York: Cambridge University Press, 1992), 87-99; James Haug, ed., *The Strategic Defense Initiative: An International Perspective* (New York: Colombia University Press, 1987).

39. *Frontline: Target America: Terrorist Attacks on Americans, 1979–1988*; "A Rallying Round for Reagan," *Time*, October 1, 1983; Weiner, *Legacy of Ashes*, 391–92; Savage, *Takeover*, 50.

40. Robert Parry, "Congressional Trip to Grenada Boosts Reagan," *Associated Press*, November 8, 1983; *Time*, "A Rallying Round for Reagan," October 1, 1983.

41. James Mann, *Rise of the Vulcans: The History of Bush's War Cabinet* (New York: Viking, 2004), 138.

42. See Mann, *Rise of the Vulcans*, 140–42.

43. Quotation in transcript, The *MacNeil/Lehrer News Hour*, Public Broadcasting Service, April 11, 1986; *BBC Transcript*, "U.S. Launches Air Strikes on Libya," April 15, 1986; Strobe Talbott, "Gong it Alone," *Time*, April 28, 1986; "Master of Mischief," *Time*, April 7, 1986; Savage, *Takeover*, 52. Also see Colonel Robert E. Venkus, *Raid on Qaddafi* (New York: St. Martin's Press, 1992), 69-103; George P. Shultz, *Turmoil and Triumph* (New York: Charles Scribner's Sons, 1993), 677-87; Christopher Simpson, ed., *National Security Directives of the Reagan & Bush Administrations: The Declassified History of U.S. Political and Military Policy, 1981–1991* (Boulder, CO: Westview Press, 1995), 638-39, 647.

44. Strobe Talbott, "Going It Alone," *Time*, April 1986.

45. Ibid.

CHAPTER 5

1. National Security Archive, "The Iran-Contra Affair 20 Years On: Documents Spotlight Role of Reagan, Top Aides," November 24, 2006; available at http://www.gwu.edu/~nsarchiv/NSAEBB/NSAEBB210/index.htm (accessed 16 September 2008); Peter Kornblum and Malcolm Byrne, eds., *The Iran-Contra Scandal: The Declassified History* (New York: New Press, 1993); Theodore Draper, *A Very Thin Line* (New York: Hill and Wang, 1991), 17–23; Weiner, *Legacy of Ashes: The History of the CIA*, 398–99.

2. Joel Brinkley and Stephen Engelberg, eds., *Report of the Congressional Committees Investigating the Iran-Contra Affair* (New York: Times Books, 1988), 144–53.

3. Brinkley and Engelberg, *Report of the Congressional Committees Investigating the Iran-Contra Affair*; George P. Shultz, *Turmoil and Triumph: My Years as Secretary of State*.

4. Brinkley and Engelberg, *Report of the Congressional Committees Investigating the Iran-Contra Affair*; Mark Danner, "How the Foreign Policy Machine Broke Down," *New York Times*, March 7, 1993.

5. Danner, "How the Foreign Policy Machine Broke Down."

6. Dubose and Bernstein, *Vice*, 70–71.

7. Iran-Contra Committee Hearing Transcripts, Vols. 1–8, Washington, DC: Library of Congress, 1987; Peter Osterlund, "GOP Congressman Warns Against Limiting Presidential Power," *Christian Science Monitor*, November 24, 1987.

8. Steven V. Roberts, "President Repeats Diversion Denial," *New York Times*, July 14, 1987.

9. Nathaniel C. Nash, "Some in Congress Express Support on Pardons for Ex-Reagan Aides," *New York Times*, July 20, 1987.

10. "Finding Comparisons Unwise," *New York Times*, July 25, 1987.

11. See Shultz, *Turmoil and Triumph: My Years as Secretary of State*.

12. David E. Rosenbaum, "On Last Day, the Panel Focuses on Summing-Up," *New York Times*, August 4, 1987; David E. Rosenbaum, "Iran-Contra Panels Are Continuing Their Inquiry, Official Says," *New York Times*, August 7, 1987.

13. See *Report of the Congressional Committees Investigating the Iran-Contra Affair*, 100th Cong., 1st sess., November 1987, H.R. Rept. 100-433, S. Rept. 100-216, 16–23.

14. See *United States v. Curtiss-Wright Export Corporation*, 299 U.S. 304 (1936).

15. *Report of the Congressional Committees Investigating the Iran-Contra Affair*, 100th Cong., 1st sess., November 1987, H.R. Rept. 100-433, S. Rept. 100-216, 16–23. Also see Brinkley and Engelberg, *Report of the Congressional Committees Investigating the Iran-Contra Affair*. Also see Sean Wilentz, "Mr. Cheney's Minority Report," *New York Times*, July 9, 2007.

16. Jane Mayer, "The Hidden Power," *New Yorker*, July 3, 2006.

17. See Mayer, "The Hidden Power"; Wilentz, "Mr. Cheney's Minority Report."

18. Cary Thatcher, "Minority Report Takes Strong Issue," *Christian Science Monitor*, November 19, 1987. Also see Brinkley and Engelberg, *Report of the Congressional Committees Investigating the Iran-Contra Affair.*

19. Richard Cheney, "Covert Operations: Who's In Charge?" *Wall Street Journal*, May 8, 1988.

20. Ibid.

CHAPTER 6

1. R. W. Apple, Jr., "Challenges for Bush: Agenda and Congress," *New York Times*, November 10, 1988; David E. Rosenbaum, "Democrats Take Solace as the Party Defies History and Adds to Majority," *New York Times*, November 10, 1988.

2. Excerpts from George Bush's acceptance speech, reprinted in the *New York Times*. See "Bush Victory Talk: 'I Mean to Be a President of All the People,'" *New York Times*, November 9, 1988.

3. Anthony Lewis, "President and Congress," *New York Times*, December 8, 1988; also see Truman, seizure case.

4. *Morrison v. Olson*, 487 U.S. 654 (1988).

5. William P. Barr, "Common Legislative Encroachments on Executive Branch Authority," July 7, 1989, 13 U.S. Op. Office of Legal Counsel 248, 1989 WL 595833 (OLC).

6. Neill Kinkopf, "Furious George," *Legal Affairs*, September/October 2005.

7. See R.W. Apple Jr., "An Attempt to Recover," *New York Times*, March 11, 1989; Dan Goodgame, "Rude Awakening," *Time*, March 20, 1989; See Maureen Dowd, "Bush's Careful Efforts Slow Selection of Pentagon Team," *New York Times*, November 30, 1988; Andrew Rosenthal, "Tower's Personal Life Is Scrutinized," *New York Times*, February 1, 1989; Robin Toner, "GOP Leaders in Senate Striving to Keep Tower Nomination Alive," *New York Times*, February 25, 1989.

8. Savage, *Takeover*, 60–61.

9. "After Tower: High Road and Low Road," *New York Times*, March 11, 1989.

10. "On the Second Shot, a Straight Arrow," *Time*, March 20, 1989.

11. Andrew Rosenthal, "Bush's Safer Choice," *New York Times*, March 11, 1989; Andrew Rosenthal, "Cheney, a Conservative Is Also a Compromiser," *New York Times*, March 12, 1989.

12. Quotation in James Mann, *Rise of the Vulcans*, 170; Andrew Rosenthal, "Bush's Safer Choice"; Andrew Rosenthal, "Cheney, a Conservative Is Also a Compromiser."

13. Andrew Rosenthal, "Cheney Rebukes Air Force Chief for Arms Talk with Legislators," *New York Times*, March 25, 1989; Dubose and Bernstein, *Vice*, 89.

14. Dubose and Bernstein, *Vice*, 96.

15. See Ronald Reagan, "Statement on Signing the Goldwater-Nichols Department of Defense Reorganization Act of 1986," *Public Papers of the Presidents of the United States, Ronald Reagan*, Book II, June 28–December 31, 1986, Washington, D.C.: Federal Register Division, GSA, 1989, 1312; Goldwater-Nichols Department

of Defense Reorganization Act of 1986. Public Law 99-433; U.S. Cong., Goldwater-Nichols Department of Defense Reorganization Act of 1986 Conference Report, House Conference Report no. 99-824. This was the final version of the bill proposed by House and Senate conferees.

16. "Why the Invasion Was Justified," *New York Times*, December 21, 1989; "Excerpts from Briefings on U.S. Military Action in Panama," *New York Times*, December 21, 1989; "Transcript of Bush News Conference on Noriega and Panama," *New York Times*, January 6, 1990; George J. Church, "The Devil They Knew," *Time*, January 15, 1990; Eytan Gilboa, "The Panama Invasion Revisited: Lessons for the Use of Force in the Post Cold War Era," *Political Science Quarterly*, 110, no. 4 (winter 1995-96), 539–60.

17. Stephen Engleberg, "Congressman Criticizes Use of Stealth Plane in Panama," *New York Times*, January 13, 1990.

18. Weiner, *Legacy of Ashes*, 424.

19. Michael R. Gordon, "Cheney Blamed for Press Problems in Panama," *New York Times*, March 20, 1990.

20. Mann, *Rise of the Vulcans*, 180.

21. Martin Tolchin, "Legislators Express Concern on the Operation's Future," *New York Times*, December 22, 1989; Ellen C. Collier, "The War Powers Resolution: Eighteen Years of Experience," Congressional Research Report, February 4, 1992; Kevin Buckley, *Panama: The Whole Story* (New York: Simon & Schuster, 1991), 14, 16, 59-60, 74; Frederick Kempe, *Divorcing the Dictator: America's Bungled Affair with Noriega* (New York: G.P. Putnam's Sons, 1990), 169-70, 223.

22. U.S. Cong., House Report no. 93-287.

23. See Ellen C. Collier, "The War Powers Resolution: Eighteen Years of Experience," *Congressional Research Report*, February 4, 1992.

24. Mann, *Rise of the Vulcans*, 180; Tolchin, "Legislators Express Concern on the Operation's Future."

25. Bob Woodward, *The Commanders* (New York: Simon & Schuster, 1991), 90.

26. Mann, *Rise of the Vulcans*, 180; James Baker III, *The Politics of Diplomacy* (New York: G. P. Putnam's Sons, 1995), 194.

27. Quotation from Cheney in Hayes, *Cheney*, 224.

28. Susanne M. Schafer, "Powell Steps into New Leadership Role," *Associated Press*, December 23, 1989; Saul Friedman, "Four Star Warrior," *Newsday Magazine*, February 11, 1990.

29. See Human Rights Watch/Middle East, "Iraq's Crime of Genocide" (New Haven: Yale University Press), 1995.

30. Clyde R. Mark, "Congress and Iraq," Congressional Research Report, January 3, 1992; U.S. Cong., House, Committee on Foreign Affairs. Subcommittee on Europe and the Middle East. The Middle East in the 1990s. Hearing, 101st Cong., 2nd sess., April 4, May 8, June 26, July 17, 1990.

31. Interview with Bernard Trainor, "The Gulf War: Oral History," *Frontline*, http://www.pbs.org/wgbh/pages/frontline/gulf/oral/trainor/1.html (accessed 16 September 2008).

32. Richard L. Russell, "CIA's Strategic Intelligence in Iraq," *Political Science Quarterly*, Summer 2002; Charles Allen, "Intelligence: Cult, Craft, or Business?" Program on Information Resources Policy, Harvard University, April 6, 2000; Evan Thomas with Margaret Garrard Warner, Douglas Waller, Thomas M. DeFrank, and Ann McDaniel, "The Search for Scapegoats," *Newsweek*, October 1, 1990; Weiner, *Legacy of Ashes*, 425–26; and Michael Gordon and General Bernard E. Trainor, *The Generals' War* (Boston: Little, Brown, 1995), 4–30.

33. See Interview with James Baker, "The Gulf War: Oral History," *Frontline*, http://www.pbs.org/wgbh/pages/frontline/gulf/oral/baker/1.html (accessed 16 September 2008).

34. See Clyde R. Mark, "Congress and Iraq, 1990," *Congressional Research Service Report*, January 3, 1992.

35. Evan Thomas with John Barry, Ann McDaniel and Douglas Waller, "No Vietnam," *Newsweek*, December 10, 1990; Interview with James Baker, "The Gulf War: Oral History," *Frontline*.

36. See Public Law 93-148, passed over President Richard M. Nixon's veto, November 7, 1973; Clyde R. Mark, "Congress and Iraq, 1990," CRS Report for Congress, January 3, 1992.

37. Interview with Dick Cheney, "The Gulf War: Oral History," *Frontline*, http://www.pbs.org/wgbh/pages/frontline/gulf/oral/cheney/1.html (accessed 16 September 2008).

38. Interview with Dick Cheney, *Meet the Press*, November 18, 1990.

39. Mark, "Congress and Iraq, 1990," CRS Report for Congress, January 3, 1992. Also see U.S. House, Cong. Record, January 10, 11, and 12, 1991, 118–485, and U.S. Senate, Cong. Record, January 10, 11, and 12, 1991, 97–403.

40. See Interview with James Baker, "The Gulf War: Oral History," *Frontline*.

41. Interview with Colin Powell, "The Gulf War: Oral History," *Frontline*.

42. Colin Powell, *My American Journey* (New York: Ballantine Books, 1995), 451.

43. Interview with Cheney, "The Gulf War: Oral History," *Frontline*; Melinda Beck, John Barry, and Rod Nordland, "For the Air Force, It's the Big One," *Newsweek*, October 1, 1990.

44. Interview with Brent Scowcroft, in Mann, *Rise of the Vulcans*, 187.

45. Interview with H. Norman Schwarzkopf, "The Gulf War: Oral History," *Frontline*, http://www.pbs.org/wgbh/pages/frontline/gulf/oral/schwarzkopf/2.html (accessed 16 September 2008).

46. See Mann, *Rise of the Vulcans*, 187; interview with Cheney, "The Gulf War: Oral History," *Frontline*.

47. Interview with Cheney, "The Gulf War: Oral History," *Frontline*; Mann, *Rise of the Vulcans*, 188.

48. Interview with Cheney, "The Gulf War: Oral History," *Frontline*.

49. "Transcript of President's Address on the Gulf War," *New York Times*, February 28, 1991.

50. Maureen Dowd, "Joint Session Applauds a 'Brilliant Victory' in Gulf Campaign," *New York Times*, March 7, 1991.

51. See Daniel Pedersen, Carrol Bogert, Bradley Martin, Michael Meyer, and Jane Whitmore, "America's Giant Step," *Newsweek*, March 11, 1991.

52. R. W. Apple, "Is Saddam Hussein a Phoenix?" *New York Times*, March 10, 1991.

53. Dick Cheney, Speech at the Discovery Institute, Seattle, Washington, August 14, 1992.

54. Interview with Dick Cheney, "The Gulf War: Oral History," *Frontline*.

55. Paul Wolfowitz, "Victory Came Too Easily," *National Interest*, 35, Spring 1994, 87.

56. Paul Wolfowitz, "The United States and Iraq," in *The Future of Iraq*, ed. John Calabrese (Washington, D.C.: Middle East Institute, 1997), 107–13.

57. Interview with Richard Clarke, "The Dark Side," *Frontline*, January 23, 2006, http://www.pbs.org.wgbh/pages/frontline/darkside/interviews/clarke.html (accessed 16 September 2008); Margaret Garrard Warner, Thomas M. DeFrank, and John Barry, "A Question of Time," *Newsweek*, December 3, 1990. Also see Weiner, *Legacy of Ashes*, 428–29.

58. Interview with Richard Clarke, "The Dark Side," *Frontline*.

59. See James Bernstein, "Dick Cheney Goes on the Offensive," *Newsday*, January 14, 1991; John H. Broder, and Ralph Vartabedian, "Cheney Cancels Navy's $57-Billion Attack Jet," *Los Angeles Times*, January 1, 1991; "Dick Cheney's Pentagon," *The Economist*, January 19, 1991; Lars-Erik Nelson, "Defense Contractors Learn Business as Usual Too Costly for Cheney," *Minneapolis Star Tribune*, January 11, 1991.

60. See Senate Committee on Armed Services, *Nominations of David S. Addington, to Be General Counsel of the Department of Defense and Robert S. Silberman, to Be Assistant Secretary of the Army for Manpower and Reserve Affairs; to Consider Certain Pending Civilian Nominations; to Consider Certain Pending Army and Air Force Nominations; and to Discuss, and Possibly Consider, Certain Pending Navy and Marine Corps Nominations*, July 1, 1992; Savage, *Takeover*, 62–63.

61. Mann, *Rise of the Vulcans*, 195–96.

62. Sidney Blumenthal, "Comment & Debate: Cheney's Vice-like Grip: Bush Has Granted His Deputy the Greatest Expansion of Powers in American History," *The Guardian*, February 24, 2006.

63. Interview with Barton Gellman, "Cheney's Law," *Frontline*, http://www.pbs.org/wgbh/pages/frontline/cheney/themes/cheneyview.html (accessed 16 September 2008).

CHAPTER 7

1. Interview with Dick Cheney, CNN Transcript No. 750, "Dick Cheney Comments on the Military Scene," *Larry King Live*, January 27, 1993.

2. "Poll: Dole Still '96 GOP Frontrunner," *UPI*, January 2, 1995.

3. Allen R. Meyerson, "Halliburton Picks Cheney to Be Chief," *New York Times*, August 11, 1995.

4. Kenneth T. Walsh, "The Cheney Factor."

5. Mann, *Rise of the Vulcans*, 227.

6. See Paul Wolfowitz, "The United States and Iraq," in *The Future of Iraq*, ed. John Calabrese (Washington, D.C.: Middle East Institute, 1997), 107–13.

7. Zalmay Khalilzad and Paul Wolfowitz, "Overthrow Him," *Weekly Standard*, December 1, 1997, 14.

8. Mann, *Rise of the Vulcans*, 237.

9. Ian Christopher, "Bush, Cheney Officially Debut the Full 2000 Republican Presidential Ticket," CNN, July 25, 2000.

10. Interview with Dick Cheney, CNN, *Larry King Live*, July 25, 2000.

11. Barton Gellman and Jo Becker, "Angler, the Cheney Vice Presidency: A Different Understanding with the President," *Washington Post*, June 24, 2007.

12. Gellman and Becker, "Angler, the Cheney Vice Presidency: A Different Understanding with the President."

13. Transcript, CNN Live Event, Bush Nominates Donald Rumsfeld as Secretary of Defense, December 28, 2000.

14. Alison Mitchell, "Powell to Head State Deparment as Bush's First Cabinet Pick," *New York Times*, December 17, 2000.

15. Mathew Rees, "The Long Arm of Colin Powell: Will the Next Secretary of State Also Run the Pentagon?" *Weekly Standard*, December 25, 2000, 17.

16. See Mann, *Rise of the Vulcans*, 270–76; Lou Debose and Jake Bernstein, *Vice*, 178–79.

17. Quotation in Savage, *Takeover*, 75.

18. *This Week*, ABC News, January 27, 2002.

19. Alison Mitchell, "Cheney Rejects Access to Terror Brief," *New York Times*, May 20, 2002.

20. See Letter from David Walker, Comptroller General of GAO, to the Vice President, August 17, 2001, http://www.energycommerce.house.gov/EnergyTaskForce/energytaskforce.shtml (accessed June 3, 2007); Also see Ellen Nakashima, "Can GAO Make Cheney Blink?" *Washington Post*, August 3, 2001.

21. See *Walker v. Cheney*, U.S. District Court for the District of Colombia, Civil Action No. 02-0340 (JDB), December 9, 2002.

22. *Walker v. Cheney*, U.S. District Court for the District of Colombia, Civil Action No. 02-0340 (JDB), December 9, 2002.

23. Federal Advisory Committee Act, 5 U.S.C.

24. *Cheney v. U.S. District Court for the District of Colombia*, 124 S. Ct. 2489 (2004).

25. See *In Re: Richard B. Cheney*, No. 02-5354 (D.C.Cir. 2005).

26. See Executive Order 13233 of November 1, 2001: Further Implementation of the Presidential Records Act; Presidential Records Act of 1978, 44 U.S.C., secs. 2201–7.

27. See *American Historical Association v. National Archives and Records Administration*, No. 01-2447; Public Citizen, "Federal Court Strikes Down Bush Executive Order on Presidential Records" (October 1, 2007), available at http://www.citizen.org/pressroom/release.cfm?ID=2524 (accessed 16 September 2008).

28. White House, Office of the Press Secretary, Executive Order 13292, "Further Amendment to the Executive Order 12958. As Amended, Classified National

Security Information" (March 25, 2003), available at http://www.fas.org/sgp/bush/coamend.html (accessed 16 September 2008); Jane E. Kirtley, "Transparency and Accountability in a Time of Terror: The Bush Administration's Assault on Freedom of Information," *Communications Law and Policy*, 11 (2006): 502–3.

29. See OMB Watch, "Vice President Refuses to Disclose Classification Data," June 13, 2006, available at http://www.ombwatch.org/article/3468/1/233?TopicID=1 (accessed 16 September 2008); Mark Silva, "Cheney Keeps Classification Activity Secret," *Chicago Tribune*, May 27, 2006; Letter from J. William Leonard, Director of Information Security Oversight Office, to David Addington, Assistant to the President and Chief of Staff to the Vice President, June 8, 2006; Letter from William J. Leonard, Director of Information Security Oversight Office, to David Addington, Assistant to the President and Chief of Staff to the Vice President, August 23, 2006; Letter from J. William Leonard, Director of Information Security Oversight Office, to Alberto Gonzales, Attorney General, January 9, 2007; http://oversight.house.gov/documents/20070621094929.pdf (accessed September 16, 2008); *Secrecy News*, "ISOO Asks Attorney General to Rule on Cheney's Role," no. 14, February 6, 2007, http://www.fas.org/blog/secrecy (accessed September 16, 2008).

30. See *Secrecy News*, "ISOO Asks Attorney General to Rule on Cheney's Role"; *Secrecy News*, "ISOO Director Leonard to Step Down" (September 28, 2007), http://www.fas.org/blog/secrecy (accessed September 16, 2008).

CHAPTER 8

1. Weiner, *Legacy of Ashes*, 480–81.
2. Quoted in Weiner, *Legacy of Ashes*, 477.
3. Weiner, *Legacy of Ashes*, 480; "When these attacks occur, as they likely will," Richard Clarke e-mail cited in 9/11 Commission Report.
4. Philip Shenon, *The Commission: The Uncensored History of the 9/11 Investigation*, (New York: Twelve, 2008), 265, 412; Final Report of the National Commission on Terrorist Attacks Upon the United States, Washington: Government Printing Office, July 22, 2004.
5. Jane Mayer, "The Hidden Power," *New Yorker*, July 3, 2006. Yoo recounted that Gonzales "was not a law-of-war expert and didn't have very developed views." (See Barton Gellman and Jo Becker, "Angler: The Cheney Vice Presidency," *Washington Post*, June 25, 2007.)
6. Transcript of interview with Dick Cheney, *Meet the Press*, September 16, 2001.
7. Quoted in Jane Mayer, "Outsourcing Torture," *New Yorker*, February 14, 2005.
8. Tom Daschle, "Power We Didn't Grant," *Washington Post*, December 23, 2005.
9. *Authorization for Use of Military Force*, Pub L. 107-40, 115 Stat. 223 (2001). Also see CRS Report RS22357, *Authorization for Use of Military Force in Response to the 9/11 Attacks*, Pub L. 107-40: Legislative History.
10. Gellman and Becker, "Angler: The Cheney Vice Presidency."

11. Pub L. 95-511, Title I, 92 Stat. 1796 (October 25, 1978), codified as amended at 50 U.S.C. sec 1805 (a) (3) (2003 & Supp. 2005).

12. John Yoo, *War by Other Means* (New York: Atlantic Monthly Press, 2006), 107.

13. Jack L. Goldsmith, *The Terror Presidency: Law and Judgment Inside the Bush Administration* (New York: W.W. Norton & Co., 2007), 181.

14. See Eric Lichtblau, *Bush's Law*, 147; Tim Weiner, *Legacy of Ashes*, 483.

15. Hayden Testimony, Senate Intelligence Committee, May 18, 2006.

16. "Press Briefing by Attorney General Alberto Gonzales and General Michael Hayden, Principal Deputy Director for National Intelligence," December 19, 2005, http://www.whitehouse.gov/news/releases/2005/12/20051219-1.html (accessed 16 September 2008).

17. Interview with John Yoo, in Charlie Savage, *Takeover*, 134.

18. John Yoo, interview transcript, "Spying on the Home Front," *Frontline*, http://www.pbs.org/wgbh/pages/frontline/homefront/interviews/yoo.html (accessed 16 September 2008).

19. Scott Shane and Eric Lichtblau, "Cheney Pushed U.S. to Widen Eavesdropping," *New York Times*, May 14, 2006.

20. Tim Golden, "Threats and Responses: After Terror, a Secret Rewriting of Military Law," *New York Times*, October 24, 2004; Savage, *Takeover*, 134–35; Jane Mayer, "The Hidden Power," *New Yorker*, July 3, 2006; Gellman and Becker, "A Different Understanding with the President," *Washington Post*, June 24, 2007.

21. Savage, *Takeover*, 137; Golden, "Threats and Responses: After Terror, a Secret Rewriting of Military Law."

22. Golden, "Threats and Responses: After Terror, a Secret Rewriting of Military Law."

23. See Gellman and Becker, "A Different Understanding with the President," *Washington Post*, June 24, 2007.

24. Tim Golden, "Threats and Responses: After Terror, a Secret Rewriting of Military Law," *New York Times*, October 24, 2004; Gellman and Becker, "A Different Understanding with the President."

25. Golden, "Threats and Responses: After Terror, a Secret Rewriting of Military Law."

26. See Remarks by Vice President Dick Cheney to the U.S. Chamber of Commerce, November 14, 2001, http://www.whitehouse.gov/vicepresident/news-speeches/speeches/vp20011114-1.html (accessed September 16, 2008).

27. See Golden, "Threats and Responses: After Terror, a Secret Rewriting of Military Law"; Savage, *Takeover*, 138–39.

28. "DOD News Briefing—Secretary Rumsfeld and Gen. Myers," December 27, 2001, http://www.globalsecurity.org/military/library/news/2001.12/12/mil-011227-dod01.htm (accessed September 16, 2008).

29. Gellman and Becker, "A Different Understanding with the President."

30. See Geneva Convention Relative to the Treatment of Prisoners of War, Adopted 12 August 1949 by the Diplomatic Conference for the Establishment of

International Conventions for the Protection of Victims of War, held in Geneva from 21 April to 12 August 1949. Entry into Force 21 October 1950.

31. See War Crimes Act of 1996 (as amended) 18 U.S.C. 2441. Also see Congressional Research Service Report, "The War Crimes Act: Current Issues," July 23, 2007.

32. Jane Mayer, "Outsourcing Torture," *New Yorker*, February 14, 2005.

33. See Alberto Gonzales to the president, memorandum re: "Decision Re: Application of the Geneva Conventions on Prisoners of War to the Conflict with Al Qaeda and the Taliban," January 25, 2002, in Dratel and Greenberg, *Torture Papers*, 118; Gellman and Becker, "A Different Understanding with the President."

34. John Yoo and Robert J. Delahunty to William J. Haynes II. Memorandum re: "Application of Treaties and Laws to Detainees," January 9, 2002. Quoted in Dratel and Greenberg, *Torture Papers*, 38; Savage, *Take Over*, 146.

35. See Geneva Convention for the Amelioration of the Condition of the Wounded and Sick in Armed Forces in the Field, 6 U.S.T. 3114; Geneva Convention for the Amelioration of the Condition of Wounded, Sick, and Shipwrecked Members of Armed Forces at Sea, 6 U.S.T. 3217; Geneva Conventions Relative to the Treatment of Prisoners of War, 6 U.S.T. 3316; Geneva Convention Relative to the Protection of Civilian Persons in Time of War, 6 U.S.T.; Convention Against Torture and Other Cruel, Inhuman or Degrading Treatment or Punishment, G.A. Res. 39/46, Annex, 39 U.N. GAOR Supp. No. 51, U.N. Doc. A/39/51 (1984). Ratified by United States in 1994; War Crimes Act of 1996 (as amended) 18 U.S.C. 2441. Also see Congressional Research Service Report, "The War Crimes Act: Current Issues," July 23, 2007.

36. Scott Shane, David Johnston, and James Risen, "Secret U.S. Endorsement of Severe Interrogations," *New York Times*, October 4, 2007.

37. "Rumsfeld: Afghan Prisoners Will Not be Treated as POWs," *Fox News*, January 28, 2002, http://www.foxnews.com/story/0,2933,44084,00.html (accessed 16 September 2008).

38. "Secretary Rumsfeld Media Availability En Route to Guantanamo Bay, Cuba," at http://www.defenselink.mil/transcripts/transcript.aspx?transcriptid=2320 (accessed September 16, 2008).

39. See Stephen Grey, "Extraordinary Rendition: Five Facts and Five Fictions about CIA Rendition," *Frontline*, http://www.pbs.org/frontlineworld/stories/rendition701/interviews/Stephen_Grey.html (accessed 16 September 2008); interview with Jack Cloonan, *Frontline*, "Extraordinary Rendition," http://www.pbs.org/frontlineworld/stories/rendition701/interviews/cloonan.html (accessed 16 September 2008); interview with Lawrence Wikerson, *Frontline*, "Extraordinary Rendition," http://www.pbs.org/frontlineworld/stories/rendition701/interviews/wilkerson.html (accessed 16 September 2008); Jane Mayer, "Outsourcing Torture: The Secret History of America's 'Extraordinary Rendition Program,'" *New Yorker*, February 14, 2005. Also see Statement of Mark Scheuer, "Extraordinary Rendition in U.S. Counterterrorism Policy: The Impact on Transatlantic Relations," House of Rep., Subcommittee on International, Organizations, Human Rights, and Oversight and Subcommittee on Europe, Committee on Foreign Affairs, April 17, 2007.

40. See President Ronald Reagan's message to the Senate and text of the Convention Against Torture and Other Cruel, Inhuman, or Degrading Treatment or Punishment, May 20, 1988.

41. Quoted in Mayer, "Outsourcing Torture."

42. See Dan Froomkin, "White House Torture Advisors," *Washington Post*, April 10, 2008; Editorial, "The Torture Sessions," *New York Times*, April 20, 2008.

43. See U.S. Department of Justice, Office of Legal Counsel, Memorandum for Alberto R. Gonzales, Counsel to the President, August 1, 2002 [otherwise known as "Torture Memo"].

44. Dan Froomkin, "White House Torture Advisors," *Washington Post*, April 10, 2008.

45. See U.S. Department of Justice, Office of Legal Counsel, Memorandum for Alberto R. Gonzales, Counsel to the President, August 1, 2002.

46. Barton Gellman and Jo Becker, "Pushing the Envelope," *Washington Post*, June 25, 2007.

47. Dana Milbank and R. Jeffrey Smith, "Memo Offered Justification for Use of Torture," *Washington Post*, June 8, 2004.

48. Barton Gellman and Jo Becker, "Pushing the Envelope."

CHAPTER 9

1. See Patrick E. Taylor and Elaine Sciolino, "A Nation Challenged: Bush's Advisors Split on Scope of Retaliation," *New York Times*, September 20, 2001; Bob Woodward and Dan Balz, "At Camp David, Advise and Dissent," *Washington Post*, January 31, 2002.

2. Taylor and Sciolino, "A Nation Challenged: Bush's Advisors Split on Scope of Retaliation"; Woodward and Balz, "At Camp David, Advise and Dissent."

3. See Mark Mathews, "The Resurrection of Colin Powell," *Baltimore Sun*, October 8, 2001; Richard A. Ryan, "Powell Resists Rumsfeld's Vision to Broaden Battles," *Detroit News*, October 7, 2001; Woodward and Balz, "At Camp David, Advise and Dissent."

4. Mann, *Rise of the Vulcans*, 303; Interview with Dick Cheney, *Meet the Press*, September 16, 2001.

5. Joseph Kahn, "Before & After; Awakening to Terror, and Asking the World for Help," *New York Times*, September 16, 2001.

6. See William Drozdiak, "Attack on U.S. is Attack on All, NATO agrees," *Washington Post*, September 13, 2001; "Old Friends, Best Friends," *Economist*, Special Report, September 15, 2001; "NATO's Rizzo at Warsaw Conference on Combating Terrorism," GlobalSecurity.org, November 7, 2001, available at http://globalsecurity.org/militarylibrary/news/2001/11/11-07[lowen]index.htm.

7. Mann, *Rise of the Vulcans*, 305.

8. William H. Arkin, "Secret Plan Outlines the Unthinkable," *Los Angeles Times*, March 10, 2002; Michael R. Gordon, "U.S. Nuclear Plan Sees New Targets and New Weapons," *New York Times*, March 10, 2002.

9. Defense Department transcript, "Secretary Rumsfeld Speaks on 21st-Century Transformation of the U.S. Armed Forces," address to National Defense University, January 31, 2002.

10. See interview with Thomas Ricks, "Rumsfeld's War," *Frontline*, http://www.pbs.org/wgbh/pages/frontline/shows/pentagon/interviews/ricks.html (accessed 16 September 2008).

11. See interview with Dana Priest, "Rumsfeld's War," *Frontline*, http://www.pbs.org/wgbh/pages/frontline/shows/pentagon/interviews/priest.html (accessed 16 September 2008).

12. George W. Bush, State of the Union address, January 29, 2002; "Text: Bush's Speech to U.N on Iraq," *New York Times*, September 12, 2002; David E. Sanger, "Bush, Focusing on Terrorism, Says Secure U.S. Is Top Priority," *New York Times*, January 30, 2002.

13. Interview with Thomas Ricks, *Frontline*.

14. David Frum, *The Right Man* (New York: Random House, 2003), 225–44.

15. See Steven Erlanger, "German Joins Europe's Cry That the U.S. Won't Consult," *New York Times*, February 13, 2002; Gerald Baker and Richard Wolffe, "Powell Shrugs Off European Dismay Over 'Axis of Evil,'" *Financial Times*, February 14, 2002; Charles Krauthammer, "The Axis of Petulance," *Washington Post*, March 1, 2002.

16. Quoted in "Mr. Smoke and Mirrors," *Progressive*, 2004, http://findarticles.com/p/articles/mi-m1295/is[lowen]/ai[lowen]n6134001.

17. Thom Shanker and David E. Sanger, "U.S. Envisions Blueprint on Iraq Including Big Invasion Next Year," *New York Times*, April 28, 2002.

18. Transcript of Remarks by the President at 2002 Graduation Exercise of the United States Military Academy, June 1, 2002.

19. See John Lewis Gaddis, "A Grand Strategy of Transformation," *Foreign Policy*, no. 103 (November-December 2002), 50–57; National Security Strategy of the United States of America, September 2002, http://www.whitehouse.gov/nsc/nss.pdf (accessed 16 September 2008).

20. Mann, *Rise of the Vulcans*, 331.

21. James A. Baker III, "The Right Way to Change a Regime," *New York Times*, August 25, 2002; Transcript of Lawrence Eagleburger, *Crossfire*, August 19, 2002; Transcript of interview with Brent Scowcroft, *Face the Nation*, August 4, 2002; Brent Scowcroft, "Don't Attack Saddam Hussein," *Wall Street Journal*, August 15, 2002.

22. White House transcript, *Vice President Speaks at VFW 103rd National Convention*, Nashville, Tennessee, August 26, 2002.

23. Dick Cheney, Speech at the Discovery Institute, Seattle, Washington, August 14, 1992. Also see interview with Dick Cheney, *Frontline*, available at http://www.pbs.org/wgbh/pages/frontline/gulf/oral/cheney/2.html (accessed 16 September 2008).

24. White House transcript, *Vice President Speaks at VFW 103rd National Convention*, Nashville, Tennessee, August 26, 2002.

25. White House transcript, *President's Remarks at the United Nations General Assembly*, September 12, 2002.

26. David E. Sanger and Elisabeth Bumiller, "Bush Presses U.N. on Iraq, Calling Action Unavoidable," *New York Times*, September 13, 2002.

27. John Burns, "Pakistan Releases 3 Scientists Questioned on Ties to Taliban," *New York Times*, November 3, 2001.

28. Mann, *Rise of the Vulcans*, 317.

29. Walter Pincus and Dana Priest, "Some Iraq Analysts Felt Pressure from Cheney Visits," *Washington Post*, June 5, 2003; Mark Hosenball, Michael Isikoff, and Evan Thomas, "Cheney's Long Path to War," *Newsweek*, February 9, 2004.

30. See U.S. Senate, 110th Cong., 2nd Sess., Select Committee on Intelligence, S. Report 110, *Report on Whether Public Statements Regarding Iraq by U.S. Government Officials Were Substantiated by Intelligence Information*, June 2008.

31. Weiner, *Legacy of Ashes*, 488–49.

32. Weiner, *Legacy of Ashes*, 490.

33. Statement of John D. Rockefeller IV, U.S. Senate, 110th Cong., 2nd Sess., Select Committee on Intelligence, S. Report 110, *Report on Whether Public Statements Regarding Iraq by U.S. Government Officials Were Substantiated by Intelligence Information*, June 2008.

34. DIA, *Knowledge of Iraqi Society: Policymaker Need for Insight and Looking at Post-Saddam Iraq*, April 2002, cited in S. Report 110.

35. See U.S. Senate, 110th Cong., 2nd Sess., Select Committee on Intelligence, S. Report 110, *Report on Whether Public Statements Regarding Iraq by U.S. Government Officials Were Substantiated by Intelligence Information*, June 2008.

36. CIA, *Can Iraq Ever Become a Democracy?* August 8, 2002, i–iv.

37. "State of the Union Address," *New York Times*, January 29, 2003.

38. Interview with Colonel Larry Wilkerson, "The Dark Side," *Frontline*, available at http://www.pbs.org/wgbh/pages/frontLine/darkside/interviews/Wilkerson.html; and Steven R. Weisman, "Powell Presents Case to Show Iraq Has Not Disarmed," *New York Times*, February 6, 2003.

39. Dexter Filkins, "Turkish Deputies Refuse to Accept American Troops," *New York Times*, March 2, 2003.

40. Interview with Dick Cheney, *Meet the Press*, March 16, 2003.

41. Redacted copies of both reports may be found as appendices in the Senate (see U.S. Senate Select Committee on Intelligence, S. Report 110-76, *Prewar Intelligence Assessments about Postwar Iraq*, May 2007).

CHAPTER 10

1. Barton Gellman and Jo Becker, "Pushing the Envelope on Presidential Power," *Washington Post*, June 25, 2007.

2. See Brief for Respondents—Appellants, *Hamdi v. Rumsfeld*, U.S. Court of Appeals for the Fourth Circuit, No. 02-6895, June 19, 2002. Also see *Hamdi v. Rumsfeld*, 296 F.3d 278 (4th Cir. 2002); *Padilla v. Rumsfeld*, 352 F.3d 695 (2nd Cir. 2003).

3. Interview with Jack Goldsmith, "Cheney's Law," *Frontline*, http://www.pbs.org/wgbh/pages/frontline/cheney/interviews/goldsmith.html (accessed 16 September 2008).

4. Ibid.

5. Eric Lichtblau, *Bush's Law: The Remaking of American Justice* (New York: Pantheon Books, 2008).

6. Interview with Jack Goldsmith, "Cheney's Law."

7. Ibid.

8. See *Youngstown Sheet & Tube Co. v. Sawyer*, 343 U.S. 579, June 2, 1952.

9. See Edward Lazarus, "How Much Authority Does the President Possess When He is Acting as Commander in Chief?" FindLaw, http://writ.news.findlaw.com/lazarus/20060105.html.

10. Daniel Klaidman, Stuart Taylor Jr., and Evan Thomas, "Palace Revolt," *Newsweek*, February 6, 2006; Jack L. Goldsmith, *The Terror Presidency: Law and Judgment Inside the Bush Administration* (New York: W.W. Norton & Co., 2007); Eric Lichtblau, *Bush's Law*, 175–76.

11. Goldsmith, *The Terror Presidency*, 182; interview with Jack Goldsmith, "Cheney's Law"; Lichtblau, *Bush's Law*, 176.

12. Benjamin Welser and Eric Lichtblau, "Manhattan U.S. Attorney in Line to Be Ashcroft Aide," *New York Times*, October 4, 2003; Lichtblau, *Bush's Law*, 176.

13. John Ashcroft, *Never Again: Securing America and Restoring Justice* (New York: Center Street Hachette Book Group USA), 231; Lichtblau, *Bush's Law*, 179; Dan Eggen, "Official: Cheney Urged Wiretaps," *Washington Post*, June 7, 2007.

14. Interview with Jack Goldsmith, "Cheney's Law."

15. Daniel Klaidman, Stuart Taylor, Jr., and Evan Thomas, "Palace Revolt."

16. Lichtblau, *Bush's Law*, 184; Klaidman, Taylor, and Thomas, "Palace Revolt."

17. *Youngstown Sheet & Tube Co. v. Sawyer*, 343 U.S. 579, June 2, 1952.

18. *United States v. Curtiss-Wright Export Corporation*, 299 U.S. 304 (1936).

19. See Susan Page, "NSA Secret Database Report Triggers Fierce Debate in Washington," *USA Today*, May 11, 2006; Bill Nichols and John Diamond, "Controversy Shadows Hayden Confirmation," *USA Today*, May 11, 2006; Dan Eggen, "Negroponte Had Denied Domestic Call Monitoring," *Washington Post*, May 15, 2006; Elizabeth Drew, "Power Grab," *New York Review of Books*, 53, no. 11 (June 22, 2006).

20. Eric Lichtblau and David Johnston, "Court to Oversee U.S. Wiretapping in Terror Cases," *New York Times*, January 18, 2007; David Johnston and Scott Shane, "Senators Demand Details on New Eavesdropping Rules," *New York Times*, January 19, 2007; Dan Eggen, "Spy Court Orders Stir Debate on Hill," *Washington Post*, January 19, 2007; James Risen, "Administration Pulls Back on Surveillance Agreement," *New York Times*, May 2, 2007.

21. Carl Hulse and Edmund L. Andrews, "House Approves Changes in Eavesdropping," *New York Times*, August 5, 2007; Carol D. Leonnig and Ellen Nakashima, "Ruling Limited Spying Effort," *Washington Post*, August 3, 2007; Michael

Abramowitz and Jonathan Weisman, "Hill, White House Draw Battle Lines," *Washington Post*, August 3, 2007.

22. Eric Lichtblau, "Congress Reaches Deal on Wiretapping," *New York Times*, June 20, 2008; Paul Kane and Carrie Johnson, "Administration, Congress Settle Dispute over Surveillance," *Washington Post*, June 19, 2008.

23. Goldsmith, *The Terror Presidency*.

24. Scott Shane, David Johnston, and James Risen, "Secret U.S. Endorsement of Severe Interrogations, *New York Times*, October 4, 2007.

25. John McCain, "Torture's Terrible Toll: Abusive Interrogation Tactics Produce Bad Intel, and Undermine the Values We Hold Dear," *Newsweek*, November 21, 2005.

26. Dana Priest and Robin Wright, "Cheney Fights for Detainee Policy," *New York Times*, November 7, 2005.

27. Colin Powell, Letter to Senator John McCain, October 5, 2005. http://i.a.cnn.net/cnn/2006/images/09/14/powell.article.pdf.

28. Daniel Klaidman and Michael Isikoff, "Cheney in the Bunker: Bloodied but Unbowed, the Veep Has a New Number Two," *Newsweek*, November 14, 2005; Dana Priest and Robin Wright, "Cheney Fights for Detainee Policy," *Washington Post*, November 7, 2005.

29. See CNN.com, "Senate Ignores Veto Threat in Limiting Detainee Treatment," November 10, 2005; at http://cnn.com/2005/POLITICS/10/06/senate.detainees/index.html; Mark Agrast and Ken Gude, "Statement on the McCain Anti-Torture Amendment," Center for American Progress, December 15, 2005, http://www.americanprogress.org/issues/2005/12/b1304419.html.

30. See Detainee Treatment Act of 2005, as included in the Department of Defense Appropriations Act of 2006 and agreed to by the U.S. House and Senate and signed by President Bush, December 30, 2005.

31. *Associated Press*, "Bush Accepts Sen. McCain's Torture Policy," December 15, 2005.

32. See Shane, Johnston, and Risen, "Secret U.S. Endorsement of Severe Interrogations."

33. George W. Bush, Statement on Signing the Department of Defense Emergency Supplemental Appropriation to Address Hurricanes in the Gulf of Mexico and Pandemic Influenza Act of 2006, December 30, 2005.

34. Charlie Savage, "Cheney Aide is Screening Legislation: Advisor Seeks to Protect Bush Power," *Boston Globe*, May 28, 2006.

35. Interview with Charlie Savage, "Cheney's Law," *Frontline*, http://www.pbs.org/wgbh/pages/frontline/cheney/interviews/savage.html (accessed 16 September 2008).

36. Charlie Savage, "Bush Could Bypass New Torture Ban," *Boston Globe*, January 4, 2006; *Associated Press*, "Bush Accepts Sen. McCain's Torture Policy," December 15, 2005.

37. Interview with Jack Goldsmith, "Cheney's Law," *Frontline*, http://www.pbs.org/wgbh/pages/frontline/cheney/interviews/goldsmith.html (accessed 16 September 2008).

38. *ABC Nightline*, interview by Terry Moran with Vice President Richard Cheney at Al Asad Air Base, Al Anbar Province, Iraq, December 20, 2005.

39. See Scott Horton, "Travel Advisory," *New Republic*, June 19, 2008.

40. Ibid.

41. *Hamdan v. Rumsfeld*, 126 S.Ct. 2796 (2006).

42. See Military Commission Act of 2006, Public Law 109-366, October 17, 2006.

43. White House, Office of the Press Secretary, "President Bush Signs Military Commissions Act of 2006," October 17, 2006, http://www.whitehouse.gov/news/releases/2006/10/20061017-1.html.

44. Tim Golden, "Threats and Responses: Tough Justice: Administration Officials Split over Stalled Military Tribunals," *New York Times*, October 25, 2004.

45. Ibid.

46. Ibid.

47. See Joanne Mariner, "A Military Commissions Cheat Sheet," at http://writ.news.findlaw.com/Mariner/20080521.html (accessed 16 September 2008).

48. See Raymond Bonner, "David Hicks: A Young Man in Search of a Cause," *International Herald Tribune*," March 28, 2007; Raymond Bonner, "David Hicks, Australian Convicted of Supporting Terrorism, to be Released," *International Herald Tribune*, December 28, 2007; Gellman and Becker, "Pushing the Envelope on Presidential Power."

49. *Boumediene v. Bush*, No. 06-1195; also see David Stout, "Justices Rule Terror Suspects Can Appeal in Civilian Courts," *New York Times*, June 13, 2008; Robert Barnes and Dan Eggen, "Court Says Guantanamo Detainees Have Right to Challenge Detention," *Washington Post*, June 12, 2008; Robert Barnes and Del Quentin Wilber, "Habeas Ruling Lays Bare the Divide Among Justices," *Washington Post*, June 15, 2008.

50. *Boumediene v. Bush*, No. 06-1195, June 12, 2008.

51. Barnes and Wilber, "Habeas Ruling Lays Bare the Divide Among Justices."

52. See John Yoo, "The Supreme Court Goes to War," *Wall Street Journal*, June 17, 2008.

53. Interview with Jack Goldsmith, "Cheney's Law."

54. See Dana Priest, "CIA Holds Terror Suspects in Secret Prisons," *Washington Post*, November 2, 2005.

55. See "Update on detainees issues and military commissions legislation," briefing by John Bellinger III, State Department Legal Advisor, September 7, 2006, http://www.state.gov/s/l/rls/71939.htm (accessed 16 September 2008).

56. See Human Rights Watch Press Release, November 7, 2005; Amnesty International Report AMR 51/051/2006, "Below the Radar: Secret Flights to Torture and Disappearance," April 5, 2006; National Public Radio, "Amnesty International Report Details Secret U.S. Prisons," April 5, 2006.

57. The Venice Commission advises the Council of Europe on constitutional issues. For full text of the opinion, see http://www.venice.coe.int/docs/2006/CDL-AD(2006)009-e.asp (accessed 16 September 2008) [hereafter "Venice Commission Report"].

58. Human Rights Committee, Consideration of Reports Submitted by State Parties under Article 40 of the Covenant, United States of America, 87th sess., July 2006.

59. National Public Radio, *All Things Considered*, "Rendition Trial Opens in Milan," January 9, 2007.

60. See Andrew O. Selsky, "US Admiral Confirms Secret Camp at Gitmo," *Washington Post*, February 7, 2008; Mark Mazzetti, "CIA Secretly Held Qaeda Suspect, Officials Say," *New York Times*, March 15, 2008.

CHAPTER 11

1. Transcript of Dominique de Villepin's Remarks, "France's Response," *New York Times*, February 15, 2003.

2. Quoted in Mann, *Rise of the Vulcans*, 355.

3. See Karen DeYoung and Colum Lynch, "Bush Lobbies for Deal on Iraq," *Washington Post*, March 12, 2003.

4. Interview with Thomas Ricks, "Rumsfeld's War," *Frontline*, http://www.pbs.org/wgbh/pages/frontline/shows/pentagon/interviews/ricks.html (accessed 16 September 2008).

5. Richard W. Stevenson, "Bush Gives Hussein 48 Hours, and Vows to Act," *New York Times*, March 18, 2003.

6. "State of the Union Address," *New York Times*, September 29, 2003.

7. James Risen, "Ex-Inspector Says CIA Missed Disarray in Iraqi Arms Program," *New York Times*, January 26, 2004.

8. See "On Point II: Transition to the New Campaign: The United States Army in Operation Iraqi Freedom, May 2003–January 2005," Washington: Government Printing Office, 2008.

9. Eric Schmitt and Edward Wong, "U.S. Study Paints Somber Portrait of Iraqi Discord," *New York Times*, April 9, 2006.

10. Samantha Powers, "The Democrats & National Security," *New York Review of Books*, LV, no. 13 (August 14, 2008), 66.

11. Zbigniew Brzezinski, "The Smart Way Out of a Foolish War," *Washington Post*, March 30, 2008.

12. Editorial, "All the Time He Needs," *New York Times*, April 13, 2008.

Bibliography

BOOKS

Baker III, James. *The Politics of Diplomacy*. New York: G.P. Putnam's Sons, 1995.

Barkley, Alben W. *That Reminds Me*. Garden City, NY: Doubleday, 1954.

Baumgartner, Jody C. *The American Vice Presidency Reconsidered*. Westport, CT: Praeger, 2006.

Belsky, Martin H., ed. *The Rehnquist Court: A Retrospective*. New York: Oxford University Press, 2002.

Brinkley, Joel, and Stephen Engelberg, eds. *Report of the Congressional Committees Investigating the Iran-Contra Affair*. New York: Times Books, 1988.

Buckley, Kevin. *Panama: The Whole Story*. New York: Simon & Schuster, 1991.

Burns, James MacGregor. *Roosevelt: The Soldier of Freedom*. New York: Harcourt, Brace Jovanovich, 1970.

Cannon, Lou. *Governor Reagan: His Rise to Power*. New York: Public Affairs, 2003.

Casserly, John J. *The Ford White House: The Diary of a Speechwriter*. Boulder, CO: Associated University Press, 1977.

Christian, George. *The President Steps Down*. New York: Macmillan, 1970.

Collier, Ellen C. *The Loss of the Legislative Veto*. Washington, DC: Government Printing Office, 1983.

Craig, Barbara Hinkson. *The Legislative Veto: Congressional Control of Regulation*. Boulder, CO: Westview, 1983.

Dallek, Robert. *Flawed Giant: Lyndon Johnson and His Times, 1961–1973*. New York: Oxford University Press, 1998.

Davis, James Kirkpatrick. *Spying on America: The FBI's Domestic Counterintelligence Program*. Westport, CT: Praeger, 1992.

DiSalle, Michael V., and Lawrence G. Blochmann. *Second Choice*. New York: Hawthorn Books, 1966.

Dubose, Lou, and Jake Bernstein. *Vice: Dick Cheney and the Hijacking of the American Presidency*. New York: Random House, 2006.

Eisenhower, Dwight D. *Mandate for Change: The White House Years, 1953–56.* Garden City, NY: Doubleday, 1963.

Eisenhower, Dwight D. *Waging Peace: The White House Years, 1956–61.* Garden City, NY: Doubleday, 1965.

Ellis, Joseph. *Founding Brothers.* New York: Alfred A. Knopf, 2001.

Feerick, J. D. *From Failing Hands: The Story of Presidential Succession.* New York: Fordham University Press, 1965.

Fisher, Louis. *Congressional Abdication on War and Spending.* College Station: Texas A&M Press, 2000.

Ford, Gerald R. *A Time to Heal.* New York: Harper & Row, 1979.

Friedman, Leon, and William F. Levantrosser, eds. *Watergate and Afterward: The Legacy of Richard M. Nixon.* Westport, CT: Greenwood Press, 1992.

Gillon, Steven M. "A New Framework: Walter Mondale as Vice President," in *At the President's Side: The Vice Presidency in the Twentieth Century,* edited by Timothy Walch. Colombia: University of Missouri Press, 1997.

Goldsmith, Jack L. *The Terror Presidency: Law and Judgment Inside the Bush Administration.* New York: W.W. Norton & Co., 2007.

Goldstein, Joel K. *The Modern American Vice Presidency.* Princeton, NJ: Princeton University Press, 1982.

Halberstam, David. *The Best and the Brightest.* New York: Random House, 1969.

———. *War in a Time of Peace.* New York and London: Simon & Schuster, 2002.

Hartmann, Robert T. *Palace Politics: An Inside Account of the Ford Years.* New York: McGraw-Hill, 1980.

Haug, James, ed. *The Strategic Defense Initiative: An International Perspective.* New York: Colombia University Press, 1987.

Hayes, Stephen F. *Cheney: The Untold Story of America's Most Powerful and Controversial Vice President.* New York: HarperCollins, 2007.

Howell, William G. *Power without Persuasion: The Politics of Direct Presidential Action.* Princeton: Princeton University Press, 2003.

Hull, Cordell. *The Memoirs of Cordell Hull,* Vol. II. New York: Macmillan, 1948.

Human Rights Watch/Middle East. *Iraq's Crime of Genocide.* New Haven: Yale University Press, 1995.

Iran-Contra Committee Hearing Transcripts, Vols. 1–8. Washington, DC: Library of Congress, 1987.

Isaacson, Walter, and Evan Thomas. *The Wise Men.* New York: Simon & Schuster, 1986.

Johnson, Loch K. *The Making of International Agreements: Congress Confronts the Executive.* New York: New York University Press, 1984.

Jones, Gordon S., and John A. Marini, eds. *The Imperial Congress: Crisis in the Separation of Powers.* New York: Pharos Books, 1988.

Kempe, Fredrick. *Divorcing the Dictator: America's Bungled Affair with Noriega.* New York: G.P. Putnam's Sons, 1990.

Kissinger, Henry A. *White House Years.* Boston: Little Brown, 1979.

———. *Years of Upheaval.* New York: Simon & Schuster, 1982.

———. *Years of Renewal.* New York: Simon & Schuster, 1999.

Kitts, Kenneth. "The Politics of Armageddon: The Scowcroft Commission and the MX Missile," in *Presidential Commissions and National Security*. Boulder, CO: Lynne Rienner Publishers, 2006.

Kornblum, Peter, and Malcolm Byrne, eds. *The Iran-Contra Scandal: A Declassified History*. New York: W. W. Norton, 1993.

Kutler, Stanley I. *The Wars of Watergate: The Last Crisis of Richard Nixon*. New York: Alfred A. Knopf, 1990.

———. *Abuse of Power: The Nixon Tapes*. New York: The Free Press, 1997.

Lichtblau, Eric. *Bush's Law: The Remaking of American Justice*. New York: Pantheon Books, 2008.

Light, Paul C. *The President's Agenda*. Baltimore: Johns Hopkins University Press, 1982.

———. *Vice Presidential Power: Advice and Influence in the White House*. Baltimore and London: Johns Hopkins University Press, 1984.

———. *Monitoring Government: Inspectors General and the Search for Accountability*. Washington, DC: Brookings Institution, 1993.

Mann, James. *Rise of the Vulcans: The History of Bush's War Cabinet*. New York: Viking, 2004.

Matusow, Allen J. *Nixon's Economy: Booms, Busts, Dollars, and Votes*. Lawrence: University Press of Kansas, 1998.

Mayer, Kenneth R. *With the Stroke of a Pen: Executive Orders and Presidential Power*. Princeton, NJ: Princeton University Press, 2001.

McCullough, David. *Truman*. New York: Simon & Schuster, 1992.

Medved, Michael. *The Shadow Presidents: The Secret History of the Chief Executives and their Top Aides*. New York: Times Books, 1979.

Mieczkowski, Yanek. *Gerald Ford and the Challenges of the 1970s*. Lexington: University of Kentucky Press, 2005.

Miller, Merle. *Plain Speaking: An Oral Biography of Harry S. Truman*. New York: Berkley Publishing Co., 1973.

Nathan, Richard P. *The Administrative Presidency*. New York: Macmillan, 1983.

Nelson, Michael. *A Heartbeat Away*. New York: Twentieth Century Fund, 1988.

Nessen, Ron. *It Sure Looks Different from the Inside*. Chicago: Playbook Press, 1978.

Nixon, Richard M. *Memoirs of Richard Nixon*. New York: Grosset & Dunlap, 1978.

———. *Six Crises*. Garden City, NY: Doubleday, 1962.

Paper, Lewis J. *The Promise and the Performance: The Leadership of John F. Kennedy*. New York: Crown Publishers, 1975.

Pfiffner, James P. *The President, Budget, and Congress: Impoundment and the 1974 Budget Act*. Boulder, CO: Westview Press, 1979.

Powell, Colin. *My American Journey*. New York: Ballantine Books, 1995.

Reiss, Edward Reiss. *The Strategic Defense Initiative*. New York: Cambridge University Press, 1992.

Rhodes, Richard. *Arsenals of Folly: The Making of the Nuclear Arms Race*. New York: Alfred A. Knopf, 2007.

Roberts, Brad. *U.S. Foreign Policy After the Cold War*. Cambridge, MA: MIT Press, 1992.

Rudalevige, Andrew. *The New Imperial Presidency*. Ann Arbor: University of Michigan Press, 2005.

Savage, Charlie. *Takeover: The Return of the Imperial Presidency and the Subversion of American Democracy*. New York: Little Brown and Co., 2007.

Schissler, Jakob. "The Impact of the War Powers Resolution on Crisis Decision Making," in *The Reagan Administration: A Reconstruction of American Strength?* edited by Helga Haftendorn and Jakob Schissler. Berlin and New York: Walter de Gruyter, 1988.

Seager, Robert, II. *And Tyler Too: A Biography of John & Julia Gardiner Tyler*. Norwalk, CT: McGraw-Hill, 1963.

Shenon, Philip. *The Commission: The Uncensored History of the 9/11 Commission*. New York: Twelve, 2008.

Shultz, George P. *Turmoil and Triumph*. New York: Charles Scribner's Sons, 1993.

Simpson, Christopher, ed. *National Security Directives of the Reagan & Bush Administrations: The Declassified History of U.S. Political and Military Policy, 1981–1991*. Boulder, CO: Westview Press, 1995.

Sorensen, Theodore C. *Kennedy*. New York: Harper & Row, 1965.

Stone, Geoffrey R. "The Reagan Amendment, the First Amendment, and FBI Domestic Security Investigations," in *Freedom at Risk*, edited by Richard O. Curry. Philadelphia: Temple University Press, 1988.

Sundquist, James L. *The Decline and Resurgence of Congress*. Washington, DC: Brookings Institution Press, 1981.

Theoharis, Alan. *Spying on Americans: Political Surveillance from Hoover to the Houston Plan*. Philadelphia: Temple University Press, 1978.

Trainor, General Bernard E. *The Generals' War*. Boston: Little, Brown, 1995.

Turner, Michael. *The Vice President as Policy Maker: Rockefeller in the White House*. Westport, CT: Greenwood Press, 1982.

Weiner, Tim. *Legacy of Ashes: The History of the CIA*. New York: Doubleday, 2007.

Wilmerding, Lucius, Jr. *The Electoral College*. Boston: Beacon Paperback, 1964.

Woodward, Bob. *The Commanders*. New York: Simon & Schuster, 2002.

Young, Donald. *American Roulette: The History and Dilemma of the Vice Presidency*. New York: Viking Press, 1974.

ARTICLES

Anderson, Keith. "Is There Still a Sound Legal Basis? The Freedom of Information Act in the Post-9/11 World." *Ohio State Law Journal* 64 (2003): 1627–75.

Bretscher, Carl. "Presidential Records Act: The President and Judicial Review under the Records Acts." *George Washington Law Review* 60, no. 5 (June 1992): 1477–1508.

Canon, Carl M. "Nixon's Revenge." *National Journal* 34, no. 2 (12 January 2002); 95–102.

Castano, Sylvia E. "Disclosure of Federal Officials' Documents under the Freedom of Information Act: A Limited Application." *Houston Law Review* 18, no. 13 (31 March 1981): 641–54.

Clarke, Richard. "Threats to U.S. National Security: Proposed Partnership Initiatives Toward Preventing Cyber Terrorist Attacks." *DePaul Business Law Journal* 12 (1999): 25–40.

Cole, David. "The Grand Inquisitors." *New York Review of Books* 54, no. 12 (19 July 2007): 50–54.

Cole, David, and Martin S. Lederman, eds. "The National Security Agency's Domestic Spying Program; Framing the Debate." *Indiana Law Journal* 81 (May 2006): 1355–1425.

Duckett, Kenneth W., and Francis Russell. "The Harding Papers: How Some Were Burned ... And Others Were Saved." *American Heritage* 16 (February 1965): 18–31.

Gilboa, Eytan. "The Panama Invasion Revisited: Lessons for the Use of Force in the Post Cold War Era." *Political Science Quarterly* 110, no. 4, 539–60.

Halstead, T. J. "The Law: Walker v. Cheney: Legal Insulation of the Vice President from GAO Investigations." *Presidential Studies Quarterly* 33, no. 3 (September 2003): 635–48.

Hersh, Seymour M. "National Security Department: Listening In." *New Yorker*, 29 May 2006, 25–26.

Karin, Marcy Lynn. "Out of Sight, But Not Out of Mind: How Executive Order 13,233 Expands Executive Privilege While Simultaneously Preventing Access to Presidential Records." *Stanford Law Review* 55 (November 2002); 529–70.

Kirtley, Jane E. "Transparency and Accountability in a Time of Terror: The Bush Administration's Assault on Freedom of Information." *Communications Law and Policy* 11 (2006): 479–509.

McDonough, John R., Gordon Hoxie, and Richard Jacobs. "Who Owns Presidential Papers?" *Manuscripts* 27, no. 1 (Winter 1975): 2–15.

Relyea, Harold C. "The Rise and Pause of the U.S. Freedom of Information Act." *Government Publications Review* 10, no. 1 (1983): 18–29.

Sims, John Cary. "What NSA Is Doing ... and Why It's Illegal." *Hastings Constitutional Law Quarterly* 33 (Winter/Spring 2006): 101–36.

Spencer, Patricia L. "Nixon v. Administrator of General Services." *Akron Law Review* 11 (Fall 1977): 368–82.

Uhl, Kristen Elizabeth. "Comment: The Freedom of Information Act Post 9/11: Balancing the Public's Right to Know, Critical Infrastructure Protection, and Homeland Security." *American Law Review* 53 (2003-4): 261–92.

Wells, Christina E. "National Security Information and the Freedom of Information Act." *Administrative Law Review* 56 (2004): 1195–1222.

NEWSPAPERS AND PERIODICALS

Associated Press, 7 June 1999–7 August 2008
Austin Chronicle, 28 September 2001

Boston Globe, 10 November 2003–28 June 2007
Buffalo News, 2 December 2002
Charlotte Gazette, 22 May 2002–16 December 2003
Chicago Tribune, 5 February 2001
Christian Science Monitor, 16 December 2003–20 August 2008
Chronicle of Higher Education, 16 November 2001
Cincinnati Post, 17 September 2002
Columbus Dispatch, 1 June 2002–1 July 2006
CQ Researcher, 4 June 1952–2 August 2008
Detroit News, 7 October 2001
Environment & Energy Daily, 18 November 2002
Financial Times, 14 February 2002
Guardian, 6 November 2002
Knight-Ridder Tribune News Service, 14 November 2002–1 August 2008
Los Angeles Times, 9 August 2002–28 June 2007
Newsday, 23 May 2002
NewsFactor Network, 27 June 2002
Newsweek, 1 January 1968–1 August 2008
New York Review of Books, 30 September 1974–14 August 2008
New York Times, 20 January 1968–7 August 2008
Ottawa Citizen, 29 December 2001
Recorder, 16 December 2002
Reuters, 3 March 2003
San Diego Union-Tribune, 5 December 2002
San Francisco Chronicle, 6 January 2002–18 August 2003
San Francisco Gate, 12 December 2005
Seattle Post-Intelligencer, 19 April 2006
Secrecy News, 6 February 2007–28 February 2007
The Hill, 19 February 2003
Time, 16 January 1974–14 August 2008
USA Today, 13 August 2003–26 April 2007
U.S. News & World Report, 29 May 2006–1 August 2008
Wall Street Journal, 16 December 2003–30 July 2008
Washington Post, 15 September 1970–3 August 2008
Yakima Herald-Republic, 21 November 2002

GOVERNMENT DOCUMENTS

U.S. Congress, Congressional Record, 1974–2008
U.S. Congress, House Hearings, 1972–2008
U.S. Congress, House Reports, 1971–2008
U.S. Congress, Senate Hearings, 1972–2008
U.S. Congress, Senate Reports, 1972–2008

COURT RECORDS

American Civil Liberties Union v. National Security Agency/Central Security Service, Complaint for Declaratory and Injunctive Relief, U.S. District Court, Eastern District of Michigan, Southern Division, Case No. 06-CV-10204 (17 January 2006).

American Civil Liberties Union, et al. v. National Security Agency, et al., U.S. District Court for the Sixth Circuit, Nos. 06-2095/2140 (6 July 2007).

American Historical Association v. Peterson, 876 F.Supp.1300, 1320 (D.D.C. 1995).

American Historical Association, et al. v. National Archives and Records Administration et al., Memorandum of Points and Authorities in Support of Plaintiff's Motion for Summary Judgment, No. 01-2447 (8 February 2002).

Armstrong v. Bush, 924 F.2d 282,288 (U.S. App. D.C.1991).

Association of American Physicians and Surgeons, Inc. v. Hillary Rodham Clinton, 813 F. Supp.82, 95 (D.C.C.1993).

Boumediene v. Bush, No. 06-1195.

Cheney v. U.S. District Court for the District of Columbia, Writ of Certiorari to the U.S. Court of Appeals for the District of Colombia Circuit, Brief for the Petitioners, Civil Action No. 03-475 (2004).

Cheney v. U.S. District Court for the District of Columbia, On Petition for a Writ of Certiorari to the U.S. Court of Appeals for the District of Colombia Circuit, Brief in Opposition of Respondent Sierra Club, Civil Action No. 03-475 (2004).

Cheney v. U.S. District Court for the District of Columbia, Civil Action No. 03-475 (2004).

David M. Walker v. Richard B. Cheney, U.S. District Court for the District of Colombia, Civil Action No. 02-0340 (JDB) (2002).

Hamdan v. Rumsfeld, 126 S.Ct. 2796 (2006).

Hamdi v. Rumsfeld, 542 U.S. 507 (2004).

Hamdi v. Rumsfeld, U.S. Court of Appeals for the Fourth Circuit, No. 02-6895, June 19, 2002.

In *Re: Richard B. Cheney, Vice President of the United States, et al.*, U.S. Court of Appeals for the District of Colombia Circuit, No. 02-5354 (May 10, 2005).

In *Re: Richard B. Cheney, et al. Petition for Writ of Certiorari*, U.S. Supreme Court, No. 03-475 (September 2003).

In *Re: Richard B. Cheney*, No. 02-5354 (D.C.Cir.2005).

Judicial Watch v. National Energy Policy Development Group, Civil Action No. 01-1530 (EGS) and *Sierra Club v. Vice President Richard Cheney*, et al., Civil Action No. 02-631, U.S. District for the District of Colombia (EGS) (12 July 2002).

Judicial Watch v. U.S. Department of Energy, et al., U.S. District Court for the District of Colombia, Civil Action No. 01-0981 (PLF).

Morrison v. Olson, 487 U.S. 654 (1988).

Nixon v. Administrator of General Services, 433 U.S. 425 (1977).

Nixon v. Freeman, 670 F.2d 346 (1982).
Nixon v. Burke, 843 F.2d 1473 (D.C. Cir. 1988).
Padilla v. Rumsfeld, 352 F.3d 695 (2nd Cir. 2003).
United States v. Curtiss-Wright Export Corporation, 299 U.S. 304 (1936).
United States v. Nixon, 418 U.S. 683 (1974).
Walker v. Cheney, Complaint for Declaratory and Injunctive Relief, U.S. District Court for the District of Colombia, Civil Action No. 1:02cv00340.
Walker v. Cheney, U.S. District Court for the District of Colombia, Civil Action No. 02-0340 (JDB) (9 December 2002).
Youngstown Sheet & Tube Co. v. Sawyer, 343 U.S. 579 (June 2, 1952).

INTERNET SOURCES

Note: All Web sites were accessed 16 September 2008, except where noted.
http://www.aclu.org
http://www.boston.com/bostonglobe
http://www.chicagotribune.com
http://chronicle.com
http://www.citizen.org
http://www.csmonitor.com
http://www.defenselink.com
http://www.fas.org
http://www.findlaw.com
http://www.firstamendmentcenter.org
http://www.gao.gov.com
http://globalsecurity.org/Military
http://www.gwu.edu/~nsarchiv.com (accessed February 20, 2008)
http://www.house.gov/reform (accessed February 20, 2008)
http://judiciary.senate.gov
http://www.latimes.com
http://library.cqpress.com/cqresearcher/php?id=cqresrre20
http://www.msnbc.com
http://www.newsweek.com
http://www.nybooks.com
http://www.nytimes.com
http://www.ombwatch.org
http://www.openthegovernment.org
http://www.pbs.org/wghb/pages/frontline/gulf/oral/baker/1.html
http://www.pbs.org/wgbh/pages/frontline/gulf/oral/cheney/1.html
http://www.pbs.org/wgbh/pages/frontline/gulf/oral/cheney/2.html
http://www.pbs.org/wgbh/pages/frontline/darkside/interviews/clarke.html
http://www.pbs.org/wgbh/pages/frontline/cheney/interviews/goldsmith.html
http://www.pbs.org/wgbh/pages/frontline/gulf/oral/powell/1.html
http://www.pbs.org/wgbh/pages/frontline/shows/pentagon/interviews/ricks.html

http://www.pbs.org/wgbh/pages/frontline/cheney/interviews/goldsmith.html
http://www.pbs.org/wgbh/pages/frontline/gulf/oral/schwarzkopf/2.html
http://www.pbs.org/wgbh/pages/frontline/gulf/oral/trainor/1.html
http://www.pbs.org/wgbh/pages/frontline/homefront/interviews/yoo.html
http://www.pbs.org/wgbh/pages/frontline/shows/pentagon/interviews/priest.html
http://www.pbs.org/frontlineworld/stories/rendition701/interviews/wilkerson.html
http://www.publiccitizen.org
http://www.rcfp.org/homefrontconfidential/foi.html
http://www.salon.com
http://www.sej.org
http://www.senate.gov
http://sfgate.com
http://www.usdoj.gov/oip/foiapost/2002foiapost10.htm
http://www.washingtonpost.com
http://www.whitehouse.gov

Index

Williams, Pete, 79
Wilson, Henry, 5
Wilson, Pete, 77
Wilson, Woodrow, 5–6
Woerner, Fredrick General, 82
Wolfowitz, Paul, 80, 91, 103–4,
    108, 143, 144, 147, 149, 152, 182,
    190
Wright, Jim, 63

Yoo, John C.: detainees, 185;
    interrogation, 133, 134–35, 136, 139,
    140, 171, 178; military commissions,
    128, 130; Office of Legal Counsel,
    161; rendition, 137; warrantless
    domestic surveillance, 122, 123, 124,
    125, 126, 162–67

Zahkeim, Dov, 104

About the Author

BRUCE P. MONTGOMERY is Associate Professor and Faculty Director of Archives at the University of Colorado at Boulder. He is the founding director of the UCB Human Rights Initiative and a founding member of the International Federation of Human Rights Centers and Archives. He has served as an analyst of classified documents for the U.S. government. He is the author of *The Bush-Cheney Administration's Assault on Open Government* (Praeger, 2008) and *Subverting Open Government: White House Materials and Executive Branch Politics*. Articles by Montgomery on the aggrandizement of the executive branch have appeared in many journals and newspapers, including *Presidential Studies Quarterly*, *Political Science Quarterly*, and *The Washington Post*.